Heaven on Earth?

## Directions in Modern Theology Book Series

Born out of the journal *Modern Theology*, the Directions in Modern Theology book series provides issues focused on important theological topics and texts in current debate within that discipline, whilst looking at broader contemporary topics from a theological perspective. It analyses notions and thinkers, as well as examining a wide spectrum of "modern" theological eras: from late Medieval through to the Enlightenment and up until the present "post-modern" movements. Attracting distinguished theologians from a world-wide base, the book series develops what is a unique forum for international debate on theological concerns.

Titles in the series include:

*Heaven on Earth? Theological Interpretation in Ecumenical Dialogue*
Edited by Hans Boersma and Matthew Levering

*Faith, Rationality and the Passions*
Edited by Sarah Coakley

*Re-thinking Dionysius the Areopagite*
Edited by Sarah Coakley and Charles M. Stang

*The Promise of Scriptural Reasoning*
Edited by David Ford and C. C. Pecknold

*Aquinas in Dialogue: Thomas for the Twenty-First Century*
Edited by Jim Fodor and Frederick Christian Bauerschmidt

*Re-thinking Gregory of Nyssa*
Edited by Sarah Coakley

*Theology and Eschatology at the Turn of the Millennium*
Edited by L. Gregory Jones and James Buckley

*Catholicism and Catholicity: Eucharistic Communities in Historical and Contemporary Perspectives*
Edited by Sarah Beckwith, L. Gregory Jones and James J. Buckley

*Theology and Scriptural Imagination: Directions in Modern Theology*
Edited by L. Gregory Jones and James Buckley

*Spirituality and Social Embodiment*
Edited by L. Gregory Jones and James Buckley

# Heaven on Earth?
## Theological Interpretation in Ecumenical Dialogue

*Edited by*
**Hans Boersma and Matthew Levering**

**WILEY-BLACKWELL**

A John Wiley & Sons, Ltd., Publication

This edition first published 2013
Originally published as Volume 28, Issue 4 of *Modern Theology*
© 2013 Blackwell Publishing Ltd

Blackwell Publishing was acquired by John Wiley & Sons in February 2007. Blackwell's publishing program has been merged with Wiley's global Scientific, Technical, and Medical business to form Wiley-Blackwell.

*Registered Office*
John Wiley & Sons Ltd, The Atrium, Southern Gate, Chichester, West Sussex, PO19 8SQ, United Kingdom

*Editorial Offices*
350 Main Street, Malden, MA 02148-5020, USA
9600 Garsington Road, Oxford, OX4 2DQ, UK
The Atrium, Southern Gate, Chichester, West Sussex, PO19 8SQ, UK

For details of our global editorial offices, for customer services, and for information about how to apply for permission to reuse the copyright material in this book please see our website at www.wiley.com/wiley-blackwell.

*Library of Congress Cataloging-in-Publication Data applied for.*

A catalogue record for this book is available from the British Library.

Cover design by Richard Boxall Design Associates.

Set in 10 on 12 pt Palatino by Toppan Best-set Premedia Limited
Printed in Malaysia by Ho Printing (M) Sdn Bhd

1   2013

# CONTENTS

# INTRODUCTION: SPIRITUAL INTERPRETATION AND REALIGNED TEMPORALITY

## HANS BOERSMA AND MATTHEW LEVERING

The current scholarly trend of increased attention to spiritual or theological interpretation of Scripture shows few signs of abating. Both by way of underlying hermeneutical reflection and in terms of biblical commentary, historical-critical interpretation appears to be on the wane as the dominant mode of biblical scholarship. The articles that comprise this special issue of *Modern Theology* are written in the conviction that this renewed attention to spiritual interpretation not only represents a positive re-appropriation of earlier modes of exegesis but also offers renewed opportunity for ecumenical dialogue, in particular between Catholics and evangelicals. While historical exegesis has impacted both Catholic and evangelical biblical scholarship, it is nonetheless possible to discern differences between the two traditions. Within the Catholic Church, spiritual interpretation has always had a privileged position, and arguably the development of doctrine within Catholicism (including at the earliest Councils) depends in part on the conviction that historical exegesis does not provide exhaustive insight into the meaning of Scripture. Evangelicals, partially out of concern with controls for a proper guidance of doctrinal development, have tended to be more reticent with regard to spiritual exegesis, and can at times be quite critical about patristic and medieval approaches to biblical interpretation. Since the renewed focus on theological interpretation cuts across traditional ecclesial divides, however, it has become necessary for Catholics and evangelicals to enter into conversation both about what spiritual or theological interpretation should and should not look like and about possible doctrinal implications

*Heaven on Earth?: Theological Interpretation in Ecumenical Dialogue*, First Edition.
Edited by Hans Boersma and Matthew Levering.
© 2013 Blackwell Publishing Ltd. Book compilation © 2013 Blackwell Publishing Ltd.

that this renewed focus may have for the relationship between Catholics and evangelicals.

These considerations were the reason for the authors of this introductory article—at the same time co-directors of the Center for Catholic-Evangelical Dialogue (www.ccedprograms.org)—to organize a conference at Regent College in Vancouver in September of 2011 on the theme of "Heaven on Earth? The Future of Spiritual Interpretation." This conference, the result of a Lilly Research Grant of the Association of Theological Schools, brought together Catholic and evangelical scholars in ecumenical discussion about the question of whether the recent flourishing of theological interpretation represents some sort of "heaven on earth" or whether we ought to be aware also of shadow sides to this recent trend. Further, since these developments raise important questions about the relationship between historical and spiritual meaning—as well as between nature and the supernatural, reason and faith, and earthly and heavenly realities—the conference theme conveys a *double entendre*, raising explicitly the most intriguing issue at stake in the question of theological interpretation.

In this introductory article, we want to offer some initial reflections on the topic of spiritual interpretation. We will focus, however, not on the spatial categories of "heaven" and "earth" but on the question of time. We have become convinced that the way in which we evaluate the relationship between historical and spiritual exegesis not only depends on our understanding of the relationship between heaven and earth but also has to do with how we understand temporality. In particular, it seems to us that when we look at time not just in chronological but also in sacramental fashion, patristic approaches to spiritual interpretation become intelligible. The first part of our article will show how this functions in the pre-modern Christian distinction between "secular time" and "higher time." In the second part of this article, we will make clear that, in their discussions of the Second Vatican Council's *Dei Verbum*, various theological voices have recently appealed to a similar sacramental understanding of time in defence of spiritual exegesis.[1]

*Temporality, Participation, and Spiritual Exegesis*

Time, for the premodern mindset, was not simply a strictly chronological affair. Charles Taylor, in his book, *A Secular Age*, draws a distinction between "secular time" and "higher time."[2] Secular time, Taylor maintains, is something we can also refer to as "ordinary time," seeing that the word "secular" is derived from the term *saeculum*, meaning "century" or "age." "People who are in the saeculum," explains Taylor, "are embedded in ordinary time, they are living the life of ordinary time; as against those who have turned away from this order to live closer to eternity. The word is thus used for ordinary as against higher time. A parallel distinction is temporal/spiritual. One is concerned with things in ordinary time, the other with the affairs of eternity."[3] Secular or ordinary time, in other words, refers to the basic chronological progression of temporal events, whereas higher time has to do with the eternal, unchanging realm of eternity, which Europe had inherited from Plato and Greek philosophy.

Taylor then makes the crucial move of insisting that the notion of "higher time" enabled various chronological moments in "secular time" to be linked to each other. Taylor mentions the example of the sacrifice of Isaac and the Crucifixion of Christ as two moments in secular time that are somehow linked together or, we could almost say, become contemporaneous:

> Now higher times gather and re-order secular time. They introduce "warps" and seeming inconsistencies in profane time-ordering. Events which were far apart in profane time could nevertheless be closely linked. Benedict Anderson in a penetrating discussion of . . . some of the same issues I am trying to describe here, quotes Auerbach on the relation prefiguring-fulfilling in which events of the Old Testament were held to stand to those in the New, for instance the sacrifice of Isaac and the Crucifixion of Christ. These two events were linked through their immediate contiguous places in the divine plan. They are drawn close to identity in eternity, even though they are centuries (that is, "aeons" or "saecula") apart. In God's time there is a sort of simultaneity of sacrifice and Crucifixion.[4]

The "simultaneity" of two chronologically distinct moments in time is a remarkable feature of premodern Christianity. And it is no coincidence that Taylor uses the example of the sacrifice of Isaac and the Crucifixion of Christ. Somehow, it appears, the two sacrifices are joined together at a "higher time," in eternity.[5] Two historical events, one of which we could describe as Old Testament type and the other as New Testament antitype are linked and become simultaneous because together they participate in the "higher time" of God's eternity.

This distinction between secular and higher time had obvious and significant implications for the interpretation of Scripture. The typological and allegorical exegesis of the church fathers generally did not result from an arbitrary imposition of alien meanings onto the biblical text, so as to avoid its more obvious historical meaning. Rather, premodern theological or spiritual interpretation resulted from the conviction that Old Testament events occurring in "ordinary time" were contiguous with (in fact, in an important sense, linked in with) their Christological fulfillment in the New Testament. This connection resulted from the fact that both events were linked in the providential rule of God in eternity. We have described this participatory understanding of time elsewhere as follows: "When history is understood as a participation in God, the words and deeds depicted in John's Gospel take on what for Christians is recognizable as their true and deepest meaning. Jesus Christ constitutes the center of linear and participatory history as the incarnate Word, the one Mediator, in whom human beings receive the Holy Spirit and are led to the Father."[6] Participatory exegesis assumes that chronologically disparate events participate, in and through the Christ event, in the "higher time" of eternity itself.

Charles Taylor rightly points to St. Augustine as an example of an exegete who recognizes that "all times are present to [God], and he holds them in his extended simultaneity. His now contains all time."[7] Augustine, however, is not the only one for whom time functioned in this manner, and for whom, as a result, exegesis both distinguished and linked historical and spiritual levels of meaning. We find much the same in several places in Gregory of Nyssa's writings. We will restrict ourselves to just one example. In his Easter homily *De tridui spatio* (*On the Three-day Period*), Gregory depicts for us the neophytes entering the church, each of them holding a burning candle. St. Gregory maintains that the light of the many candles is derived from the one light of Christ himself. The one light of Christ thus sheds its light forward to the many lights of the neophytes. As he reflects on the many Old Testament passages that foreshadow this one light of Christ, Nyssen maintains that they, too, function like many little candles that derive their light from the Christ candle himself. Thus, the one light of Christ also sheds its light backward to the many lights of the Old Testament Scriptures. Comments Gregory: "And just as in the scene before our eyes one light blazes about our vision, though constituted by a multitude of candles, so the whole blessing of Christ, shining by itself like a torch, produces for us this great light compounded from the many and varied rays of scripture."[8] It appears that for Gregory, both the many lights of Old Testament history and the many lights of today's neophytes participate in Christ, while in and through him they participate in the "higher time" of the eternal light of God's providential life.

### Temporality in Francis Martin, Joseph Ratzinger, and Denis Farkasfalvy

In their discussions of Vatican II's Dogmatic Constitution *Dei Verbum*, several contemporary theologians present understandings of time that are remarkably similar to that of Gregory of Nyssa. The biblical scholar Francis Martin credits his fifteen years in a Cistercian Monastery with giving him the awareness that "the native home of Scripture is the Liturgy."[9] Martin, like Gregory, in convinced that saving realities revealed in Scripture continue to be present today in a way that strictly time-bound realities could not be. Drawing upon a range of thinkers, including Henri de Lubac and Matthew Lamb, Martin proposes thinking of history in terms of "temporality" and thus of presence.[10] He notes that modern historiography conceives of time solely as a succession of moments, whereas from a more biblical perspective Augustine argues that time is a participation in infinite presence: "Temporality, the proper mode of creation's existence, is not just succession; it is succession with the dimension of presence."[11] Martin's claim is that when time is understood as "temporality" in Augustine's biblical sense, the saving mystery can be seen to be intrinsic to the event that occurs in history.

What about historical-critical reconstructions that seek to move behind the biblical text in order to explore critically the text's historical referents (or lack thereof)? Indebted to his teacher Luis Alonso-Schökel, Martin finds these reconstructions to be valuable, so long as one recognizes that the biblical authors' narrative techniques are the means by which the Holy Spirit enables humans to interpret the actions of God in history. These narrative techniques disclose the mystery in the event, the way in which the temporal reality participates in God's infinite presence. Martin observes that it is this relationship between word and event that *Dei Verbum* describes as follows: "This economy of Revelation is realized by deeds and words, which are intrinsically bound up with each other. As a result, the works performed by God in the history of salvation show forth and bear out the doctrine and realities signified by the words; the words, for their part, proclaim the works, and bring to light the mystery they contain."[12]

On this view, historical-critical reconstructions can illumine the biblical text but cannot, if interpretation is to succeed, become a norm that displaces the biblical text. Historical reconstruction can set forth hypotheses about the temporal progression but cannot (unlike the inspired narrative) mediate understanding of temporality's presence to God. This is all the more the case when the temporal moment involves the Word incarnate, the Creator of all things who sustains all things by his presence and who guides all things by his providence, and whose actions thereby constitute the very center of history.[13]

The approach taken by Joseph Ratzinger (Pope Benedict XVI) moves along lines quite similar to Martin's. Ratzinger describes *Dei Verbum* as "a decisive step forward" in terms of the relationship between theology and historical-critical method in Catholic biblical interpretation.[14] Agreeing with *Dei Verbum* §12, he argues for the necessity of the historical-critical method, especially since the historicity of God's saving work is a central claim of the Christian faith. At the same time he notes that the historical-critical method, given its understanding of history as a succession of temporal moments with no metaphysical or providential relationship to God, must leave the history that it seeks to reconstruct strictly in the past. Although it can demonstrate the intra-biblical exegesis that relates the texts to each other, the historical-critical method cannot defend the unity of the diverse texts as one "Bible." In the ability of biblical words to be appropriated by later biblical authors, Ratzinger identifies an openness of the words themselves to a fulfillment or deeper value unknown to the original authors. This openness of the words corresponds to the openness of the community in which they were written: the people of God journeys forward in faith, and the sacred writings live within this community of believers. The words have their full, trans-historical meaning within the presence of God to his people and of his people to God.

In an earlier essay, Ratzinger argues that the modern understanding of history as "pure facticity, which is composed of chance and necessity,"[15] needs to be augmented by a metaphysical understanding of time as participating in God's eternity, with a resulting openness to providential teleology and to analogous relationships between past, present, and future events. Indebted to Thomas Aquinas, he finds that this understanding of history allows for God's action (above all God's action in Christ) to be recognizable as "the principle of the intelligibility of history."[16] Given this understanding of history, one can affirm in faith that "the deeds that occurred in the Old Testament have their basis in a future deed."[17] Among other things, this perspective unites word and event as participating in God's creative and providential work and thus recovers the teleological unity of Scripture with Christ at the center.

Indebted to Brevard Childs's canonical exegesis, Ratzinger envisions two phases of interpretation, the first of which seeks to understand the texts' ancient near-Eastern contexts, while the second of which locates the texts within "the entire historical movement and in terms of the central event of Christ."[18] Without openness to completion in the second phase, the first phase of interpretation—which, it should be noted, cannot prescind from metaphysics—can see only parts rather than the whole. The exegete of the Bible, which is a whole, does not therefore "occupy a neutral position above or outside the history of the Church."[19]

A third significant contemporary effort to develop the insights of *Dei Verbum* for Catholic biblical exegesis comes from Denis Farkasfalvy. Citing Oscar Cullmann, he remarks that "[t]he literary heritage of the apostolic Church represented by the books of the New Testament is so closely and organically related to the Eucharist that one is entitled to state that all New Testament Scripture has a Eucharistic provenance."[20] The Gospels were written and proclaimed within the context of early Christian worship, as believers assembled to hear about Jesus and to share in table fellowship with him through the breaking of the bread. In this way, the encounters with Jesus depicted in the Gospels extend to the community of believers. Jesus is the one who comes and who is coming, not only to persons in his earthly life but now eucharistically to believers. Farkasfalvy also argues for the liturgical framework of the Book of Revelation, which he links with the Resurrection appearances presented in the Gospel of John. The Book of Revelation confirms the New Testament's emphasis on "the coming of God in the coming of Jesus, both complete and to be completed," an emphasis that locates interpretation of the texts within the eucharistic task of building up the Church in relationship to the Lord.[21]

*Conclusion*

Several conclusions may be drawn from the above reflections. First, each of the authors discussed holds that from a Christian viewpoint, one cannot limit a proper understanding of time to a purely linear, chronological progression. God's providential action in history—and particularly in Jesus Christ—opens up spiritual registers that are not limited to a purely historical progression of events. Second, several of the authors reviewed above point to the liturgy as the event through which time is opened up, as it were, to a deeper dimension. Or, to put it in terms of the conference theme, it is particularly through the liturgy that heaven impinges on earth, and that earthly, historical events can be said to participate in heavenly realities. Third, the implication of such an understanding of time would appear to be that historical exegesis is incomplete when the Christological, spiritual dimensions of historical events are ignored. Spiritual exegesis, then, is founded on the conviction that the biblical events recorded in Scripture find their climax and true reality in God's self-revelation in Jesus Christ. It is in him that heaven and earth are truly joined together.

Of course, in developing this argument, we are not speaking on behalf of the authors of this issue of *Modern Theology*. As the various articles will make clear, while each of the authors supports spiritual interpretation in one form or another, they do not all arrive at their respective positions in the same way, and differences remain about what constitutes legitimate theological exegesis. Nonetheless, it is our hope that by reflecting on the notion of temporality in Gregory of Nyssa and various contemporary theologians, we have presented an approach to temporality that offers a potentially fruitful way of dealing with spiritual interpretation.

With respect to the articles that follow in this issue, we will be brief. We have asked five Catholics (Lewis Ayres, Brian E. Daley, Matthew Levering, Francesca A. Murphy, and Michael Maria Waldstein) and six evangelicals (Hans Boersma, David Lyle Jeffrey, Peter J. Leithart, Peter W. Martens, Kevin J. Vanhoozer, and Jens Zimmermann) to contribute an article on the topic of spiritual interpretation. Part I ("Reading the Fathers") deals with patristic exegesis. Brian Daley argues from a broad-ranging discussion of patristic authors that while we are to take original authorial intent as the starting-point and guide for our exegesis, we are to look also for the greater depth of history, which is rooted in God's reality, comes forth from God, and leads to God. Lewis Ayres looks to the second-century Christian adaptation of classical reading practices in order to discern what reading the letter of the text meant for subsequent patristic exegesis. In the process, he argues that we need to read doctrinally not only the establishment of the canon *per se*, but also the emergence of the Christian community's practices and patterns of reading that allowed people to see Scripture as Scripture. Peter Martens subjects the objections to Origen's alleged neglect of history to detailed analysis and critique. He argues that these criticisms of Origen have rarely hit their intended target, and that when they have, they do not appear to be particularly troubling. Hans Boersma turns to the issue of slavery in Gregory of Nyssa and notes that his opposition to slavery is one of the fruits of his spiritual exegesis. Thus, his theological approach to Scripture does not imply a disinterested otherworldliness but a genuine concern to bring heaven to earth.

Part II ("Reading Scripture") consists of three articles that focus specifically on biblical and exegetical matters. Here, Peter Leithart finds typological links between the book of Revelation, on the one hand, and the Song of Songs and Daniel, on the other hand. He argues that the political hope expressed in Revelation is for an imperial lover whose love is better than wine and who confers his kingdom upon his saints. David Jeffrey shows that many of our contemporary Bible translations reduce theological mysteries to mundane analogies. The result is a tacit desacralization of Scripture, which hinders our ability to engage in spiritual interpretation. In light of Paul's typological exegesis, Matthew Levering argues that typological exegesis cannot be denied its place as a valid way of interpreting Scripture in the Church, not only for the purposes of moral exhortation but also for instruction about the realities of salvation history. The truth of particular instances of typological exegesis requires the discernment provided by the Church's liturgy and magisterial tradition.

Part III ("Reading in Contemporary Context") looks at the functioning of theological or spiritual interpretation in today's context. Here, Michael Waldstein sets the stage by drawing attention to Joseph Cardinal Ratzinger's 1988 Erasmus Lecture. Waldstein builds on Ratzinger's critical engagement with Raymond Brown's use of historical criticism, and he cautions against the narrowing of our epistemological horizons inherent in Brown's approach. Francesca Murphy sheds light on how to read the Psalms of abandonment by drawing on analogies taken from the cinema. She concludes that we need to read these Psalms both in their historical setting as referring to David and also as having a further Christological reference. Jens Zimmermann draws on Dietrich Bonhoeffer to argue for the legitimacy of theological interpretation, as he shows that Bonhoeffer offers a consciously sacramental and Christological hermeneutic. Finally, Kevin Vanhoozer lucidly defends Protestant typological exegesis. He argues that such "transfigural" interpretation does not add additional meanings to the literal sense but rather extends the latter, so that spiritual interpretation renders the Spirit's intended transfigural meaning, an intention that includes the reader's own transfiguration.

The first and last articles originally functioned as the two keynote addresses in the conference where this collection originated. Brian Daley, as the Catholic keynote speaker, makes a significant observation toward the end of his article: "To read Scripture figurally, as well as critically and analytically, is not to abandon a modern sense of the history in which we live, but simply to see history in greater depth, as having 'spiritual' significance—as rooted in God's reality, coming forth from God, leading to God." Vanhoozer, our evangelical keynote presenter, comments poignantly in his article: "Christ's physical body is to his transfiguration what the literal sense is to its spiritual rendering. It is not a matter of leaving the body, or the verbal sense behind, but of penetrating more deeply into their intrinsic nature. The glory (i.e., the divine discourse) that was formerly implicit has become explicit." The two comments show a remarkable convergence. Where Daley refuses to abandon history, Vanhoozer declines to leave behind the body. Where Daley maintains that a figural reading means to recognize history's "greater depth," Vanhoozer suggests that spiritual reading penetrates "more deeply" into the intrinsic nature of the verbal sense. This is not to suggest that no differences remain, either between these two authors or among the various articles in this *Modern Theology* issue. Nonetheless, it seems fair to suggest that this ecumenical endeavour has arrived at a great deal of convergence regarding the need for Christian biblical exegesis to find ways of recognizing the work of the living God in the very fabric of history and temporality. If some of this may be achieved also among our readers, our editorial labour will have been worth the effort.

*NOTES*

1 The material below on contemporary Catholic scholars will also be published in Matthew Levering, "'The Scriptures and Their Interpretation," in *The Oxford Handbook of Catholic Theology*, ed. Lewis Ayres and Medi Ann Volpe (Oxford: Oxford University Press, forthcoming).
2 Charles Taylor, *A Secular Age* (Cambridge, MA: Belknap—Harvard University Press, 2007), p. 54.
3 *Ibid.*, p. 55.
4 *Ibid.* Taylor is referring to Benedict Anderson, *Imagined Communities* (London: Verso, 1983), pp. 28–31.
5 Cf. the discussion in Hans Boersma, *Heavenly Participation: The Weaving of a Sacramental Tapestry* (Grand Rapids, MI: Wm. B. Eerdmans Publishing Company, 2011), pp. 126–127.
6 Matthew Levering, *Participatory Exegesis: A Theology of Biblical Interpretation* (Notre Dame, IN: University of Notre Dame Press, 2008), p. 33.
7 Taylor, *Secular Age*, p. 57.
8 Gregory of Nyssa, *On the Three-day Period of the Resurrection of Our Lord Jesus Christ*, trans. S. G. Hall in Andreas Spira and Christoph Klock (eds.), *The Easter Sermons of Gregory of Nyssa: Translation and Commentary: Proceedings of the Fourth International Colloquium on Gregory of Nyssa; Cambridge, England: 11–15 September, 1978*, Patristic Monograph Series, 9 (Cambridge, MA: Philadelphia Patristic Foundation, 1981), pp. 273–274. For further discussion of *De tridui spatio*, see Hans Boersma, *Embodiment and Virtue in Gregory of Nyssa: An Anagogical Approach* (Oxford: Oxford University Press, 2013).
9 Francis Martin, *Sacred Scripture: The Disclosure of the Word* (Naples, FL: Sapientia Press, 2006), p. xii.
10 *Ibid.*, p. 239.
11 *Ibid.*, p. 240.
12 Vatican Council II, *Dogmatic Constitution on Divine Revelation, Dei Verbum*, in Austin Flannery (ed.), *Vatican Council II*, Vol. 1, *The Conciliar and Post Conciliar Documents* (Northport, NY: Costello Publishing Company, 1975), §2.
13 Cf. Martin, *Sacred Scripture*, p. 272.

14  Joseph Ratzinger, *Jesus of Nazareth: From the Baptism in the Jordan to the Transfiguration*, trans. Adrian J. Walker (New York, NY: Doubleday, 2007), p. xiv.
15  Joseph Ratzinger, "Biblical Interpretation in Conflict: On the Foundations and the Itinerary of Exegesis Today," in José Granados, Carlos Granados, and Luis Sánchez-Navarro (eds.), *Opening Up the Scriptures: Joseph Ratzinger and the Foundations of Biblical Interpretation* (Grand Rapids, MI: Wm. B. Eerdmans Publishing Company, 2008), p. 23.
16  *Ibid.*, p. 24.
17  *Ibid.*
18  *Ibid.*, p. 25.
19  *Ibid.*, p. 29.
20  Denis Farkasfalvy, *Inspiration and Interpretation: A Theological Introduction to Sacred Scripture* (Washington, DC: The Catholic University of America Press, 2010), p. 63; cf. *ibid.*, p. 75.
21  *Ibid.*, p. 86.

# Part I

# Reading the Fathers

# 1

# "IN MANY AND VARIOUS WAYS": TOWARDS A THEOLOGY OF THEOLOGICAL EXEGESIS

BRIAN E. DALEY, SJ

Texts are everything in the modern (and post-modern) world. Since the rise of philosophical hermeneutics with Heidegger and Gadamer and Ricoeur, since the days of deconstructivist literary criticism and the growth of contemporary theories of philosophical and literary interpretation, scholars in the humanities have tended, increasingly, to see their work as dealing above all with written productions as their objects of study: texts that conceal as well as disclose the writer's intended meaning in written, time-bound, culturally determined words; texts that always involve both the reception and the destruction of older traditions of thought and language; texts that challenge the readers who come after them to enter and rearrange their world, like the furniture in a living-room.

For Christians, this focus on hermeneutics and textual theory can feel both natural and alienating. On the one hand, Jews and Christians and Muslims—perhaps more than any other set of religious traditions—regard their holy texts, their "Scriptures," not just as the historic monuments of a sacred heritage, but as the place of God's continuing revelation: the foundation of their faith's present understanding of the reality of God, the chief guide towards how God calls us to act now. Our holy Scriptures form a book constantly in the process of being understood for the first time, a collection of writings that, by its very significance for their religious tradition, requires constant re-interpretation and re-application. On the other hand, for the faithful of all of these traditions, the text of what they regard as Scripture is not an object to be toyed with or even objectified, but a human, linguistic set of voices witnessing to an ultimate reality that is the reason all the other

*Heaven on Earth?: Theological Interpretation in Ecumenical Dialogue*, First Edition.
Edited by Hans Boersma and Matthew Levering.
© 2013 Blackwell Publishing Ltd. Book compilation © 2013 Blackwell Publishing Ltd.

realities we know exist at all. The book of Scripture, unlike all other books, is something sacred, human words communicating the Word of God; as such, it transcends time, and even its own original historical context. So the text of Scripture, precisely *as* Scripture, acquires for what are sometimes called "the religions of the book" both an urgency, a religious normativity, that no other writings in those traditions, however valuable, possess, and at the same time a translucency—an invitation to continuing reflection and interpretation— that other religious works can never have. What believers seek in them is not simply information, or historical evidence of ancient religious thought, but the reality of God as he speaks and acts in our midst.

Reading and interpreting Scripture correctly, then—discovering its meaning correctly so that we can understand it and live by it—presents us with unique challenges, if only because the one whom believers take to be speaking in and through the text is *God*, not simply a historical human author or editor. At the same time, human authors and editors, as well as translators and interpreters through the ages, have clearly been involved in the production of Biblical texts from their remotest origins. To know what the Biblical text *means* requires that, as far as possible, we know what these *authors* meant, and take that "original meaning" as a starting-point and guide for determining what it might mean for us today.

So reading the Bible and understanding it, in a way that allows us to take its content and meaning seriously, is clearly a complex, even paradoxical process that calls into play both a sophisticated conviction of God as creator, mysteriously yet really involved in human thoughts and actions, and of the ordinary human circumstances of literary authorship and the communication of meaning. In the words of the Second Vatican Council's Constitution on Divine Revelation, *Dei Verbum*, from 1965:

> Those things revealed by God, which are contained and presented in the texts of Holy Scripture, were written under the influence of the Holy Spirit. . . . In the process of composition of the sacred books, God chose and employed human agents, using their own faculties and powers, in such a way that while he was acting in them and through them, they committed to writing, as genuine authors, everything which he willed— but only what he willed. Since, then, everything that the inspired authors or "sacred writers" affirm should be considered to be affirmed by the Holy Spirit, the books of Scripture should be confessed as teaching firmly, faithfully, and without error that truth which God wished to be sealed in the sacred books for the sake of our salvation. . . . But since God, in Sacred Scripture, has spoken in a human way through human beings, the interpreter of Sacred Scripture—in order to grasp what God has wished to communicate to us—must carefully investigate what the sacred writers really intended to signify, and what it has pleased God to reveal to us in their words.[1]

This paragraph tries to walk a fine line between a more traditional under-standing of divine inspiration, which saw the authors of the Biblical books as passive instruments for communicating the thoughts of God, and a more modern, historical and critical approach to the Biblical text, which approaches these works first of all as human compositions, written by particular writers in particular circumstances that inevitably frame their range of possible meaning for future readers.

The long tradition of Christian theology, East and West, has regarded the books of the Bible, and the various layers and sections that make them up, as being the definitive norm for our understanding of who and what God is, and how God acts in our world. For thinkers of the Western Enlightenment, however, the very notion of a God, who is genuinely transcendent, actually communicating in direct, intelligible and specific terms with creatures, seemed awash in contradictions; there may be a transcendent first cause of beings in the world whom we call God, it was sometimes argued, but infor-mation is communicated to human minds through language, action, and symbol, all of which are enacted within history, by finite historical agents. This emphatically inner-worldly understanding of historical reality, and of how history is investigated and facts ascertained, still stands in the back-ground of the modern historical criticism of Biblical texts. Yet to many believ-ers today who read Biblical texts in a spirit of faith, simply seeking to reconstruct the circumstances and possible "original intention" of Biblical texts is not enough to let us discover their meaning as *Scripture*: their signifi-cance through the centuries, and today, for the community of faith.

To conceive of the works contained in the Bible—narrative, moral and ritual commands, praise and lament, wisdom teaching and theological reflec-tion—as embodying God's Word to humanity in more than simply a meta-phorical sense requires, first, an understanding of how God acts in the world that allows for him genuinely to sustain and steer human speech and action for his own purposes, without infringing on the full, conscious activity of human prophets, poets and redactors. And it implies, too, that the ideas expressed in Biblical books, or the events narrated by Biblical authors, may well take on new significance, beyond the "surface" meaning of fact or law, when received as Scripture by the community of faith in later generations. So to understand the Bible as the Word of God—to read it as Bible, and not simply as a collection of disparate religious texts of varying ages—the inter-preter needs to understand both God and the continuing meaning of human words: to be both a theologian and a linguistic, literary and historical scholar.

## I. Oral Traditions

For early Christian writers, in fact, it was clearly the understanding of Jewish faith in which they shared, the faith heard and professed in their Churches—centered on the conviction that God's promise to Abraham and God's covenant at Sinai had found their fulfillment in Jesus—which was the primary claimant to being the vehicle of God's saving revelation. Justin, for example, in his lengthy *Dialogue with Trypho* (written probably in Rome in the early 160s) makes relatively little direct reference to written documents about Christ,[2] although it is clear he is familiar with at least the sayings of Jesus recorded in the Synoptics. What he declares, in the dialogue's opening narrative, is that he has come to Christianity as a result of looking for the best available "philosophy," the way of life best suited to lead a person to happiness and hope.[3] Having been directed eventually to the Christian way, Justin is able to interpret the corpus of Israel's Scriptures as finding their true, if hitherto hidden, meaning in Jesus' life. Scripture, as written text, is for him the confirmation of a preached and lived message about who Jesus is.

Irenaeus of Lyons, writing his monumental treatise *Against the Heresies* some twenty-five years later, emphasizes that the disciples of Jesus first proclaimed the Gospel of salvation verbally (*praeconaverunt*), and only "afterwards, by the will of God, handed it down to us in written form (*in Scripturis*)."[4] As Irenaeus tells the story, Matthew wrote his Gospel text in Hebrew, while Peter and Paul were preaching the same Gospel orally in Rome; Mark, who was Peter's "interpreter," "handed on to us in writing what had been proclaimed by Peter," while Luke did the same for Paul's message.[5] The priority in the formation of the Christian message, in Irenaeus's view, clearly also lies with oral, rather than with written witness—the oral witness preserved in the living traditions of the Churches around the world through the leadership of the Twelve and their successors.[6]

> And if a discussion should arise on some issues of reasonable importance, should one not have recourse to the most ancient Churches, in which the Apostles were active, and take from them whatever is certain and substantially clear on the issue at hand? But what if the Apostles themselves had not left us written accounts (*scripturas*)? Should we not follow the order of tradition, which they entrusted to those to whom they gave responsibility for the Churches? Many peoples of those foreign tribes (*barbarorum*) who believe in Christ show their agreement with this arrangement: they have salvation written on their hearts, through the Spirit, without parchment or ink, and by carefully preserving the ancient tradition they believe in one God, maker of heaven and earth, and of all that is in them, through Christ Jesus, the Son of God . . .[7]

Irenaeus goes on to summarize the story of Jesus' life and death, and of his coming appearance as judge and savior, as it is contained in the "rule of faith," and concludes:

> Those who have come to profess this faith without written documents are, as far as our language is concerned, "barbarians," but as far as what they hold, and their customs and behavior, are thoroughly wise because

of their faith, and are pleasing to God, behaving in all righteousness and purity and wisdom. And if anyone were to announce to them, speaking in their own language, the things that have been fabricated by the heretics,[8] they would immediately block their ears and flee as far away as they could, not even enduring to hear such blasphemous talk.[9]

The final criterion for recognizing the authentic Christian message, in other words—the interpretation of the world and human history that is genuinely based on the teaching and works of Jesus—is not any written text in itself, for Irenaeus, but rather the tradition of faith, maintained in properly constituted communities of faith, in which the texts that summarize that tradition are received and understood. Those who have been trained in this tradition develop, in his view, an ability to recognize Christian teaching intuitively, simply on the basis of living it.

It was Origen, however, writing a generation after Irenaeus, who recognized that this very process of maintaining and recognizing the faith is more complicated than it sounds. Origen's life's work was principally the careful interpretation of the texts used by the mainstream Christian Churches as Scripture. In his time, this included both the generally accepted Hebrew canon, as contained in the Septuagint and its various corrected versions, and the four Gospels and Pauline corpus, which by this point had almost reached a canonical status parallel to that of Israel's Bible in the Christian Churches.[10] In his influential and comprehensive treatise *On First Principles*—a work which, as I have argued elsewhere, seems really to be an attempt to sketch out the foundations and methods of Christian Biblical interpretation[11]—Origen begins the preface with a clear affirmation that the source of saving wisdom for all Christians ought simply to be the written teaching of Scripture:

All who believe and are convinced that "grace and truth have come into being through Jesus Christ" (John 1.17) and recognize Jesus as the truth, according to his own saying, 'I am the truth,' receive the knowledge which invites men and women to live well and happily from no other source than from the very words and teaching of Christ. But by "the words of Christ" we mean not only those by which he taught when he had been made human and was placed in flesh; even before [his incarnation], after all, Christ the Word of God was in Moses and the prophets.[12]

The problem facing Christians, however, even in the third century, as Origen sees it, was not the availability of Scripture, but its correct interpretation. There were many Christian sects, many individual lines of understanding; everyone understood the Bible according to his or her prior assumptions about God and the world. What the community of believers needed was a set of criteria for making sense of the Bible itself, as the ultimate criterion of faith. He continues:

> Because, then, many of those who profess faith in Christ are in disagree-
> ment, not only in small, insignificant things, but even in large, very
> significant ones—for instance, on God or on the Lord Jesus Christ
> himself, or on the Holy Spirit; and not only on them but also on other
> creatures, that is, on the dominations and the holy powers—for this
> reason it seems necessary first to lay down a clear line and an obvious
> rule on these details, one by one, and then to ask also about the other
> things.[13]

For Origen, this "clear line and obvious rule" can only be found in actively
following Christ, and in understanding Christ in the way the Apostles have
taught the Churches:

> So since there are many who think they hold in their hearts what Christ
> holds—and some of them are of very different opinions from their fore-
> bears—yet the preaching of the Church is preserved, handed down
> through the order of succession from the Apostles and remaining in the
> Churches up to the present time, only that truth is to be believed that in
> no respect departs from the tradition of the Church and the Apostles.[14]

Concretely, this means that the "rule of faith," which is itself distilled from
Biblical teaching—the ancestor of what we think of as the great baptismal
creeds—is the community's common framework, within which the form of
Christian life and the meaning of individual Biblical passages can be discerned. The Bible is the originating norm, by which the rule of faith is first
formed; but the rule of faith—summarizing the Bible's teaching as a
whole—is in turn the interpretive norm, by which individual Scriptural
passages are understood consistently with the Bible's whole message.

So Origen sets out, in the first three books of this treatise, to explain the
details and implications of the Church's rule of faith. Going, not once but
twice, through the assertions of the common creed—the affirmation of faith
in a single, all-powerful God who has created all things from nothing in time;
faith in God's involvement in the history of salvation, as recounted in the
story of Israel, and in the mission of Jesus, his eternal Son, to bring that
history to fulfillment in his death and resurrection; faith in the role of the
Holy Spirit, who "shares in honor and dignity with the Father and the Son,"
inspiring the "saints, prophets and apostles" of Israel and the Church; faith in
the reality and moral freedom of the human soul, in the certainty of God's
judgment on human actions, in the promise of bodily resurrection, in the role
of other created spirits in our lives; and finally, faith in the divine origin and
spiritual character of the whole of Scripture, as received in the Church. All of
this, as teased out by Origen in the first three books of *On First Principles*,
enables him, by constantly interweaving and interpreting Biblical texts from
both Testaments, to reject the Gnostic understanding of Christian faith—
which saw the laws and practices of ancient Israel as overturned by the news

of redemption in Christ, and which rejected the importance of the material world and the body we live in, as the work of a lesser creator. It also allowed Origen to open the way for a more synthetic understanding of the Christian Scripture as a single whole. In the final book, he then lays out some principles for interpreting the Christian Scripture authentically, "spiritually," in a way that will let us hear God's Word as it really is and be assimilated to his "incorporeal" nature.[15]

## II. Interpretation and Theology

The heart of Christian interpretation of Scripture, obviously, is the realization that all of its books and layers, with their variety in age, message, and literary form, constitute a single book and tell a single story—a story that includes *us*, as disciples of Jesus today, and receivers of his Spirit. The center of the story, for the Christian, is Jesus himself: he is the norm by which the story of Israel is understood, the unexpected fulfillment who gives meaning to the promises made to Abraham; and it is the faith and history of Israel, conversely, that allowed his followers, in the confusing days after his resurrection and in the early decades of the Christian community, to interpret Jesus within God's history, and to discern both breaches and continuities in their own relationship with God's original elect. At the heart of such an understanding of the Scriptures, then, is an understanding of God—a *theologia*—that sees in Jesus the key to understanding the story of God's relationship to the world. Christian faith sees Jesus primarily as God's creative and revealing Word, eternally active in a mysteriously "personal" way, and now made flesh and raised from the dead.

Irenaeus, once again, is the first to articulate his understanding of divine revelation precisely in terms of an incipient sense that the mystery of Israel's God must be different—more complex within its radical monotheism, more inclusive in its relation to creation—from what previous generations of Jews or Christians had guessed, if Jesus is really to play the crucial role Christian believers attributed to him, as the final revealer of God and the agent of God's saving work in the world. Both creation and revelation are the work of God's "Word," his *Logos*, which the prologue to John presents precisely as the key to Jesus' personal identity. In a dense passage of Book IV of *Adversus Haereses*, which is centered precisely on the attempt to point out the continuity of God's saving history in both the story of Israel and the story of Jesus, Irenaeus builds on Matthew 11:25–27 to articulate Christianity's new sense of God's being:

> No one can know the Father without the Word of God—that is, unless the Son reveals him (Matt. 11.27)—nor can anyone know the Son without the approval of the Father. But the Son realizes the good will of the Father, for the Father sends, but the Son is sent and comes. . . . And for this reason

the Father has revealed the Son, that through him he might [himself] be manifested to all, and might rightly receive those who believe in him into incorruptible and everlasting comfort—for to believe in him is to do his will. . . . For the Father has revealed himself to all, by making his Word visible to all; and again, the Word has shown to all the Father and the Son, since he was seen by all. . . .

So through [the fact of] creation itself, the Word reveals God to be the Creator; and through the world, the Lord who has made the world. . . . Through the Law and the Prophets the Word proclaims at the same time both himself and the Father; and all the people have indeed heard in the same way, but all have not believed in the same way.[16] And through the Word, made visible and palpable, the Father has been shown forth; and even though all do not believe him in the same way, still all have seen the Father in the Son. For surely the Father is the invisible side of the Son, but the Son is the visible side of the Father (*invisibile etenim Filii Pater, visibile autem Patris Filius*). And for this reason, everyone spoke with Christ when he was present, and called him God. . . .[17]

What Irenaeus struggles to say here is that God's own Word is constantly active as God's mediator with the world of time and space: bringing into being God's designs, and articulating within those designs God's purpose of life and healing. In the person of Jesus, the Word made flesh, this active force within God's being has become audible and visible to us. Jesus' role, as Son and Word, is to make God accessible to the world—a role that includes the formation of matter and living beings, the communication of Scripture, and ultimately the reconciliation of a fallen humanity through the sacrifice of the Cross. To see a continuity between creation, revelation and salvation, all as coming from the God who is ultimate Reality, demands a distinctive notion of what God is. It is on this basis that Christian faith ultimately would speak of that God as Trinity.

## III. The Meaning of the Whole

Throughout the Patristic period, in both East and West, this sense of the unity of revelation and salvation as grounded in the complex, embracing unity of God grew to be a central assumption of Biblical interpretation—one not often articulated with full clarity, but clearly implied for the perceptive reader. The Church's strong rejection of Marcion, who refused to acknowledge the Hebrew Scriptures as pertinent to the Gospel of freedom in Christ, led to the growing sense within the mainstream community of a distinctively Christian canon of Biblical books—including the Hebrew canon and adding to it the Gospels and the letters of Paul—by the turn of the third century. It also led to the insistence of theologians like Irenaeus and Origen that the correct use of the Christian Scriptures both implies and requires a distinctive way of interpreting the Bible, beginning in the acknowledgement that Jesus is the final fulfillment of Israel's faith and hope. As so often is the case, however, it was really Augustine, two centuries later—Augustine as rhetorician, classical philosopher, pastor and preacher, and tireless reader of Scripture—who articulated most clearly and constantly this sense that the whole Bible, as Christians recognize and use it, is really about Christ.

In a dense and moving passage from his treatise on basic Christian instruction, for instance—the *De catechizandis rudibus*—written about 399 for an overworked Carthaginian deacon named Deogratias, Augustine emphasizes that Christian catechesis always is a matter of telling the full story spread out in all the books of the Bible, precisely as the proclamation of the Gospel of Christ:

> Indeed, everything we read in the holy Scriptures that was written before the coming of the Lord was written for the purpose of drawing attention to his coming and of prefiguring the future Church. That Church is the people of God throughout all the nations [i.e., not just Israel or the present community of the baptized]; it is his body, and also included in its number are all the faithful servants who lived in this world even before the Lord's coming, believing that he *would* come even as we believe that he *has* come.[18]

Augustine insists, in the pages that follow, that the only reason God has intervened in the history of fallen humanity, the only reason for the incarnation of the Word and the teaching and life of Jesus, is "that God intended to reveal his love among us, and to prove it with great force."[19] There is a kind of rhetoric, he suggests, implicit in the whole story of Israel and reaching its climax in the story of Jesus, which is intended to persuade humanity to love in return:

> Thus, before all else, Christ came so that people might learn how much God loves them, and might learn this, so that they would catch fire with love for him who first loved them, and so that they would also love their neighbor as he commanded and showed by his example—he who made himself their neighbor by loving them when they were not close to him but were wandering far from him. And all of the divine scripture that was written before the Lord's coming was written to announce that coming; and everything that has since been committed to writing and invested with divine authority tells of Christ, and calls to love. If this is so, then it is plain that on the two commandments of love for God and neighbor hinge not only the whole law and the prophets—the only holy scripture that existed when the Lord spoke these words—but also all the other books of divine writings which were later set apart for our salvation and handed down to us. Hence, in the Old Testament is concealed the New, and in the New Testament is revealed the Old.[20]

The message of the Bible is love, in Augustine's view: the astonishing news that we and our world exist because God loves us; the reminder that we have been called away from the idolatry and falsehood of self-love by God's ceaseless involvement of himself in the world; and the practical conclusion that therefore the only way to live well in the world is to love God above all things, and our neighbor as ourselves. To see this as the point of Scripture and of all the Church's preaching is to grasp also the unifying principle of correct Scriptural interpretation—the meaning of the whole that must shape and correct our attempts to make sense of every verse. Towards the end of Book I of *De Doctrina Christiana*, a broad but stunningly concise summary of the Church's moral and doctrinal teaching that sets the framework for effective Christian exegesis and preaching, Augustine expands on what we might call his "hermeneutic of love":

> So what all that has been said amounts to while we have been dealing with things [taught by Scripture], is that 'the fulfillment and the end of the law' and of all the divine Scriptures 'is love' (Rom 13.8; I Tim 1.5). . . . So in order that we might know how to do this and be able to, the whole ordering of time was arranged by divine providence for our salvation. This [sense of time] we should be making use of with a certain love and delight that is not, so to say, permanently settled in, but transitory, rather, and casual—like love and delight in a road, or in vehicles . . . , so that we love the means by which we are being carried along, on account of the goal to which we are being carried.[21]

As a result, Augustine here suggests a distinction between levels of correctness in Scriptural interpretation that appears throughout his own exegesis and preaching: between the attempt to find out the "original" meaning of any given passage, as intended by its human author and as we can identify it from what we know about the author's language, culture, and situation in history, and the more ambitious attempt to see this "micro-meaning" of a passage within the "macro-meaning" of the Scriptural narrative as a whole. Augustine continues:

> So if it seems to you that you have understood the divine Scriptures, or any part of them, in such a way that by this understanding you do not build up this twin love of God and neighbor, then you have not yet understood them. If on the other hand you have made judgments about them that are helpful for building up this love, but for all that have not said what the author you have been reading actually meant in that place, then your mistake is not pernicious, and you certainly cannot be accused of lying. . . . Any who understand a passage in the scriptures to mean something which the writer did not mean are mistaken, though the scriptures are not deceiving them. But all the same, as I had started to say, if they are mistaken in a judgment which is intended to build up charity,

which is 'the end of the law' (I Tim 1.5), they are mistaken in the same sort of way as people who go astray off the road, but still proceed by rough paths to the same place as the road was taking them to. Still, they must be put right, and shown how much more useful it is not to leave the road, in case they get into the habit of deviating from it, and are eventually driven to take the wrong direction altogether.[22]

The exegete in the Church must always make real efforts to identify what a given text was originally meant to say; but we can misunderstand passages in Scripture, in their humanly intended and even their inspired meaning, and still grasp the sense of the larger Biblical context, in which their meaning comes to fullness.

## IV. Multiple Meanings?

Augustine, in fact, along with a number of other great exegetes from early Christianity, seems to have been quite comfortable with the assumption that a given passage in Scripture might be capable of a number of different interpretations, all of which might be correct within the larger context of Scripture's overall message. Although determining the author's "original intention" is ideally the goal of exegesis when we are dealing with any passage, this may not always be possible to do with certainty, and the ecclesial preacher may sometimes be left with the alternative of allowing a generous pluralism. A classic example of this in Augustine's work is Book XII of his *Confessions*. Here, near the end of his great, experientially focused meditation on what it is to be a human being who yearns for God, Augustine turns his attention, in the last three books, to the first chapter of Genesis: a set of three guided reflections—sermons, perhaps—on the world of time and space, where human creatures must find the Creator. In Book XII, he is specifically trying to explain the relationship of Genesis's account of God's creation of "heaven and earth" (Gen. 1:1), as the dwelling place of living creatures, with the reference in Psalm 113:24 (Hebrew: Ps. 115:16) to "the heaven of heavens," which belongs to the Lord alone. With great ingenuity, Augustine argues that this special, highest part of creation could well be a world of intelligences and intelligible objects that is created, and so not eternal, but still free from the vicissitudes of matter and time, and always united with God in contemplation.[23] Yet he readily admits that there are a number of other, simpler interpretations of the Biblical language of "the heavens," all of which are plausible, yet none of which we can definitively assign to the original author.[24] Augustine concludes, with disarming frankness:

> What difficulty is it for me when these words can be interpreted in various ways, provided only that the interpretations are true? What difficulty is it for me, I say, if I understand the text in a way different from someone else, who understands the scriptural author in another sense?

In Bible study, all of us are trying to find and grasp the meaning of the author we are reading, and when we believe him to be revealing truth, we do not dare to think he said anything which we know or think to be incorrect. As long as each interpreter is *endeavoring* to find in the holy Scriptures the meaning of the author who wrote it [a crucially important condition!], what evil is it if an exegesis he gives is one shown to be true by you [i.e., God], light of all sincere souls, even if the author whom he is reading did *not* have that idea and, though he grasped a truth, had not discerned that seen by the interpreter?[25]

His point here is clearly *not* to say that any interpretation we assign to a text of Scripture is equally authentic, as long as it fits within the larger context of the Biblical narrative, as we understand it; it is simply that even if we assume the author was guided, in what he wrote, by the Holy Spirit, and that the Spirit's purpose is to guide us on the way of love—which is the way of Christ—we, as readers, may still legitimately disagree on how to read the details, yet still be in agreement about the guiding, overall message.

Assuming that the book of Genesis was authored by Moses, Augustine readily admits that he cannot say with certainty what Moses was thinking of when he laid out the steps of creation in the book's first chapter,[26] although he is convinced that Moses, too, intended to call his readers to obey the double commandment to love God and neighbor.[27] In fact, Augustine concludes,

Had I been Moses—had I been what he was, and had been commissioned by you to write the book of Genesis—I would have wished to be granted such skill in eloquence and facility of style that those unable to understand how God creates would not set aside the language as beyond their power to grasp; that those who had this ability and by reflection had attained to some true opinions would find in some terse words used by your servant that their true perceptions were not left out of account; and that if, in the light of the truth, another exegete saw a different meaning, that also would not be found absent from the meaning of the same words.[28]

## V. Some Principles

We have discussed here a few key passages from some of Christian antiquity's most celebrated interpreters of the Bible, to help us identify the main principles—fundamentally *theological* principles—those interpreters implicitly brought to bear on the text of Scripture, as they searched for its meaning. Let us now try to bring these principles together into a few simple theses, in the hope of discovering how the "spiritual" or "theological" exegesis they practiced might differ from the approach of modern historical and critical study.

1) They assumed that *the Bible is a single book*, with a single overall message, despite the great variety of authors represented in it. What makes it a single book is simply that it is accepted as such by the Church, in a canonical collection whose contents were not finally established, in East and West, until the mid-fourth century, but which in general outline was already widely recognized, in an implicit but operative way, by the end of the second. This included the Hebrew canon of Torah, prophets and "writings"—in Greek translation—that Christians came to call the "Old Testament," and the collection of Gospels, epistles, and the Book of Revelation they called the "New." By seeing this double set of works as a single, normative collection or book to be used within the life of the Church, by giving it a privileged position in liturgy and theological argument, and by making it—as a whole—the endless object of serious interpretation within the community, early Christian writers sought to find in their Scriptures a single, coherent message. This message may not always have been apparent, but they assumed it was there.

2) They assumed, too, that the object of Biblical interpretation was to discover *the truth about the world* we live in, and *about ourselves*. Truth, for ancient thinkers, was generally understood to be first of all a quality of language, insofar as it accurately reflected the situation in the world to which that language refers;[29] for Augustine, as for most Christian writers, the truth is not only "what is, being just as it appears to the one who knows,"[30] but also is grounded in the infinite reality of God, who is "eternal truth, and true love, and beloved eternity."[31] So to search for truth in the Bible was to seek what really is *so*, as it is rooted in God who is always *just so*, yet always beyond the grasp of language and ideas, and who Jews and Christians believe *speaks* the truth to us—in human language and idioms—in the Biblical texts. The Bible is about God, about the reality God has created, and about what God does in his creation, based on God's self-disclosure.

3) The early Christians were convinced that *Bible texts are "inspired,"* at least in the sense that God was purposefully at work in their composition. This is not immediately obvious in the Biblical texts themselves, however. In Book IV of *On First Principles*, Origen offers an indirect approach to recognizing the divinely inspired character of Scriptures: in seeing passages from the Hebrew Bible "fulfilled"—given a fullness of application beyond their original context—in the words and actions of Jesus, and in recognizing the impact and broad acceptance of Jesus' mission now throughout the world, one discovers that God is real, present, and at work in the whole process of Biblical narrative.

> Having demonstrated, in a concise way, the divinity of Jesus, and making use of the prophetic words about him, we have also shown that the writings that prophesy about him are inspired by God, and the writings that proclaim his coming and his teaching were set forth with full power

and authority, and therefore have taken hold of those chosen from among the nations. We must say that the *divine* element of the prophetic words and the spiritual part of the law of Moses came to light when Jesus was among us.[32]

Just as we only come to recognize the working of divine providence in human history retrospectively, and God's guidance is seldom evident in the moment when it is actually operating,[33] so the inspiration of Scripture—the fact that God is guiding human writers to speak his truth for the salvation of all peoples—is something that is only fully known in retrospect, when promises are fulfilled. The insight of Christian faith is that the focus of that fulfillment is *Jesus*, and with him the community of his disciples now gathered and led by his Holy Spirit.

4) The real *mystery* behind Scriptural meaning, for both the early Church and for exegetes today, is the mystery of *how God acts in the world*: how God can be seen as directing and guiding both natural events and human free acts, without eliminating either the laws of nature or full human intentionality. The world follows its inbuilt regularities, humans (and other spirits) freely determine their own acts, yet God is present in all these actions as ultimate cause, goal, and sustaining guide. Origen speaks, in the same fourth book of *De Principiis*, of the Holy Spirit's having "managed" (*ōkonomēsen*) the authorship of both the Old and the New Testament in such a way that both the truth needed by human beings to live well is eventually made sufficiently clear, and that enough "stumbling blocks"—inaccuracies, implausibilities—are left in the text to spur on the sensitive reader to seek a deeper meaning by reading those texts figurally.[34]

The real theological mystery, then, is again not simply the inspiration of Scripture but God's action in created history; and the challenge—as *Dei Verbum* suggests in the passage we quoted at the start—is to grasp that God's action is never a competitor with the natural activity of creatures, since it is God, as first cause of all things, who has given created natures the ability to function in the first place. In creating, understood as a constant active presence, God allows other beings to be what they are in fullness, and shapes and guides their activity without infringing on their proper, if limited, autonomy. In the language of medieval Western scholasticism, God's "primary" causality, as creator and first cause, almost never eliminates the functioning of the "secondary" causes he wills to be operative in nature; rather, God supports and steers those created causes in such a way that his will for the well-being of creation as a whole is achieved, while individual living beings continue to develop and work as genuine agents, using their own natural powers and even their own intelligence and freedom.[35] In terms of Biblical inspiration, this means that the Christian reader must take it for granted that the books we regard as constituting the Bible were freely written by human beings at various points in history, who used their own intelligence and languages and literary traditions to compose works that they believed represented, in some way, a part of God's story with humanity. The guidance of the Holy Spirit, which we call inspiration, means simply that God caused the whole complex and growing collection to form, first of all, the faith of the Jewish people in himself as creator and Lord, but also that the collection—enlarged by the documents that witness specifically to the early disciples' faith in Jesus— pointed, in the end, to Christ and the Church.

5) This multiplicity of authors and historical settings for the texts and works that make up the Christian Bible, all guided by God's loving purpose in a way that only gradually comes to light for believers, is really the reason that early Christian interpreters saw in the Bible not just a straightforward narrative (which, in large part, they assumed it was), but also *a "book of signs."* As history unfolds, the people faithful to God discover his plan of healing and salvation in ever-greater depth and detail, and—to their delight—find their own place within it. As this happens, they continually discover more about how God acts, and what his dealings with humanity really signify. So Jesus, on the road to Emmaus, gently upbraids two of his distraught disciples for not recognizing that God's word to Israel had been fulfilled in the events of his death and resurrection: "and beginning with Moses and all the proph- ets, he interpreted to them in all the Scriptures the things concerning himself" (Luke 24:27).

Within this understanding of what the Biblical text, as a continuous whole, can signify, the traditional Jewish and Christian practice of *figural interpreta- tion* makes, I think, perfect sense: not as a replacement for the careful attempts of ancient or contemporary scholars to establish what a text may have been understood to mean in its original context, or to discover what the author's or redactor's intent was in building the original elements into the text that we have, but rather as a way of seeing a text, or even a reported event or person, within the larger, specifically *Biblical* (and not simply the empiri- cally verifiable) context of *telling what God does.* Thomas Aquinas, in an article of the first question of his *Summa Theologiae*—the question where he reflects on the "science" of "sacred doctrine" and its sources—wonders aloud "whether in Holy Scripture a Word may have several senses." Acknowledg- ing the difficulties such an understanding of Biblical meaning presents to the discerning reader, Thomas nevertheless argues, with his usual common sense, that this is clearly possible, because *God* stands behind the human authors as the ultimate source of Scripture:

> The author of Holy Scripture is God, in whose power it is to signify his meaning, not by words only (as humans also can do), but also by things themselves. So, whereas in every other science [= logically ordered branch of human learning], things are signified by words, this science has the property that the *things* signified by the words have themselves also a signification. Therefore that first signification, whereby words

signify things, belongs to the first sense: the historical or literal. That signification whereby things signified by words have themselves also a signification is called the spiritual sense, which is based on the literal and presupposes it.[36]

Thomas goes on to subdivide this "spiritual sense" Christian interpreters find in Scripture into three kinds: what he calls "allegorical," which sees Old Testament passages as pointing not just to their own immediate objects but to Christ; the "moral" sense, which indicates for the Christian reader how he or she must live now; and the "anagogical" sense, pointing beyond the practicalities of Christian life now to a hope for the eschatological future. Still, if one sees the Bible as written not just by human authors but by God, who guides them, then all of these "spiritual" senses can themselves also be seen as "literal," in the context of the whole Bible, because all are providentially intended by God. They are all what the *real* author—the Holy Spirit—meant to say. So, alluding to *Confessions* 12, Thomas writes:

Since the literal sense is that which the author intends, and since the author of Holy Scripture is God, who by one act comprehends all things in his intellect, it is not unfitting, as Augustine says, if, even according to the literal sense, one word in Holy Scripture should have several senses.[37]

From God's perspective, in other words, all the signs that the faithful Christian reader finds in the pages of Scripture—signs in the Old Testament pointing to Jesus, signs in the New pointing to us and to our future—may well be understood as part of what the Bible, as intended by God, *really means*.

To be able to read the Bible responsibly as a book of living signs, without disregarding the importance of finding the original intent or historical context of any passage, demands of us first of all a deep sense of the reality of God, and a deep commitment to understanding the Bible as God's Word. This is what we mean, I think, by *theological* interpretation: we begin our approach to the text from what we know of God, in the hope that it will lead us still closer to him. This, too, is what it really means to read it not simply as a collection of texts reflecting various evolving stages of ancient Mediterranean literary and religious history, but as *the Bible*: a single book or canon, manifold in origin yet—for the Christian reader—generally homogeneous in message, the book that is as a whole the normative witness to faith.[38] And this, in turn, is why the figural interpretation of Scripture, in the traditional Christian sense, is always by definition a *theological* way of understanding texts, not simply a literary method.

In his great early work, *Catholicism*, the influential mid-twentieth-century Jesuit theologian Henri de Lubac draws a clear, if perhaps unexpected, connection between the universal, socially incarnate character of the Church and Patristic exegesis.

God acts in history and reveals himself through history. Or rather, God inserts himself in history and so bestows on it a 'religious consecration' which compels us to treat it with due respect. As a consequence, historical realities possess a profound sense, and are to be understood in a spiritual manner: *historika pneumatikōs;* conversely, spiritual realities appear in a constant state of flux and are to be understood historically: *pneumatika historikōs.* The Bible, which contains the revelation of salvation, contains, too, in its own way, the history of the world. In order to understand it, it is not enough to take note of the factual details it recounts, but there must also be an awareness of its concern for universality, in spite of its partial, schematic, and sometimes paradoxical mode of expression. It was in this way that the Bible was read by the Fathers of the Church. From Irenaeus to Augustine, by way of Clement of Alexandria and Eusebius, they all found in it a treatise on the history of the world. . . . If salvation is social in its essence, it follows that history is the necessary interpreter between God and humanity.[39]

To read Scripture figurally, as well as critically and analytically, is not to abandon a modern sense of the history in which we live, but simply to see history in greater depth, as having "spiritual" significance—as rooted in God's reality, coming forth from God, leading to God. It is to read history in faith, and to see faith as the key to understanding history's comprehensive meaning. Genuine faith is not an alternative to historical study or scientific explanation, but an awareness of the ultimate origin and purpose, the meaning beneath the surface, of the phenomena our empirical sciences investigate. So the world, as well as the Bible, can best be read both in its "literal sense" and as a book of signs, promising the community of faith both a deeper understanding of the reality around us, and "the assurance of things hoped for, the conviction of things not seen."[40] Christ, in whom God has finally spoken to us, after speaking through history "in many and various ways,"[41] offers us nothing less!

## NOTES

1  *Dei Verbum* 11.
2  See, however, *Apology* 1.66.3 and *Dialogue* 100.4, where he refers to the Gospels as *apomnē-moneumata* (written "memoirs") of the Apostles concerning Jesus.
3  For an argument that ancient philosophy was primarily understood by its practitioners as a way of asking questions and cultivating mental practices that led to a freer, more intentionally ethical form of life, see especially Pierre Hadot, *Philosophy as a Way of Life* (Oxford: Blackwell, 1995); *What is Ancient Philosophy?* (Cambridge, MA: Harvard University Press, 2002).
4  Irenaeus, *Adversus Haereses* 3.1.
5  *Ibid.*
6  *Ibid.* 3.3.1.
7  *Ibid.* 3.4.2.

8 Irenaeus is referring, of course, to the Christian "Gnostic" sects whom he is refuting here, such as the Valentinians, whose understanding of Jesus, and of the material world and the human person, is substantially different from that of the main body of Christian believers in his time, despite the fact that they, too, can claim to have written Gospels containing versions of the story of Jesus, on which to base their faith.

9 *Adv. Haer.* 3.4.2.

10 On the historical development of the Christian Scriptural canon, see Bruce M. Metzger, *The Canon of the New Testament: Its Origin, Development, and Significance* (Oxford: Oxford University Press, 1987); Lee M. McDonald, *The Formation of the Christian Biblical Canon* (Peabody, MA: Hendrickson, 1995). An older work, still valuable for its details, is Hans Freiherr von Campenhausen, *The Formation of the Christian Bible* (Philadelphia, PA: Fortress Press, 1972).

11 "Origen's *De Principiis*: A Guide to the 'Principles' of Christian Scriptural Interpretation," in John Petruccione (ed.), *Nova et Vetera: Patristic Studies in Honor of Thomas Patrick Halton* (Washington, DC: Catholic University of America Press, 1998), pp. 3–21.

12 Origen, *De Principiis* I, preface 1.

13 *Ibid.* preface 2.

14 *Ibid.*

15 See also my article, "Incorporeality and 'Divine Sensibility': the Importance of *De Principiis* 4.4 for Origen's Theology," *Studia Patristica*, Vol. 41 (2006), pp. 139–144.

16 See Rom. 10:16–18.

17 Irenaeus, *Adv. Haer.* 4.6.3; 4.6.5–6.

18 Augustine of Hippo, *De catechizandis rudibus* 3.6 (trans. Raymond Canning, *Instructing Beginners in Faith* [Hyde Park, NY: New City Press, 2006], p. 65).

19 *Ibid.* 4.7 (Canning, *Instructing Beginners in Faith*, p. 67).

20 *Ibid.* 4.8 (Canning, *Instructing Beginners in Faith*, p. 70).

21 *De Doctrina Christiana* 1.35.39 (trans. Edmund Hill, *Teaching Christianity* [Hyde Park, NY: New City, 1996], p. 123).

22 *Ibid.* 1.36.40 (Hill, *Teaching Christianity*, p.124).

23 *Confessions* 12.xv.19.

24 *Ibid.* 12.xv.22-xvii.26.

25 *Ibid.* 12.xviii.27 (italics mine).

26 *Ibid.* 12.xxiv.33.

27 *Ibid.* 12.xxv.35.

28 *Ibid.* 12.xxvi.36.

29 See, for instance, Aristotle, *De Interpretatione* 9 (19a33): "Since propositions are true in the same way that the facts (*ta pragmata*) are, it is clear that if things are in such a situation that whatever happens, the opposite is also possible, the denial will be equally necessary as the affirmation."

30 *Soliloquies* 2.5.8.

31 *Confessions* 7.10.16.

32 *De Principiis* 4.1.6.

33 *Ibid.* 4.1.7.

34 *Ibid.* 4.2.9. Cf. 4.2.7–8, where Origen makes clear his conviction that what the Spirit primarily was concerned to bring about, in the composition of Scripture, was an understanding of basic doctrine: about God, Christ and his work, rational natures, and the nature of evil. Since not everyone is equally capable of investigating and understanding these matters in depth, God has brought it about that the teaching of Scripture, since the beginning, has been "wrapped" in stories and laws that are, in themselves, often true and helpful, but that invite the more curious and determined readers to move beyond them and seek deeper doctrines.

35 See, for instance, Thomas Aquinas, *Summa Theologiae* I, q. 105, a.5, where Aquinas writes: ". . . the active powers which are seen to exist in things would be bestowed on things to no purpose, if these did nothing through them. Indeed, all things created would seem, in a way, to be purposeless if they lacked an operation proper to them; since the purpose of everything is its operation. . . . We must therefore understand that God works in things in such a manner that things have their proper operation."

36 Thomas Aquinas, *Summa Theologiae* I, q. 1, a.10 (trans. English Dominican Province [Westminster, MD: Christian Classics, 1911/1981], p. 7 [altered]).

37 *Ibid.*

38  See again Thomas Aquinas, *Summa Theologiae* I, q. 1, a. 8, resp. ad 2: "Sacred doctrine makes use of the authority of philosophers in those questions in which they were able to know the truth by natural reason. . . . Nevertheless, sacred doctrine makes use of these authorities as extrinsic and probable arguments; but properly uses the authority of the canonical Scriptures as an incontrovertible proof, and the authority of the doctors of the Church as one that may properly be used, yet merely as probable. For our faith rests upon the revelation made to the apostles and prophets, who wrote the canonical books, and not on the revelations (if any such there are) made to other teachers" (trans. English Dominican Province, p. 6 [altered]).

39  Henri de Lubac, *Catholicism: Christ and the Common Destiny of Man* (San Francisco, CA: Ignatius Press, 1988), pp. 165–166 (trans. altered).

40  Hebrews 11:1.

41  Cf. Hebrews 1:1–2.

## 2

# "THERE'S FIRE IN THAT RAIN": ON READING THE LETTER AND READING ALLEGORICALLY

## LEWIS AYRES

"Scripture [is] the medium in which the mind of the Church
has energized and developed."
                              Blessed John Henry Newman[1]

I offer this article as a complement to Brian Daley's "'In Many and Various
Ways': Towards a Theology of Theological Exegesis." I do this in part simply
because I agree with his main thrust: a Catholic vision of scripture and its
interpretation can always fruitfully return to its sources in the early Christian
period. The patristic vision of how God, through the Word, uses scripture to
draw us into the divine life should form the skeleton that gives shape to all
the flesh of subsequent reflection on scripture. But I also want to offer this
article as a complement, because I think there are a couple of further points
that can and should be made.

   At the heart of Brian's argument is an elegant reassertion of the Patristic
insistence that Christians read scripture as a unified story, and in the light of
the gospel as it is known in the life of the Church. In the course of expound-
ing this theme Brian also speaks powerfully of the relationship between
reading the text literally and reading the text spiritually. Scripture is a unity,
and a unity in the specific sense that it tells a consistent story of God's
action in history. Scripture tells a story in which God works in and through
the events of history and the choices of human beings, in and through a
world intended to signify its creator. Because scripture tells this story, and
because it points always forward to include us within that story, it seems to
follow naturally that Christians should read scripture as both a trustworthy

*Heaven on Earth?: Theological Interpretation in Ecumenical Dialogue*, First Edition.
Edited by Hans Boersma and Matthew Levering.
© 2013 Blackwell Publishing Ltd. Book compilation © 2013 Blackwell Publishing Ltd.

account of God's dealings with the cosmos, and as a world of signs. Thus Christians legitimately find signs in the Old that point toward Christ, and signs in the New that speak of our situation now. To attend to both literal and spiritual senses is to attend to what scripture's divine author intends, and thus to do so is not simply still a possibility for modern Christians, but a necessity.

My supplement to this argument will proceed primarily by suggesting that some rethinking of the manner in which we narrate the development of early Christian exegesis is necessary. I will suggest that re-conceiving the second-century adaptation of classical reading practices by Christians allows us to grasp with new clarity the character of what reading the letter of the text means for subsequent Patristic exegesis, and then allows us to see even more clearly why reading allegorically flows naturally from reading the letter of scripture. To be honest, I will have only a little to say about allegory *per se*, but by the end of the article why so much time needs to be spent achieving clarity about what it means to read literally should be clearer. I must also beg some indulgence as this represents something of an interim report on my main current research project, and I make a number of sweeping historical judgments here that will need much detailed proof at some future stage.[2]


*I*

In his article Brian Daley emphasized that it took Christians a good while to decide what it would mean for them to be a scriptural community. The most common example given to demonstrate the inseparability of Church and scripture in the first few centuries is the process by which the community of Christians gradually agreed on and authorized a canon of scripture, a list of books that would count as scripture.[3] My own interests are, however, not focused on the Church's developing sense of the canonical "list".

Indeed, I suspect that the process of "choosing" texts is frequently misunderstood. In a longer account, I would argue that by the 50s and 60s of the second century we can fairly suppose wide-spread assumptions concerning which Gospels could be read out in the liturgical assembly (though "suppose" should indicate that we deal only with matters of probability). There may have been some dispute in some places about the use of John, and there is at least one documented occasion on which a bishop allowed the reading of another text that would not make it into later canon lists alongside the inherited plurality of Gospels. But overall I think we have sufficient evidence to speak of a widely accepted tradition that a plural set of Gospels could be used in the liturgical assembly, and that this set was constituted by the synoptics and, in many places, also by John.[4] Thus, when we ask ourselves how were the Gospels "chosen" one of the best answers we can give begins with wariness about the concept of "choosing". I do not think we should imagine an act of "choosing" parallel to that made when we walk into a bookstore and pick from a large array of equally plausible possibilities. In the middle decades of the second century it seems better to think of Christians gradually distinguishing between the long used and plausible memoirs of the apostles, and other more recent and often localized texts.[5]

But, even if such an account is right, I have said nothing about one of the most important developments in the Christian community during the second century. Christians became the scriptural community that they did not merely by choosing books and marking distinctions between those books and others, but also by choosing to *use and read* those books in a certain way, by means of certain reading practices. It is *this* act of choosing that is my concern here. To understand the sort of practices to which I refer, consider briefly the fourth century. One condition of possibility for the famous Trinitarian controversies of that century was a set of reading practices that disputants on all sides applied to both Old and New Testaments. Some examples of such practices include: careful attention to whose voice a given section of text should be understood to represent; close attention to patterns of word use and expression within the text of scripture (or in a particular scriptural author or text); close comparison of phrases and titles taken to be parallel and mutually illuminating; close attention to common tropes used by an author; etymological analysis of names; explanations of possible meanings of terms by the use of contemporary scientific and philosophical material. Such exegetical practices are not only the foundation for doctrinal controversy, but for the reading of scripture toward almost all ends. Note that many of these reading practices assume that a text should be interpreted where possible from within its own resources. When these methods are applied to a set of texts they can only have the force of pressing the need for clear distinctions between that set and other texts and sets; it is thus that these reading practices may also have formed a significant extra pressure toward the adoption of a clear canonical list.

These reading practices were accompanied by a series of assumptions about how the text of scripture revealed and yet remained sometimes mysterious. To describe how Christians in the fourth century were scriptural we need not only to note *that* they valued and argued over a particular set of texts, but also to describe the particular reading practices they used and the assumptions about the text to which they held. Such practices and assumptions played a fundamental role in constituting a set of texts as "scripture". But these practices and assumptions were not self-evident, nor were they fundamental for the earliest Christian writers. (I return to the differences between these practices and those we find in the earliest Christian authors a little later in the article.)

If, then, we are to understand the history and character of Christian exegesis, we need to see how the Church developed these shared practices and assumptions. Allow me to take some space to sketch that story before reflecting doctrinally upon it. The story that I will tell concerns the gradual adoption by Christians of reading practices developed in ancient Greek and Latin traditions of literary commentary.[6]

My story begins, possibly in Rome, and probably in the 150s and 160s. These decades saw the appearance of texts written by writers in the Valentinian tradition and commenting on texts of the New Testament.[7] "Valentinianism" has frequently in modern scholarship been considered as a species of the wider genus "Gnosticism".[8] Scholarship of the past thirty years has, however, offered an extensive discussion of whether it is possible or useful to unify a diverse set of texts and movements under this latter term. For our purposes I do not need to offer a wide-ranging judgment about these debates, only to state that I still think it possible to speak of a Valentinian tradition or school in the second half of the fourth century, for whom Valentinus was a central and originating figure, however one conceives the relationship between this tradition and the others that have frequently been grouped under the title "Gnostic". Valentinus himself seems to have commented in various ways upon texts that would be incorporated into the emerging scriptural canon, but it seems to be only with his successors that we see the appearance of commentaries that take form as a detailed and dense analysis of grammar and styles of expression, and do so in order to argue that the texts they consider must be read as fundamentally enigmatic or parabolic discourse.[9]

To understand the character of Valentinian interest in the parabolic it is worth bearing in mind that the first two centuries of the Christian era saw the decline of Stoic traditions of allegory and the gradual rise of accounts of the allegorical and enigmatic that emphasized its role in shaping and reforming the intellect toward the divine. Stoic allegorical practice had focused on reading the poets as speaking of metaphysical realities rather than of the Gods that are frequently mentioned in the letter of the text. In the first couple of centuries AD, authors as diverse as Cicero and Plutarch criticize Stoic allegory as implausible and virtually blasphemous in its atheism.[10] In criticizing Stoic allegory as implausible such authors could draw on a long tradition of literary criticism suspicious of the allegorical—a tradition honed in Hellenistic Alexandria and perhaps drawing inspiration from Aristotle, *Poetics* 25.[11] And yet, this criticism of Stoic allegory could be accompanied by a celebration of the allegorical as an acceptable practice when used to uncover the symbolic structure of religious texts and practices. Thus Plutarch provides us with both an excellent witness to critiques of Stoic allegory in his *How The Young Should Study Poetry,* and to a reconstructed pious allegory in his *On Isis and Osiris.* This latter tradition is then the precursor to the more well-known Neo-platonic tradition that would be such a prominent feature from Porphyry onward.[12]

The Valentinian exegetes that are our concern here wrote within this transitional period. It is, however, vital to note that styles of reading which treat texts as parabolic or enigmatic (and these terms were far more prominent until the second century than "allegory") were supported by the use of many of the same techniques of classical literary commentary that we see in non- or anti-allegorical tradition. In a manner that reflects a well-established tradition, Valentinian exegetes of the supposedly enigmatic justify their readings in part by using techniques of literary analysis to show that an author's patterns of speech, ambiguities of expression and word order, leave a trail that the educated and discerning may follow into the teaching lying beyond the actual words. It is thus that the New Testament texts are taken to provide clues that they point toward those truths Jesus taught directly only in private (and further warrant for such a vision is found in such texts as Matt. 13. 10–17 and Mark 4. 33–34[13]). That fuller truth may then be sketched by references to the texts and teaching of Valentinian faith. Thus, just as generations of allegorical interpreters had done before them, these Valentinian exegetes tried to claim the cultural capital of ancient literary commentary as warrant for their vision of the Savior's higher teaching.

It is in response to this particular current of Valentinian exegesis that we see Christian exegetes developing the foundations for the Classical patristic exegesis of the fourth and fifth centuries. I include in this anti-Valentinian group Irenaeus, Clement of Alexandria, Origen, Tertullian and many texts of the Hippolytan corpus. In the small amount of space available here, I want to focus on Irenaeus, who, I would in any case argue, represents a fundamental turning point. At the beginning of his *Against Heresies* Ireaneus's expressed concern is with precisely these figures. He culminates his account of his opponents' system with a tirade against their attempts to interpret the scriptures in line with their beliefs, which Irenaeus sees as fundamentally drawn from other textual sources. He quotes a fairly extensive example to prove his point, and the example is of a Valentinian commentary to John's prologue. Valentinian scriptural exegesis thus seems to be at the heart of what he seeks to controvert—not simply Valentinian doctrine.[14]

Some features of Irenaeus's response are well known: a call for interpretation to occur within the context of the publically attested and apostolic rule of faith, a call for interpretation of any given passage to occur within the context of the overall plot or *hypothesis* of scripture.[15] But it is important to understand that these prescriptions are part of a wider strategy. Irenaeus frequently claims that the meaning of the text is "clear", and he then performs this clarity by applying some of the basic tools of literary critical analysis to show the meaning apparent in the letter of the text. Time and again Irenaeus suggests his opponents do not know how to punctuate a sentence, how to identify in whose person a particular text is spoken, how to interpret a term by its use elsewhere in scripture, how to recognize a figure of speech or a quirk of personal style, or how to read a statement in its immediate context (and in this last sense he is as much concerned with the importance of identifying the *hypothesis* of passages within which individual sayings and statements are located, as he is with the one *hypothesis* of the Bible as a whole).[16] Irenaeus thus participates in the tradition of anti-allegorical rhetoric and performs the fact that the scriptural text provides on its face keys to its interpretation. This is to reclaim the cultural capital of ancient literary critical techniques for the anti-Valentinian project of those many scholars frequently term the "proto-orthodox".

But Irenaeus (and those who followed in his wake) did not simply *adopt* this tradition of commentary, they also *adapted* it to suit their own theological needs. This adaptation is visible in particular in the prominence given a particular set of literary tools, and the frequency with which they are used to demonstrate the unified teaching of the scripture. Some general observations are here possible, although it requires extensive justification in the future. If one looks at surviving commentaries by non-Christian authors of the period, while it is easy to see a range of similar literary critical techniques used to those we find in Irenaeus (to continue with this one example), non-Christian commentary often focuses far more on piecemeal observation than on the performance of the unity of the scriptures that we find in the Bishop of Lyons. The observation must, of course, be made with great care because Irenaeus is not writing in a formal commentary genre. Nevertheless, it is fairly clear that Irenaeus gives prominence to those techniques that will serve his end of showing that the scriptures tell a unified and consistent story whose basic meaning is "clear". Thus clarity about the *hypothesis* of passages, and about the flow of the words of a given passage, is frequently used against piecemeal exegesis of particular sayings or phrases. Similarly, Irenaeus insists that we best understand the number and inter-relationship of divine realities by attending to the patterns of predication (especially of the terms "God" and "Lord"[17]) that we find through scripture as a whole. To give a last example, we might note that Irenaeus's emphasis on interpreting numbers and possible numeric symbolism by reference to well-established symbolic and harmonic patterns, and on interpreting parables by reference to other clear statements in scripture, has the effect of emphasizing the whole "surface" of the text as the key to its meaning.[18] At the same time, for example, we do not find him using text-critical skills to excise problematic texts, and we very rarely find him making use of extra-canonical textual evidence to fill out his account of Christ's teaching (although such material is certainly used throughout the period in offering accounts of where, how and why Gospel writers wrote). Thus, we see emerging a set of concerns and practices that not only assert but also perform the unity of the text.

It may help to forestall an obvious question if I note at this point that appropriating an anti-allegorical tradition of literary criticism did not mean that allegory was eschewed by Christian writers. Anyone possessing even a brief acquaintance with the exegesis of Clement of Alexandria or Origen knows this to be so, but the peculiarity of Christian allegory as developing within the context of an exegesis that saw the plain meaning of the letter as foundational has not been sufficiently considered. Thus, to provide one example, at one point in the fifth book of the *Stromateis*—often taken to be a defense of the esoteric inimical to the sort of exegetical project we find in Irenaeus—Clement uses his variant of Ps. 77:1–2 to assert "hear, my people, my law, incline your ear to the words of my mouth. I will open my mouth in parables, I will speak my riddles from the beginning." But in the following discussion Clement insists that there are actually only two types of enigma in scripture, prophetic enigmas revealed in Christ, and enigmatic references to that which constitutes the higher faith or knowledge in Christ.[19] This attempt follows on from a number of assertions that Christian thought is founded on the faith given to us through the scripture that God has spoken—and from many examples in which Clement uses the same techniques as Irenaeus to counter Valentinian exegesis.[20] Thus, even from these initial comments it should be clear how one might plausibly argue that Christian "spiritual" exegesis develops inseparably with Christian emphasis on close attention to the letter of the text as foundational.

We must, for a moment, take a step back in time. At one level the techniques that figure so strongly in his anti-Valentinian polemic are not first used by Irenaeus. In many ways that honour may go to a figure Irenaeus knew personally and on whom he drew—Justin Martyr. And yet, noting the manner in which Irenaeus innovates will reinforce the argument I have made so far. When he is discussing texts from the Hebrew scriptures Justin makes use of classical literary critical techniques a number of times—asking, for example, who is speaking in a particular passage as a way of emphasizing that the *Logos* is presented as a distinct divine agent.[21] And yet, only very rarely does Justin ever subject the sayings of Jesus he quotes from what he terms the "memoirs of the apostles" to close textual analysis. For Justin the texts that will come to form the canon of the "New Testament" are only coming to be treated as parallel to the texts of the Jewish scriptures. Irenaeus thus innovates because he treats Old and New Testaments as two sections of a unified body of texts, to be read and analyzed by the same close methods. From one perspective the rise of those methods may be seen as the inevitable result of textual arguments among those who value the same literary culture. And yet the timing and form of that rise results from the particular challenges raised by dispute over Valentinian readings.

If reflection on the difference between the exegesis of Justin and Irenaeus helps to make clear the character of Irenaeus's innovation, comment on the distinction between both and exegesis in the period between the first Christians and 150 will help to make clear the character of the continuity that identifying this innovation should not mask. If we take as examples two representative pieces of Christian exegesis from this very early period, Hebrews 1–4 and 2 Clement, we find some common features that can be paralleled in Irenaeus. The authors of these texts at a number of points quote scriptural texts and then offer short explanations; they also parallel texts from different places in order to illuminate. But in neither case is it possible to identify with clarity any particular technical terminology and thus to be clear how we might relate these exegetical styles to prior Greek or Hebrew literary traditions. Neither text makes a self-conscious claim on the cultural capital of a particular exegetical school or tradition. Thus, there is both a clear distinction between the self-conscious techniques of Irenaeus—especially in his extension of those techniques to the body of the "New" Testament—and the earlier more inchoate exegesis of the Jewish scriptures; yet there is also a basic continuity. In the same way, that earlier exegesis takes form also as an explanation of how prophecy is fulfilled in Christ, even if the unity of the two covenants is not yet placed in the foreground as it will be in and subsequent to anti-"Gnostic" polemic.

I have focused on Irenaeus for the sake of space. But let me note at the end of this section that these practices soon become the standard way of opposing Valentinians and indeed, Gnostics of all forms. Moreover, these practices become the standard fare of doctrinal definition and argument through the centuries that follow: the creeds and definitions of later centuries, as well as many of the texts that become central to later Christian liturgy, are constructed by means of these tools.[22] The prominence of these reading practices is seen in Irenaeus's contemporary, Clement of Alexandria, and then in the writers of the following generation: in Origen, Tertullian and in the Hipploytan corpus. I do not think, however, that these later writers simply copied Irenaeus. Many of them knew these techniques—especially as they were developed in the higher study of rhetoric and philosophy—even better than Irenaeus (Origen is paradigmatic here). Thus there is both a certain inevitability about the adoption of classical reading practices by Christians, and yet a contingent quality; the adaptation of those practices occurred because of a particular doctrinal context. Indeed, had we more time it would be important to note how similarly these authors adapt these practices—in large part, perhaps, because of seeking to serve common ends, in small part because of mutual awareness of each other's work.[23]

Some of the ways in which I envisage this article as a complement to Brian Daley's article should now be apparent. Classical patristic exegesis indeed insists that we read the scripture as a whole and in the light of the Church's faith. To make further progress we need to see that those who emphasized the importance of reading the scriptures as whole also argued for the reading practices I have explored here as the best means of performing that overall unity. The adaptation of these reading practices was not an act extrinsic to the Christian community's gradual acceptance of a canon of scriptural texts, but an intrinsic one that both influenced that acceptance and shaped how that text would be seen as revelatory.

In this regard, it is worth reminding ourselves how the literal reading practices Irenaeus shapes overlap but are not identical with modern historicist notions of the literal sense.[24] One reason why Irenaeus claims that the scriptures are not all to be interpreted as enigmatic discourse is that he thinks the basic story they tell to be historically real. Similarly he thinks that the claims that the scriptures make about the structure of things are on their face true. But belief in the historicity and basic truthfulness of the letter is accompanied by belief that the text is publicly handed down by divine providence and stands as the source of our basic doctrine (in both senses of the Latin *doctrina*), needing only the application of literary techniques that foreground "the way the words run". For Irenaeus, our basic faith and deeper understanding of what God accomplished in Christ stems not only from our participation in a public ecclesial body that is continuous with the apostolic community, and from our confession of a "rule" that has been handed down, but also from our participation in a certain kind of textual interrogation—and from our acceptance that we are shaped by the character of the text's speech and refusal to speak.[25] When Brian Daley speaks of Christians treating scripture as a world of signs pointing back toward the prophetic structure of Israel and forward to our own day, it is this textual culture, as it developed in a number of forms between Irenaeus and the fourth and fifth centuries, that was the means of entering and being shaped by that world of signs.

## II

At this point I want to pause from my historical story to offer a few brief doctrinal comments on the process I have described. How might my account of the development of the Church's own notion of the literal sense affect the manner in which we theologically describe the Father using scripture to draw us—and the manner in which we conceive of the practice of scriptural interpretation in the twenty-first century?

In his article, Kevin Vanhoozer draws attention to the recent writing of John Webster on the relationship between scripture and Church, and I will do likewise.[26] When Webster carefully separates the authority of scripture from the Church he does so expressly in order to preserve God's freedom in action. For him, to emphasize the role of the historical community of Christians in forming the canonical scripture is to undercut the true relationship between God's giving of the canon and the church's acknowledgment and reception of that divine gift.[27]

Two comments suggest themselves in response. The first is to reiterate a point made by Daley. To see the Church as *given* its ability to distinguish the canon of scripture from other texts that might have been included, may be understood as God's gracious giving to humanity of free and appropriate actions that serve the unity of the body of Christ as a faithful, contemplative and speculative community. Viewing the actions of those drawn into the body of Christ as necessarily in competition with the "direct" action of God, is not a road we need travel if we also have an account of redemption in which human beings are drawn by grace into true freedom. My second comment is that the very project of separating so clearly the gift of scripture and human recognition of that gift becomes much more complex once one recognizes that scripture grew more and more fully into being what we may call classically scripture not simply when it was "recognized" but when the Church learned how it was to be read. Church and scripture once again become deeply interwoven.

While these comments certainly suggest some of the questions I have about some Reformed ways of relating scripture and church, they betray only a little of how I would approach the theological questions raised by the historical account I have suggested. Some progress may, I hope, be made by pointing to the debates among Catholic theologians writing at the time of the Second Vatican Council and attempting to describe the inter-relationship between scripture and tradition. Congar's extensive treatment of tradition is one of the great monuments to this project, but for me some of the most promising if inchoate suggestions of the period are in two early essays by the young Ratzinger.[28] For my argument here I will note only two themes of his argument. In the first place, Ratzinger argues for the importance of understanding the structure of God's revelation as a speaking, as a word that does not return empty-handed because it is a word that, in the Spirit, always also calls forth a response. The depths and meaning of the Word spoken by the Father are seen in the response that comes forth, but there is no sense here of the Word passing somehow under human control—not because those who respond are puppets in the hands of the divine—but because the nature of divine action brings about our free actions. Expanding a little on what Ratzinger himself says there, the "response" brought forth by the Word is also an act of proclamation. The act of proclamation is from one perspective an act of distillation, identifying the core of the gospel message. To distill is also, I suspect, to witness that the present time is within, governed by, the time of the gospel. It is to link this time with the time between Ascension and Eschaton, and thus this response is also a testifying and witness to the living reality of God's redemptive action in Christ.

In the second place, Ratzinger attempts to root this theme in a nuanced account of the character of tradition's presence in scripture itself. The New Testament's proclamation of the gospel, Ratzinger suggests, always points in two directions at the same time. On the one hand, the text proclaims by interpreting the Old Testament as pointing toward the event of Christ. On the other hand, the text proclaims Christ himself and the Spirit living among us; the text proclaims the living reality of Christ's body. Ratzinger then argues that his proclamation of Christ's work among us has a particular form following from the apostles' recognition that their expectations of converting the Jews and hastening the Kingdom were being transformed through the Spirit's work. In Acts 15, for Ratzinger, we see the culmination of a process begun after Christ's resurrection. The assembled "council" in Jerusalem listens to Paul and Barnabas recounting what "signs and wonders God has done through them among the Gentiles" (Acts 15:12); James's response is to quote the prophecy in Amos 9 of the rebuilt temple inspiring the Gentiles to seek the Lord, and to suggest a strict limitation on those things demanded of Gentile converts. In these events, the prophets are interpreted in the light of Christ's work in his body, but in so doing the beginning of the Church as a phenomenon beyond the bounds of Israel begins to be announced. To proclaim the fulfillment of the prophets now becomes an act of pointing to the living reality of Christ's body, not simply to the Christ who has risen and ascended.

This reinterpretation of the gospel as addressed to all beyond the bounds of Israel is what Ratzinger calls an "ecclesial interpretation of the New Testament", and at this point he offers a summary of four different layers in the material form of revelation. In the first place, there is "an Old Testament theology of the Old Testament"; the historian may ascertain layers of interpretation that are constitutive of a developing structure. In the second place, there is "a New Testament theology of the Old Testament" by which phrase Ratzinger refers to the original layers of Christ's own interpretation of himself in the light of the Old. In third place, there is "a New Testament theology of the New Testament", which is also constituted by layers of commentary and reinterpretation of earlier layers of the gospel, culminating in the ecclesial reinterpretations that we mentioned in the case of Acts 15. In reality, the middle two "theologies" merge into each other, creating a series of layered interpretations prompted by growing awareness of the true quality and expansiveness of Christ's mission.

Lastly, in fourth place, there is "an ecclesial theology of the New Testament, which we call dogmatics."[29] Following one of the fundamental lines of his essay, Ratzinger argues that just as the New Testament theology of the Old involves a reading of the Old and yet also radical newness, continuing the internal trajectories of the Old but not in a predictable manner, so the ecclesial theology of the New is the continuation of dynamics and trajectories begun in the New Testament itself, and yet not always in obviously predictable ways. The parallel between the New Testament theology of the Old and this ecclesial theology of the New is possible for Ratzinger because of his insistence that this ecclesial theology occurs through the Spirit's work in the body of Christ. That link may be seen here in his further comment that properly speaking only dogma should be identified with this "ecclesial theology".[30]

Thus receiving the Word and proclaiming our response may be understood not only as an act of submission before the canon as dogmatic fact, but also by accepting that one belongs to a community, a body whose reception and answer—in the form of the Church's dogma, the lives of the saints, and the history of biblical interpretation—is the work of the Spirit within Christ's body. Within such a perspective we may (and perhaps must) read doctrinally not only the establishment of the canon *per se*, but also the emergence of those practices and patterns of reading that made scripture scripture in the second century and beyond, and which were the work of the Spirit enabling the body of Christ to grasp the character of our knowing and not knowing the divine. It is this process that formed the context and condition of possibility for the emergence of the foundational creeds and conciliar statements of the fourth through the eighth centuries.[31]

Now, on the one hand, I have made some strong claims for a specific understanding of reading the letter of scripture being intrinsic to early Christianity's scriptural culture, and consequently as a central part of any subsequent theological interpretation. But, on the other hand, I would be misunderstood quite seriously if I were thought to be implying a complete antipathy between this manner of reading and modern historical-critical modes. Modern modes of biblical study are highly diverse and no global judgment should be made. In some cases modern concerns can directly help enhance what the Church has long done: it is no accident that concern to identify literary forms and genre has long been identified as a central feature of a modern Catholic biblical study. There is much in such an emphasis that resonates with an exegesis founded upon the modes of reading that the Church adapted from ancient literary techniques.

At the same time, concern with interpreting texts in the contexts of their production and first hearing can help open a discursive theological space between the speaking of the Word in the first century and the penetration of its mysteries as responses to the Word are shaped by the work of Son and Spirit over subsequent centuries. Thus historical reconstruction of how scriptural texts were heard in the first century may help us to see the process of Word and response at work, and this may be a real gain in our understanding even as texts must also be read in the light of the Church's being led by the Spirit.[32] In some cases this discursive space may enable us to discuss the emergence of a defined interpretation from a context of ambiguity (clear continuity and/or clear difference may emerge in such a conversation). In other cases, seeing historical change and continuity in interpretation, in the light of new appreciation of original contexts, may help to suggest new interpretations. This is to suggest only two from among many types of conversation one can envisage; through all of course runs the need to accept that scriptural texts are fruitfully the subject of a plurality of meanings, and the need to accept the close relationship between Church and exegesis. Through all, also, will run the need for a careful conversation about the philosophical and theological commitments of the exegete. I make these rather gnomic points only to suggest possible lines of conversation for the future.[33]

*III*

I have now offered both a brief historical sketch of how the Church's own literal sense emerged, and some doctrinal reflections on this emergence. At the end of this article I would like to turn very briefly to a third topic, the relationship between interpretation and ascent into the mysteries of Christ. Again as a complement to Brian Daley's article, I will note further aspects of his argument that there is an intrinsic link between reading the letter of scripture as a whole, and reading scripture in ways that emphasize how every part may help us enter into the depths of the mystery of Christ.

In the story that I have told the complex structure of mature Patristic exegesis grows from an earlier and more basic form with which it shows clear lines of continuity. At the core of that continuity lies the relationship between Christ as the fulfillment of prophecy and textual interpretation as a fundamental structure of thought. Much of the earliest Christian exegesis takes the form of demonstrating and exploring ways in which Christ (and the Spirit who follows him) fulfills the prophetic structure of Israel's scripture. The necessity of scriptural interpretation to Christianity if fulfillment is to be shown finds its counterpart in the newness and surprising character of the manner in which Christ fulfills. Under the power of the Spirit, the developing proclamation of the Church gradually came to treat the texts that formed the core of the New Testament as also the subject of a detailed textual exegesis. This shift embodied a fundamental continuity because the fount of exegesis remained the confession of the continued work of Christ and Spirit. Exegesis of Israel's prophecy involved not only showing how the life of Christ fulfilled that prophecy, but showing how the resurrected, ascended and yet constantly present Christ (and his Spirit) fulfilled. And thus exploring the manner in which Christ fulfills intrinsically involves using that prophetic material to describe the character and progress of life in Christ. There is, then, a sense in which however one narrates the rise of different forms of allegorical reading and assesses their relative strengths and weaknesses, we deal here with a form of scriptural exegesis that is intrinsic to the very life of Christianity as a confessing and interpreting community.[34]

Let me point to one example of a text illustrating this point, the *Epistle of Barnabas*, a text probably dating from the first two decades of the second century.[35] The letter claims not only that Christ, the master, has fulfilled the prophets, but that he speaks through them directly to us, foretelling what has now happened and giving us a foretaste of the eschaton. We see here a lovely example of the insistence on the significance of the text and yet also on the text being significant because of the presence of the living Christ in the Church. As Christians, Christ's fulfillment of prophecy is a tenet of our faith and it is, for *Barnabas*, our consequent task to search the prophets as an offering to God, and in order to shape our faith, righteousness and love.[36]

In the body of the letter Barnabas performs for us the search he encourages. In many cases he turns to material well known: he interweaves, for example, sections of Isaiah 50, Psalms 22 and 118 to tease out how Christ fulfills and is established as a rock and cornerstone in his suffering for us.[37] These connections flow easily from the New Testament's own usage, but push beyond the precise connections found there. At times Barnabas turns also to material that will help us understand the character of the faithful life that Christ shapes for us. He asks, for example, what Moses the prophet means by speaking of the land of milk and honey in Exodus 33. Moses, he suggests, offers a "parable of the Lord" that refers to our gradual nourishment by faith and then by the Word directly when we are perfected:

> Why then does he say "Into the good land, a land flowing with milk and honey?" Blessed is our Lord, brothers, who placed the wisdom and knowledge of his secrets within us. For the prophet is speaking a parable of the Lord. Who will understand it, except the one who is wise and learned, who loves his Lord? Since, then, he renewed us through the forgiveness of our sins, he made us into a different type of person, that we might have the soul of children, as if he were indeed forming us all over again.[38]

For Barnabas, Christ lives and works in the Church leading us to ever-greater understanding. Through the experience of that life within the Christian community Barnabas hazards the interpretation that we can take the reference to our movement toward a land of milk and honey as a reference to the process and goal of our transformation in Christ. But note that this is no simple case of "experience" enabling an imaginative reading of text; the life from which Barnabas interprets is already one described in biblical terms as one of forgiveness, one of a new childhood, one described in relationship to the dynamic between creation and new creation. Thus the interpretation of the Jewish scriptures as fulfilled in Christ both seamlessly draws us also to see our own Christian life in those prophetic texts, and we undertake that reading within the circle of a life in Christ already being described and explored in scriptural terms.

Barnabas's vocabulary for the interpretations he offers varies. He speaks of types, he speaks of parables and he speaks frequently of interpreting a text "in the Spirit". Barnabas wrote long before the battle against Valentinian exegesis led to the emergence of a new clarity about the Church's own methods of reading, and long before Clement and Origen offered more technical reflection on the relationship between literal and allegorical reading practices. But the links he demonstrates show how naturally those later reading practices flow out of a well-established set of theological links between confessing the living voice of Christ in the Church and reading the Jewish scriptures as speaking of the Christian life. Those links form the foundations for the complex later traditions of allegorical reading that will emerge as Christian exegetical culture develops and grows.

Connections between the first and third sections of this article thus emerge, and may perhaps be summarized thus. If we are to understand the scope of theological interpretation—and the nature of "spiritual" exegesis—we must first get straight the character of the literal reading with which it is intertwined. What it means to speak of the "letter" of scripture is shaped in part by the methods one thinks appropriate in the task of elucidating it, and during the late second century the Church adapted a set of reading practices drawn from existing literary-critical traditions in opposition to Valentinian exegetes. It was this adaptation that founded the classical Patristic exegesis we have come to value again in recent years. At the heart of this style of scriptural reading beats a relationship between reading the scriptural canon as one whole in which Christ fulfills and reveals the meaning of prophecy, and assuming that one best performs this wholeness and explores the resources of scripture by the application of close grammatical reading practices to the details of the text as it is given to us.

This is a development that follows on from the earliest Christians' emphasis on seeing their experience of the risen and ascended Christ (and the given Spirit) as the context for and guide to understanding ever more closely how Israel's prophecy has been fulfilled, and how the teachings of Jesus are now to be interpreted. But during the second century the Spirit led the Church to a new role for those texts that became the "New Testament"; engagement with their details in the light of the publicly professed gospel gradually formed Christian argument, teaching and worship. As I have suggested in the second part of the article, this process is one that we must also read theologically, and it is one we can read in such a way as to open a fruitful dialogue between the methods of modern biblical study and those of Patristic exegesis.

As Brian Daley has indicated, in the textual culture of early Christianity, the scriptural world of signs both leads us ever further into a reflection on the accomplishment of God in Christ, and simultaneously on into a reflection on the ways in which the prophecy of Israel's scripture speaks also directly to and about us. The texts of the New Testament claim Christian readers as members of that original community now spreading into all the earth, and as such invite readers to use those texts—including those which speak parabolically and symbolically—to describe their own lives. However one might judge the various different styles of allegorical reading that do develop, the germ of the allegorical strains within the letter; it is released not unnecessarily by the idleness of Christians merely playing with textual ambiguity, but necessarily by the careful attention of Christians who learn to read as members of Christ's body.

My title alludes to the mighty voice of Brother Claude Ely, the Gospel Ranger. When he sang "send down that latter rain" he spoke of the promised sending of the Spirit, coming to wash and baptize; when he sang "there's fire in that rain Lord" he points to the multi-valence of the rain as that which both washes and burns away impurity. I suggest the relationship as an analogy for the various kinds of reading scripture that should be ours. In his Word the Father has sent down upon us the rain of the scriptural text and led us to read its letter. But in that letter there lies also the fire that burns when we follow the paths that Christ himself has opened up, reading the text to ascend into his mysteries.

## NOTES

1  John Henry Cardinal Newman, *An Essay on the Development of Christian Doctrine*, sixth edition (Notre Dame IN: University of Notre Dame Press, 1989), p. 339.

2  A more extended historical justification for my account may be found in my forthcoming "At the Origins of Patristic Exegesis: Anti-Valentinian Polemic and Grammatical Practice in Irenaeus and Clement".

3  For useful introductions to current scholarly debate on this question see Lee Martin McDonald, *The Biblical Canon: Its Origin, Transmission and Authority*, third edition, (Peabody MA: Hendrikson, 2007) and the essays collected in *idem* and J. A. Sanders (ed), *The Canon Debate* (Peabody MA: Hendrikson, 2002). It is also important to note that my discussion here concerns the canon of the New Testament; McDonald's *The Biblical Canon* offers a useful introduction to what we know of the canon of Jewish scriptures that Christians inherited. (Note that throughout this article I have provided some basic bibliographical orientation, mostly to literature available in English, rather than full bibliographies of all the topics discussed.)

4  The strongest recent argument for John being included in this set during this period, and for their being such a set, is provided by Charles Hill, *The Johannine Corpus in the Early Church* (Oxford: Oxford University Press, 2004), pp. 294–359. These pages constitute his discussion of the 150–170 period; my claim here makes no judgment about his treatment of the pre-150 period (pp. 360 ff). My own argument about the importance of particular reading practices in the development of what it means to speak of early Christianity as "scriptural" may well mark a significant difference between our positions. In addition to there being a widespread use of the four-fold gospel, I also think it likely that much of the Pauline corpus was similarly widely used, but this is a matter for separate discussion.

5  Obviously enough I make no comment on how we might conceptualize the period between the gradual composition of those texts that would be incorporated into the canon and the 130s. That is beyond my purview here.

6  The most important account of this process available in English is that of Frances M. Young, *Biblical Exegesis and the Formation of Christian Culture* (Cambridge: Cambridge University Press, 1997). See esp. pp. 49–76 for her fundamental narrative. I differ from her in arguing for the importance of particular disputes concerning Christian doctrine and self-definition in shaping the history of exegesis.

7  The two main fragments remaining of these works are the fragments of Heracleon preserved in Origen and the fragment of a commentary on John's prologue preserved at Irenaeus, *Adv. haer.* 1.8. This latter may be by the same Ptolemy who also composed the *Letter to Flora* which, although it is not a commentary, witnesses to Valentinian use of some of the same techniques. A number of other reports and short fragments of this literature survive.

8  Christoph Markschies, "Valentinian Gnosticism: Toward The Anatomy of a School," in John B. Turner and Anne McGuire, eds., *The Nag Hammadi Library After Fifty Years* (Leiden: E. J. Brill, 1997), pp. 401–438 offers a particularly sophisticated treatment the Valentinians as possibly conceiving of themselves as parallel to a philosophical school, and the shifts in doctrine that could be accepted within such a fluid tradition. Cf. also the excellent discussion of Peter Lampe, *From Paul to Valentinus: Christians at Rome in the First Two Centuries*, trans. Michael Steinhauser, (Minneapolis MN: Fortress Press, 2003), pp. 292–318. For Valentinian belief see also Einar Thomassen, *The Spiritual Seed: The Church of the 'Valentinians'* (Leiden: E. J. Brill, 2006). Thomassen offers little comment on Valentinian exegetical techniques. For an overall sketch of the relationship between this tradition and others that have frequently been placed in modern writing under the name of "Gnostic" see Bentley Layton, *The Gnostic Scriptures: A New Translation with Annotations and Introductions* (New York, NY: Doubleday, 1987), pp. 5–22. For many Layton's clear distinctions and groupings, however

carefully presented, find insufficient warrant in the texts he describes. Such a critique is now classically presented in Michel A. Williams, *Rethinking "Gnosticism": An Argument for Dismantling a Dubious Category* (Princeton NJ: Princeton University Press, 1999).

9   Valentinian attempts to co-opt the cultural capital of ancient literary culture to support their religious project are paralleled in a number of other quarters. We know, from Eusebius, of figures making use of various ancient reading and commentary practices to advance particular positions within the Christian community during the latter half of the second century. When we try to find clear evidence of those who did so before the Valentinian commentators with whom I am concerned here, we can point to Valentinus himself, to Basilides and to Marcion. One of the best introductions to these other figures is provided by Robert M. Grant, *Heresy and Criticism: The Search for Authenticity in Early Christian Literature* (Louisville KY: Westminster/John Knox Press, 1993). Grant does not, however, recognize the place of Irenaeus, and the role of anti-allegorical literary critical traditions.

10  For an excellent introduction to this tradition see David Dawson, *Allegorical Readers and Cultural Revision in Ancient Alexandria* (Berkeley, CA: University of California Press, 1992), pp. 52–72.

11  For an overview of literary activity in ancient Alexandria sympathetic to the idea of Aristotelian influence see P. M. Fraser, *Ptolemaic Alexandria*, 3 vols. (Oxford: Oxford University Press, 1972).

12  Fundamental for this narrative remains the classic study, Jean Pépin, *Mythe et allégorie. Les origines grecques et les contestations judéo-chrétiennes* (Paris: Aubier, 1958). That story is told in even more clear cut fashion in Luc Brisson, *How Philosophers Saved Myths: Allegorical Interpretation and Classical Mythology*, trans. Catherine Tihanyi (Chicago IL: University of Chicago Press, 2004). For a rather different account that achieves much by focusing on the broader category of "symbol", see Peter Struck, *Birth of the Symbol: Ancient Readers at the Limits of their Texts* (Princeton, NJ: Princeton University Press, 2004), here esp. chps. 3–5. A number of the essays in Robert Lamberton and John J. Kearney (eds.) *Homer's Ancient Readers* (Princeton, NJ: Princeton University Press, 1992) are also very helpful for our period. On Stoic allegory see also the very helpful G. R. Boys-Stones, "The Stoics' Two Types of Allegory," in G. R. Boys-Stones (ed.) *Metaphor, Allegory and the Classical Tradition* (Oxford: Oxford University Press, 2003), and his earlier discussion in *Post-Hellenistic Philosophy* (Oxford: Oxford University Press, 2001), chps. 1–3.

13  Note the parallel quoted by Clement at *Excerpts from Theodotus* 66: "The Savior taught the apostles, at first in types and mystically, later parabolically and enigmatically, thirdly clearly and openly when they were alone". Trans. adapted from Robert Pierce Casey (ed and trans), *The* Excerpta ex Theodoto *of Clement of Alexandria* (London: Christophers, 1934), p. 83.

14  See Irenaeus, *Adv. haer. pref.* & 1. 8–9. Cf. 2, *pref.*

15  A good introduction to this aspect of Irenaeus's thought and exegesis is provided by Robert M. Grant, *Irenaeus of Lyons* (London: Routledge, 1997), pp. 1–53. Grant does not, however, discuss the techniques that are the main focus of my concern here.

16  For assertions of clarity see e.g., *Adv haer.* 2.25–7 and 3.10.6, then the attribution of clarity to Peter and Paul at 3.12.3 and 3.14.2. For the use of prosopological exegesis see 3.6.1 and 3.10.1; for etymological discussions see 2.24-2 and 2.35.3; for extensive discussion of knowing how to "punctuate" a text and the importance of observing personal patterns of speech see 3.7 and 4.6.

17  See e.g. *Adv. haer.* 3.6.1.

18  For discussion of number theory see *Adv. haer.* 2.24.2. The *locus classicus* for Irenaeus's assertion of the need to read the surface of the text in the light of publicly available knowledge is 2. 25–7, a passage already noted.

19  Clement, *strom.* 5. 4. 25 and 5. 10.61.

20  E.g. Clement, *strom.* 2.8.38 ff. For an assertion of the importance of following the letter and order of the scriptural text see *strom.* 7.16.96.

21  Eg, Justin, *Dial.* 59–60, cf. *Apol.* 36.1–36.3.

22  Lewis Ayres, *Nicaea and Its Legacy: An Approach to Fourth-Century Trinitarian Theology* (Oxford: Oxford University Press, 2004), p. 386, with reference to Andrew Louth, *Discerning the Mystery: An Essay on the Nature of Theology* (Oxford: Clarendon Press, 1983), p. 100: ". . . the Fathers, and creeds, and councils claim to be interpreting Scripture. How can one accept their results if one does not accept their methods?"

23   Over the centuries that followed the set of practices used by Christian exegetes certainly shifted, and the manner in which they saw the text as revealing the divine and yet revealing as mystery also developed. But that story—and the continuities that are evident throughout it—lies beyond my scope here.

24   The adjective "historicist" is important here; the areas of overlap between Irenaeus's literal sense and modern notions may well be different where modern notions have come to question the identity of "literal" sense and the sense that a text had for its authors of first hearers.

25   The manner in which disputes over doctrine and exegesis gradually shaped a sense of the text as both reliable in its letter and also mysterious will be treated at some length in the monograph toward which I am currently working.

26   During the conference at which these papers were originally delivered I also had the pleasure of responding to Kevin Vanhoozer's paper, which now appears in article form in this issue. Two of my responses may be worth repeating here. In the first place, I was not convinced by his assumption that it is possible to offer a theological distinction between allegory and typology without getting involved in historical judgments. Vanhoozer's arguments seem to rest on the assumption that there *is* or *was* something called "allegory" that may be characterized as bad. Whatever he says, were there no instance of it, then his argument *for* something called typology would have far less bite. But as a historical argument his account seems to me to fit with a narrative that is now no longer widely accepted by historians of the period. And thus, in the second place, I am not at all convinced that one should pursue his idea of pursuing those typological trajectories apparent in the New Testament, but without getting caught up in playing with the details of the text. It is the text and its details that have been given us and that textuality is woven through our confessions and liturgies (and I think this argument could be made to bite even with reference to the classical Reformed confessions). In discussion it seemed to me that a further difference resulted from Vanhoozer's commitment to a model of the relative tasks of biblical scholarship and "systematic" theology that I do not share. The wide-spread antipathy of those trained in the methods of modern biblical studies to allegorical engagement with the text given to us seems to me a reason for encouraging a supplementation in how we conceive the particular and relative tasks of the biblical scholar and the dogmatic theologian, rather than accepting the bifurcation that is so common at present. But, as I say at a little more length in this second part of the present article, I am not making a veiled call for rejection of modern biblical methods; there is both too much overlap with ancient methods, and such a position can hardly be made by a Catholic theologian attentive to *Dei Verbum*! It is at this point that I would like to thank the organizers and hosts of the conference for enabling and nurturing such an interesting exchange.

27   See John Webster, *Holy Scripture: A Dogmatic Sketch* (Cambridge: Cambridge University Press, 2003), chp. 2.

28   Joseph Ratzinger, "The Question of the Concept of Tradition: A Provisional Response," in *God's Word: Scripture, Tradition, Office*, trans. Henry Taylor, (San Francisco, CA: Ignatius Press, 2008), pp. 41–89 (originally published in 1965 in *Quaestiones Disputatae* 25). Yves Congar, *Tradition and Traditions: An Historical and a Theological Essay* (New York, NY: Macmillan, 1967), pp. 160–164. Debates about the relationship between scripture and tradition are closely related to those concerning how we theorize a concept of the Fathers. On this theme see the complementary approach of Joseph Ratzinger, "Die Bedeutung der Väter für die gegenwärtige Theologie," *Theologische Quartalschrift*, Vol. 148 (1968), pp. 257–282; trans. in *Principles of Catholic Theology: Building Stones for a Fundamental Theology*, trans. Sr. Mary Frances McCarthy, (San Francisco, CA: Ignatius Press, 1987), pp. 133–152.

29   Ratzinger, "Concept of Tradition," p. 61.

30   Ratzinger, "Concept of Tradition," p. 62. For our purposes I do not need to go through the second half of Ratzinger's essay in any detail. There he argues that behind the final form of Trent's discussion of revelation we should see hints of the position advocated by Cardinals Cervini and Seripando, as well as the Jesuit Fr. Claude Lejay present as a theological consultor. All three argued for a conception of scripture and tradition that saw continuity based on the fact that tradition is "the way the word is made real in Christian living" and that in this sense tradition surrounds and is found within Scripture (pp. 79–80). LeJay in particular, argued for many aspects of the Church's dogmatic language as part of tradition,

and argued that these were of a wholly different order from mere ceremonial custom which could be changed.

31 There is hidden behind this paragraph the complex theological question of why God chooses that such a mode of textual engagement will be central to our teaching and worshipping. There is no room here to face this question head-on, only to indicate that I would face it in part along the route laid out (in their different ways) by Augustine and Thomas, who both see the complexity of the text as a) most appropriately conveying the simplicity of divine truth in a manner that allows our intellects to ascend and b) most appropriate for healing the peculiar failures of thought and imagination that follow from our fallen state. Such arguments are, of course, *ex convenientia.*

32 In other words, this theological discursive space may serve the purpose not only of allowing a fruitful dialogue between modern and ancient modes of interrogating scriptural texts; it may provide a way of describing theologically the gain represented by modern methods of biblical study without succumbing to an overly simply narrative of progress in "scientific" terms.

33 Modern Catholic discussion of the relationship between the Church's traditional patterns of reading and modern methods have done an increasingly good job of stating the tensions that exist, but have rarely reflected well doctrinally on these tensions. The suggestion made here I explored at more length in my 2011 Fisher Lectures at Cambridge, which I hope to offer as a small book in the next couple of years.

34 I intentionally use the general phrase "different forms", as I am fully in accord with those who have in recent years refused the idea of a clear distinction between "typology" and "allegory". But this refusal does not yet mean that we have any clear sense of what better distinctions should be used to replace this older (if still modern) model.

35 I make use here of the new Loeb edition and translation, Bart D. Ehrman, *The Apostolic Fathers, Volume II*, Loeb Classical Library 25 (Cambridge, MA and London: Harvard University Press, 2003), pp. 3–83.

36 *Ep. Barn.* 1. 6–7.

37 *Ep. Barn.* 6. 3–7.

38 *Ep. Barn.* 6. 10–19.

# 3

# ORIGEN AGAINST HISTORY? RECONSIDERING THE CRITIQUE OF ALLEGORY

## PETER W. MARTENS

### I. Introduction

As most everyone knows, Origen had little interest in history. While this allegation could easily appear to be the invention of the modern, historically conscious mind, this criticism was already forcibly leveled in late antiquity. Approximately fifty years after his death, Pamphilus and Eusebius co-authored the *Apology for Origen*, in which they defended his biblical interpretation against this very accusation. More famously, in the fourth and fifth centuries a number of figures (and not simply "Antiochenes") repeatedly juxtaposed Origen's penchant for allegory with a simultaneous distaste for history. While appraisals of theologians invariably fluctuate over time, Origen has met little success in evading this long-standing charge. It is still a common practice to highlight how his allegorization of Christian Scripture evinced an animosity to history. "[A]s the result of his fantastic interpretations, the history itself, of course, disappears."[1] Origen's method of scriptural interpretation "despises the history, ignores the poetry, and turns all that is warm and human into frigid intellectual reasonings."[2] "Origen always assumed that any purely historical information was irrelevant."[3] There is "the temptation, inherent in Origen's love for allegory, to empty history of its meaning."[4] Nor is this view confined to the Origenian scholarship. In a curial document from 1941, the Pontifical Biblical Commission warned of "the grave exaggeration of the Alexandrian School, that they wished to find a symbolic meaning everywhere, even to the detriment of the literal and

*Heaven on Earth?: Theological Interpretation in Ecumenical Dialogue*, First Edition.
Edited by Hans Boersma and Matthew Levering.
© 2013 Blackwell Publishing Ltd. Book compilation © 2013 Blackwell Publishing Ltd.

historical meaning of the text."[5] In short, scholars have leveled many different criticisms against Origen's allegorical interpretation, but its antipathy to history is invariably regarded as its chief flaw. This is arguably the central plank in the modern case against the allegorical interpretation of Christian Scripture.

But how well have we understood this critique? "Origen against history," I will argue, is a misleadingly vague charge. While it suggests a specific, even focused criticism, close inspection demonstrates that this persistent charge has been remarkably diffuse. There are, in fact, a variety of ways in which Origen's allegory has been thought to undermine history. In this article, I will identify three prominent criticisms.[6] For some, this charge has meant that he denied the historicity of events narrated in Scripture. For others, "Origen against history" has meant that his allegories yielded "timeless" or "anti-historical truths." Finally, Origen's dogged twentieth-century critic, R. P. C. Hanson, contended that he gravely reduced the "significance" of history. Rather than envisioning the past as the field of God's own revelatory activity, Origen viewed it as little more than an "acted parable" for truths he wished to assert about God.

Part of my task in this article is to demonstrate that when Origen has been accused of being inimical to history, this charge has been anything but uniform. The corresponding task is to determine if this charge in its various iterations has accurately described Origen's approach to scriptural interpretation. As we will see below, it was *Origen himself* who distinguished between an "historical" and a "spiritual" interpretation of Scripture. And it was Origen who often privileged the latter over the former. But did he mean by this what his subsequent critics have meant? The Origen-against-history campaign has been conducted posthumously, yet enough of his corpus survives to give us a reliable sense as to how he might have crafted his response to his later critics. In what follows, then, I will present each of the aforementioned criticisms, before turning to Origen's own writings where I will examine in what manner, if at all, his allegorical project was antipathetic to history.

## II. Origen Against History (Part I)

### A. Diodore and Theodore: Allegory against Historicity

The grievances registered against Origen's biblical interpretation in antiquity were hardly monolithic. His critics targeted not simply his allegorical, but also his literal interpretations. His dubious motivations, his extra-ecclesial sources, his sensitivity (or lack thereof) to the language of Scripture, his eagerness to shape (and not be shaped by) its message—these, as well as other criticisms, were directed against Origen as scholars wrestled with his monumental, influential, and contentious exegetical legacy. Nevertheless, if there was a stock criticism of his scriptural interpretation in antiquity, it was that his allegorizing denied the historicity of the events narrated in Scripture. This critique came from several quarters: Eustathius of Antioch, Epiphanius of Salamis, Theophilus of Alexandria, and Jerome, for instance, all explicitly directed it against Origen.[7] Yet the two authors who leveled this charge most forcefully were Diodore of Tarsus (†394) and his pupil, Theodore of Mopsuestia (ca. 350–428). Several surviving writings from each author make explicit this critique of Origen's allegorical exegesis.

In Diodore's preface to his *Commentary on the Psalms*, he announces his intent to interpret the Psalter "according to the historical record and the letter [κατὰ τὴν ἱστορίαν καὶ τὴν λέξιν]" and that he will "not stand in the way of an ascent and more elevated insight. The historical record," he continues, "is not in opposition to the more elevated insight; on the contrary, it proves to be the basis and foundation of the more elevated meanings."[8] A few lines later, Diodore illustrates this relationship between a past episode and its higher meaning: according to the historical account, Cain and Abel both offered sacrifices, but when elevated, these events point respectively to the synagogue and the church.[9] Diodore presents this approach to Scripture as a "middle ground." It avoids the dangers of Judaism, "suffocating us by forcing us to settle for the literal sense alone and attending only to it," but also frees us from a "Hellenism that says one thing in place of another and introduces absurdities."[10]

How exactly did Diodore distinguish this "Hellenistic" exegetical strategy—allegory—from authentic insight? In the preface to his *Commentary on the Psalms* he articulates the thesis that he likely developed in greater depth in a work now lost, *What is the Difference between Theoria and Allegoria?* He explains:

> One thing alone is to be guarded against, however, never to let insight be seen as an overthrow of the underlying sense [μή ποτε ἀνατροπὴ τοῦ ὑποκειμένου ἡ θεωρία ὀφθῇ], since this would no longer be insight but allegory. For what is spoken otherwise than should be [Τὸ γὰρ ἄλλως ἀγορευόμενον], in defiance of the content, is not insight but allegory.[11]

Diodore later offers two illustrations of this problematic Hellenistic allegory. According to the mythographers, Zeus mutated into a bull and carried Europa across the sea to a foreign land. But allegorists recognize that a "real bull could not possibly swim such a distance across the ocean," and so they interpret the bull as a symbol of a ship with a bull as a figurehead. Or again, Zeus calls Hera his sister and wife. Allegorists, however, are worried about the moral implications of Zeus having intercourse with his sister, and so they transform the couple into air and ether.[12] Both illustrations highlight how allegorical interpreters, as Diodore understood them, overthrow the underlying sense: they deny the historicity of what they interpret.[13]

By casting allegory in such a negative light, however, Diodore needed to account for Paul's approving use of the term in his Letter to the Galatians

(4:24). The apostle, Diodore insists, "never overturned the historical record," but rather chose to label what he was really doing, *theoria*, "allegory."[14] It is otherwise with "those who make innovations in the divine Scripture and consider themselves wise, but who are either lazy or vicious with history."[15] They use the term *allegoria* with the apostle, but they do not mean what he did by the label. Instead of acknowledging the historicity of what was narrated, these interpreters force readers to "substitute one thing for another—for example, by taking 'abyss' as demons, 'dragon' as the devil, and the like."[16]

Diodore's pupil, Theodore of Mopsuestia, explicitly associated Origen with history-denying allegory.[17] In *A Tractate against the Allegorists*, Theodore singles out Philo and Origen as "truly dependent on the pagans" who themselves had turned to allegory since their fables about the gods were "contrived" and "contain no truth."[18] In his *Commentary on Galatians*, Theodore elaborates on this anti-historical tendency of allegory by attempting to exonerate Paul's use of allegory as Diodore had done.[19] Like his teacher, Theodore criticizes those who use the term allegory, but "do not understand how they differ from what the apostle is saying here. For the apostle neither eliminates the history nor explains events that happened a long while ago [*apostolus enim non interimit historiam, neque euoluit res dudum factas*]. Rather, he indicates the events just as they happened then, and makes use of the history of those things that occurred for his own understanding."[20] Theodore resumes his argument a few lines later, noting that Paul likened Hagar—who actually existed—to the present Jerusalem.

> Paul gives history priority over all other considerations. Otherwise, he would not say that Hagar "corresponds to the present Jerusalem," thus acknowledging that Jerusalem does exist now. He would also not use the expression "just as," if he was referring to a person he thought did not exist. For in saying "just as" he pointed to a similarity; but similarity cannot be established if the elements involved do not exist. . . . Those people, however, turn it all into the contrary, as if the entire historical account of divine Scripture differed in no way from dreams in the night. When they start expounding divine Scripture spiritually—"spiritual interpretation" is the name they like to give to their folly—they claim that Adam is not Adam, paradise is not paradise, the serpent not the serpent.[21]

Theodore concludes his reflection on Paul's use of the term allegory by underscoring that the apostle's use of allegory did not deny historicity: "He calls an allegory the comparison that can be made between what happened long ago and what exists at present."[22]

### B. Historicity Denied?

For Theodore, like Diodore, what rendered Origen's allegorical interpretation of Scripture problematic was that it denied ("overturned," "undermined," "repudiated," "did violence to") the historical reality that a passage signified, thereby allowing them to portray him as no different from some pagan allegorists. As noted above, this was also one of the persistent criticisms of Origen's exegesis throughout the late fourth century. But did Origen deny the historicity of events that were narrated in the Scriptures? Pamphilus and Eusebius were the first authors to defend Origen against this charge. In their *Apology for Origen* they responded to this accusation by citing two lengthy passages in which Origen affirmed the historicity of biblical figures and events, thereby leaving their readers with the impression that this charge was largely, if not entirely, fabricated.[23] However, their response ignored those passages where Origen clearly *did* deny historicity. In book four of *On First Principles*, he alerts his readers to several episodes in Genesis 1–3 that, while narrated as actual historical events, simply could not have occurred:

> Now what intelligent person will believe that the first and the second and the third day, and the evening and the morning existed without the sun and moon and stars? And that the first day, if we may so call it, was even without a heaven (cf. Gen 1:5–13)? And who is so silly as to believe that God, after the manner of a farmer, "planted a paradise eastward in Eden" (Gen 2:8), and set in it a visible and palpable "tree of life" (Gen 2:9), of such a sort that anyone who tasted its fruit with his bodily teeth would gain life; and again that one could partake of "good and evil" by masticating the fruit taken from the tree of that name? And when God is said to "walk in the paradise in the cool of the day" and Adam to hide himself behind a tree (Gen 3:8), I do not think anyone will doubt that these are figurative expressions which indicate certain mysteries through an apparent and not actual historical record [διὰ δοκούσης ἱστορίας καὶ οὐ σωματικῶς γεγενημένης].[24]

In the lines that follow, Origen explains how literary fictions were not restricted to the Old Testament, but also occurred in the New—for instance, that there was a high mountain from which Jesus could show the devil all the kingdoms of the world (Matt. 4:8).[25] The careful reader, he concludes, "will detect thousands of other passages like this . . . which will convince him that events which did not take place at all are woven into the records of what literally did happen."[26] For Origen, the point behind these fictions was clear: that the divine authors who helped compose Scripture did not want readers to "accept only what is found in the letter; for occasionally the records taken in a literal sense are not true, but [are] actually absurd and impossible."[27]

It is not hard to imagine how these lines would have invited the critique that Diodore, Theodore, and others later leveled again Origen. Yet a wider reading of book four of *On First Principles* complicates the picture. It indicates that Origen was a far less critical reader of Scripture than his opening comments about the implausibilities in Genesis might suggest. In fact, in the following passage he anticipates the very criticisms Diodore and Theodore would later direct against him:

> But someone . . . may suspect us of saying that because some of the history did not happen, therefore none of it happened; and because a certain law is irrational or impossible when taken literally, therefore no laws ought to be kept at the letter; or that the records of the Saviour's life are not true in a physical sense; or that no law or commandment of his ought to be obeyed. We must assert, therefore, that in regard to some things we are clearly aware that the historical record is true; as that Abraham was buried in the double cave at Hebron . . . and thousands of other facts. For the passages which are historically true [τὰ κατὰ τὴν ἱστορίαν ἀληθευόμενα] are far more numerous than those which are composed with purely spiritual meanings.[28]

As he closes this section of his treatise on scriptural interpretation, Origen admits that it is sometimes difficult to determine "whether a particular incident, believed to be history, actually happened or not." The ideal reader, he insists, will "search the Scriptures" (John 5:39) as Jesus admonished, carefully scouring them to "investigate how far the literal meaning is true and how far it is impossible."[29]

This more moderate stance on the fictive component of biblical narratives is corroborated by Origen's actual exegetical writings where he rarely denies the historicity of biblical figures, institutions or episodes, even when he is allegorizing them. He preaches about the Babylonian captivity as follows: "Therefore, when you hear about the captivity of the people, to be sure you should believe that the captivity really happened in accordance with the reliable testimony of history. Yet," Origen continues, "it came first as a sign of something else."[30] Or again, in his second homily on Genesis:

> As we begin to speak about the ark which was constructed by Noah at God's command, let us see first of all what is related about it literally. . . . When we have laid foundations of this kind, we can ascend from the historical account to the mystical and allegorical understanding of the spiritual meaning. . . .[31]

Statements like these are far closer to Origen's exegetical program than his infrequently voiced skepticism. They indicate that when allegorizing Scripture he did not, as a rule, call into question the historicity of what it narrated.[32] Indeed, a careful investigation of his corpus reveals writings that teem with explanatory comments about what he thought actually transpired—we find detailed philological comments on the customs and histories of peoples, as well as chronological, geographical, topographical and ethnographical remarks.[33] Perhaps the strongest indication of Origen's commitment to historicity was his willingness to *defend* episodes others attacked as fictional.[34]

In sum, the criticism leveled by Diodore and Theodore has only limited traction. There were certainly occasions when Origen thought biblical narratives were fictional and, thus, required an allegorical interpretation to elucidate a useful sense. But neither critic acknowledged that Origen's general policy, even when allegorizing, was *to affirm* the historicity of the figures and events narrated in Scripture. A careful reading of book four of *On First Principles* or of his wider exegetical corpus would have quickly confirmed that allegorizing did not go hand-in-hand with a denial of historicity. Diodore and Theodore were, thus, inviting their readers to confuse an occasional feature of Origen's philology with a global characterization of it. In so doing, they also misleadingly insinuated a far greater distance between their announced exegetical program and Origen's. As we saw above, Diodore insisted in the preface to his *Commentary on the Psalms* that "the historical record" ought to serve as the "the basis and foundation of the more elevated meanings." Yet what Diodore would later promote under the label of *theoria* was clearly anticipated by Origen when he claimed, as we already saw above, that historical realities like the ark should serve as "foundations" for the ascent to a loftier, spiritual interpretation.

## III.  Origen Against History (Part Two)

### A.  Timeless Allegories
Origen's allegory is claimed to have undermined history in yet another way. Unlike the previous criticism that focuses on *what* the allegorist interpreted, this charge focuses on the resulting interpretation: the allegorical referent. This criticism surfaces prominently in the modern allegory/typology distinction. While it is important to underscore that this distinction has not been uniformly understood in the scholarship, one of the ways in which it *has* been invoked questions the historical character of the allegorical referent.[35] For much of the modern era, reaching back at least to the early seventeenth century, a current in the scholarship has identified two broad classes of Old Testament symbols: there are symbols that point to future "facts," and symbols (sometimes the same) that point to "doctrines."[36] This trajectory has invariably defined typology as the establishment of a correspondence between the persons, events or institutions of Old Testament narratives, and later "facts," i.e., persons, events or institutions either in the New Testament itself or in subsequent Christian salvation history stretching forward to the eschaton.[37] This typological referent is historically specific, or as E. Auerbach puts it, within "the flowing stream which is historical life."[38]

The contrast between allegory and this understanding of typology has neither been uniformly nor clearly drawn. Sometimes the allegorical referent is simply considered a "doctrine" or "idea," without an indication of where a fact ends and a doctrine begins. Most scholars, however, have chosen to circumscribe this referent more narrowly: for instance, it concerns only "vertical" themes about heavenly realities,[39] "speculative" teachings,[40] "abstract" doctrines,[41] or commonly held "cosmological, psychological, or ethical truths" that would have found a widely receptive audience in the late antique world.[42] Moreover, this allegorical referent is often described as "timeless," "not historical" or even "anti-historical." Thus, for instance, we are told that, "it is the object of the allegory itself to convey a moral, not a historic truth."[43] In the entry on "types" in the *Oxford Dictionary of Christian Church*, we learn that "[a] Christian type differs from an allegory in that the historical reference is not lost sight of."[44] Or elsewhere: "Typically, allegorical interpretation shows little interest in meanings that are historically specific, preferring those that disclose timeless truths."[45] When this version of the allegory/typology distinction is applied to Origen,[46] there is almost always a normative judgment implied: to the extent that he practiced typology, his exegesis was commendable (or at least harmless), since it remained rooted in history and was identifiably Christian. To the extent, however, that Origen ventured into allegory, he abandoned historical particulars in pursuit of timeless, ahistoric or anti-historical doctrines with usually only a pale shade of Christian conviction.

## B. Historical Allegories

How might Origen have responded to this two-fold classification of his nonliteral referents into facts and doctrines, the former derived through typology and the latter through allegory? Only in a restricted sense is this scholarly construct useful. He certainly saw in the Old Testament symbols of particular individuals, events and institutions of the Christian dispensation within the stream of historical life. He also saw in the Old Testament symbols of every variety of doctrine, whether it was vertical (or horizontal), speculative (or conventional), abstract (or specific), concerned cosmological, psychological and ethical truths (or any other truth), or bore traces of non-Christian learning (or did not).[47] At the same time, there are two important ways in which this schema is unhelpful, if not misleading. The first concerns the nomenclature of "allegory" and "typology." As I have argued elsewhere, Origen's exegetical lexicon does not support the usage of these terms as sketched out in the previous section. He did not employ the Greek families of terms that stand behind the English terms "allegory" (ἀλληγορία and ἀλληγορέω) and "typology" (τύπος, τυπικός and τυπικῶς) to distinguish between two classes of referents, doctrines and facts respectively (or any other pair of referents for that matter).[48] Second, Origen firmly resisted parsing Scripture's *nonliteral* referents into "facts" and "doctrines." He recognized that Scripture contained narratives full of the sorts of details that some modern scholars have wished to label "facts." Yet these facts were not symbolic of more "facts." Rather, the scriptural authors sought to symbolically communicate "doctrines," "mystical revelations," or "unspeakable mysteries" through these historical narratives.[49] On a terminological level, then, it is neither easy nor advisable to enforce the aforementioned schema for his symbolic exegesis.

Nevertheless, we can still ask: when Origen interpreted Old (or even New) Testament narratives figuratively, were any of the resultant doctrinal referents "a-" or "anti-historical"? The answer hinges, of course, upon how we define "historical." Part of the problem is that scholars have rarely defined this term, thereby contributing to the lack of clarity in this discussion. In what follows, I will consider Origen's figurative referents to be "historical" when they concern created realities circumscribed by space and time. Angels, demons, the church, particular people, generic people (i.e., the soul), virtuous principles for living, etc., would all count as historical referents. I do not think that this is a particularly controversial definition, and it seems to capture the concern of those who, with E. Auerbach, locate historical referents with the "stream" of "historical life."

On a surface reading, admittedly much of Origen's allegorical exegesis appears to be non-historical. English translators have traditionally rendered his expression κατὰ τὴν ἱστορίαν as "according to the history" or "according to the historical sense," and thus facilitated the very critique outlined in this section of the article, especially since Origen often proposed an allegorical interpretation distinct from, and usually superior to, this "historical" interpretation. However, such a translation of the noun ἱστορία easily misleads. Its two basic senses were "inquiry" and the "written result of one's inquiries," i.e., a "report," "account," or "narrative."[50] It is this latter sense that Origen invokes in exegetical contexts when he interprets Scripture's ἱστορίαι, i.e., its "records" of past events.[51] When he contrasts an interpretation κατὰ τὴν ἱστορίαν to a nonliteral interpretation, the distinction is *not* between an interpretation that has an historical referent and some timeless referent that transcends this plane of existence. The distinction, rather, is between an interpretation that recounts the details of what has been recorded about the past, and one that proposes a new referent—still historical—that the recorded past figuratively symbolizes. A few illustrations will establish this point.

In his *Homilies on Jeremiah*, Origen preaches that the southern kingdom was exiled to the king of Babylon who is identified κατὰ μὲν τὴν ἱστορίαν— "according to the narrative report" in the Bible—as Nebuchadnezzar. But "according to the elevated meaning [κατὰ δὲ τὴν ἀναγωγὴν]," this king is the "Evil one" to whom the sinner is handed over.[52] Nebuchadnezzar and the devil are both historical realities, but since the Babylonian king is the one actually named in the biblical account, only this interpretation is κατὰ μὲν τὴν ἱστορίαν. In his *Commentary on John*, Origen notes that the Word of God was sent to the prophet Hosea, κατὰ μὲν τὴν ἱστορίαν, but κατὰ δὲ μυστικὸν λόγον the Word "was sent to the one who is saved—for Hosea means 'saved.'"[53] Here again, an interpretation "according to the mystical sense" is contrasted to one "according to the historical record," but the contrast is not between a referent that is historical (Hosea) and one that is not: in subsequent lines Origen identifies those who are saved as prophets like Isaiah and Jeremiah and the saints. In his first *Homily on Genesis*, Origen comments on Gen. 1:29–30: "The narrative account, at least, of this sentence indicates clearly [*Historia quidem huius sententiae manifeste indicat*] that originally God permitted the use of foods from vegetation, that is, vegetables and the fruits of trees." Origen continues: "But allegorically [*Secundum allegoriam*] the vegetation of the earth and its fruit which is granted to men for food can be understood of the bodily affections. For example, anger and concupiscence are offshoots of the body. . . . "[54] Here the "narrative account" [*Historia* = ἱστορία] is contrasted to its allegorical interpretation, but the allegorical referent is hardly ahistorical—it concerns our bodily affections. And finally, consider an illustration from Origen's interpretation of a New Testament narrative. He is commenting on the verse, "There was a man sent from God, whose name was John" (John 1:6), and remarks that it is clear where he was sent κατὰ μὲν τὴν ἱστορίαν, "namely he was sent to Israel." But "according to the deeper meaning [κατὰ δὲ βαθύτερον λόγον] he was sent into the world ('world' being taken as the earthly place where there are men)."[55] Yet again, both referents are historical, but only one re-states what the Gospel record indicates.

In each of these examples, Origen distinguishes between an interpretation that is κατὰ τὴν ἱστορίαν and one that is nonliteral (or in his fluid language, "elevated," "mystical," "allegorical," or "deeper"). As we have seen, the contrast is not between historical and unhistorical referents: both sets of referents are created realities that exist in space and time. Rather, the distinction is between what the narrative record (ἱστορία) of Scripture literally reports, and another, different referent symbolized by this record. It is true that Origen often speaks critically of an interpretation κατὰ τὴν ἱστορίαν, and thus proceeds to supplement it with a figurative interpretation. Concerning the birth and weaning of Isaac, for instance, he asks:

> Do we think that it is the Holy Spirit's intention to write stories [*historias scribere*] and to narrate how a child was weaned and a feast was made, how he played and did other childish things? Or should we understand by these things that he wishes to teach us something divine and worthy that the human race might learn from the words of God?[56]

Or concerning the places the Hebrews visited while leaving Egypt, Origen writes: "If we follow only the simple record of fact [*Si historiam solam sequamur*], it does not edify us much to know what place they came to first and to what place second."[57] When Origen poses questions of this sort in his homilies, he is not denying historicity, as if there was no child born to Abraham and Sarah or no exodus. Nor does his pejorative coloration of the historical details serve as a pretext (as seen above) for proposing a symbolic meaning that is somehow non-historical. Rather, his objection is to the mere re-telling of the details of an episode long past *when* this episode is devoid of obvious religious significance for him.[58]

For Origen, the highest task of the scriptural commentator was not to provide audiences with *information* about the past (historical trivia, archival details, narratival minutiae, etc.). Rather, the task was to provide them *insight*, i.e., doctrinal or ethical precepts that would inform how they thought about and conducted their Christian lives.[59] It is for this reason that he rarely settled solely for an interpretation κατὰ τὴν ἱστορίαν, since the goal of the interpreter was to discover how Scripture's historical narratives, that on their surface often appeared to contain pointless details, symbolically conveyed teachings that were edifying or useful for "humanity's salvation."[60]

The Scriptures teemed, then, with stories about figures, events and institutions, but through these narratival details they conveyed a panoramic and far more important message: about God and his Wisdom and Spirit, the creation of rational beings and their descent into three classes (the good powers, human souls, and wicked powers), the subsequent creation of this physical world, and the means by which all created things made their gradual ascent, through free will and God's educative providence, to that original state from which they fell. The Scriptures conveyed, in short, a way of understanding the world and one's place in it.[61] How accurate, then, is it to call Origen's doctrinal referents "timeless" or not "historical"? More often than not, this language is intended to insinuate Origen's doleful indebtedness to Platonism.[62] Yet whatever we want to say about his relationship to Plato and the Platonic traditions of his day, Origen did not advocate a world of eternal, immaterial, and changeless forms that transcended this world of change and becoming.[63] The most one could say is that many of his allegorical referents were *generic*. Origen often saw in scriptural narratives the theme of the soul's ascent to God (and not some specific person's ascent to God), or a virtue or vice (and not some particular person's virtue or vice). These generic allegories pertained to the features (like a soul) that a group of particulars shared in common, but they were not for this reason unhistorical or timeless allegories.[64] In fact, these themes were historical precisely because they extracted commonalities from particulars who were created and flourished within the stream of time. It would be more accurate to describe a generic allegory as "departicularized," but still historical.[65]

If we take "historical" as an adjective describing any created reality that occupies a place and time—and there is no indication from the literature surveyed above that this term is being used differently—it becomes clear how misleading this moniker is. These allegorical referents were advocated by a person who was conditioned by his late antique context. They were promulgated not in a vacuum, but to specific people who were encouraged to accept them as true. And with the exception of God and his pre-incarnate Word, and perhaps the Holy Spirit as well, Origen's symbolic universe was coterminous with this created world.[66] Whatever sort of allegorized doctrine Origen drew out of Scripture—whether it was about individuals or classes of individuals, about vertical or horizontal themes, speculative or more conventional, uniquely scriptural or not—each of these topics concerned created realities existing within the confines of space and time.[67]

## IV. Origen Against History (Part Three)

### A. Allegory and the Insignificance of History

R. P. C. Hanson has arguably been the fiercest detractor of Origen's allegory. On the opening page of *Allegory and Event* he posits his book's animating question: "Has the interpretation of the Bible as it is practiced today anything seriously in common with the interpretation of the Bible as Origen, and indeed as the early Church generally, practiced it?"[68] As the study unfolds, it becomes increasingly clear that the answer to this question is, with few exceptions, "no."[69] Origen's biblical interpretation, characterized above all by the "alchemy of allegory," is vastly inferior to contemporary biblical scholarship whose "guiding principle" is "the question of what any given text meant when it was first written or uttered to the first audience for which it was intended."[70] Modern scholars succeed, Hanson insists, where Origen failed. They grasp the authorial intent of the biblical writers on one critical issue: that history was "significant."

Origen's chief shortcoming as a biblical scholar is that unlike the great expositors of the past who "successfully put themselves into the minds of the biblical author whom they are interpreting," he "on countless occasions gives the opposite impression, that he is reading into the mind of the biblical author thoughts which are really his own."[71] "The critical subject," Hanson continues,

> upon which Origen never accepted the biblical viewpoint was the significance of history. To the writers of the Bible history is *par excellence* the field of God's revelation of himself. The Jewish historians may not have achieved the accuracy of a modern historian, but they did believe that in the events of history God's will and purposes were made plain.[72]

While Hanson is clear that Origen did not "reject or abandon history" as some scholars insist, he did not have a deep respect for it.[73] The writing prophets, on the other hand, demonstrated such a respect when they saw God's judgment and salvation in historical crises, as did the gospel writers who portrayed the life and ministry of Jesus as God "moving into history." "History," Hanson summarizes, "is therefore an essential ingredient of revelation; it is an inseparable part of the manner in which God reveals himself. One might almost say that in the Incarnation God has in a sense taken history into himself. To this insight Origen is virtually blind."[74]

If Origen fails to grasp history as significant in this way—as the place of God's self-disclosure—how *does* he view, and correspondingly treat, the past? "In his view history, if it is to have any significance at all, can be no more than an acted parable, a charade for showing forth eternal truths about God."[75] Again: "In history as event, in history as the field of God's self-revelation *par excellence*, Origen is not in the least interested. He is only interested in history as parable. . . ."[76] For Origen history is not, "as it is in the prophets, the place where through tension and uncertainty and danger and faith men encounter God as active towards them." The incarnation "is not the final and unique event, contemporary to all men and women, whereby God speaks to them for salvation or ruin," but rather "a necessary stage early in the long process of souls learning essential truths about God." Origen's mind, Hanson insists, "could never completely assimilate biblical thought because it approached the Bible with one presupposition which closed to it many doors of understanding, the presupposition that history could never be of significance."[77]

Hanson's argument, then, is that there are two different views of history: history as "event" and history as "parable." Contemporary biblical scholarship (as he understood it) is commendable because it captures the Hebraic view of history's significance, where the past becomes an event, i.e., the place of God's revelation of himself. For those with this view of the past, there is no need for allegorical interpretation: all that is required is careful attention to God's "plain" or "literal" self-revelation.[78] Allegory, on the other hand, rests upon a Hellenistic view of history not original to the biblical authors. History is not "significant" since it is no longer the place where one encounters God's direct self-revelation. Instead, interpreters like Origen distort the past into a parable, so that they can assert their own "eternal truths about God." According to Hanson, Origen rejected history as event and was only interested in history as parable.

## B. Allegory and the Significance of the Past
Hanson's critique of Origen raises a number of issues that merit a more detailed response than I will offer here. I will restrict myself to two larger points as they pertain to Origen's ostensible rejection of the "significance" of history. First, Hanson repeatedly asserts that Origen had no interest in history as event, i.e., history as the place of God's self-disclosure. This claim is perplexing, since one wonders where else Origen would think God's self-disclosure took place! It is important to note, moreover, that the examples Hanson provides of God's revelatory presence in history can readily be found in Origen's own writings. For instance, the "writing prophets saw God as judging and saving through historical crises," like Nebuchadnezzar's destruction of the southern kingdom.[79] Yet here is how Origen opens his *Homilies on Ezekiel*:

Not everyone who is a captive endures captivity on account of his sins. For though a multitude was forsaken by God because of their sin, and was seized by Nebuchadnezzar to endure captivity, and was cast out of the holy land and "was led to Babylon" (cf. Jer. 24:1), yet there were a few among the people who were just. They endured the captivity not because it was their own fault, but so that the sinners who were oppressed by the yoke of captivity would not be entirely deprived of support. For let us imagine that the just had remained in the old territories when the sinners were led away to Babylon. The result would have been that the sinners would never have attained a remedy. Therefore, God, who is clement and kind and lover of human beings, arranged it so that along with the punishments by which he punishes sinners, he intermingles the goodness of his visitation as well. He does not overwhelm the poor sufferers with punishment without limit. God is always like this, he torments those who do harm, but as a good father he joins clemency in with the torments.[80]

Hanson also points to the proper depiction of Jesus in the New Testament: he is "not merely an epiphany of divine truth" but "*the* act of God."[81] It is not clear how Origen would disagree with this assertion:

But of all the marvelous and splendid things about him [the Son of God] there is one that utterly transcends the limits of human wonder and is beyond the capacity of our weak mortal intelligence to think of or understand, namely, how this mighty Power of the divine majesty, the very Word of the Father, and the very Wisdom of God, in which were created "all things visible and invisible" (Col. 1:16), can be believed to have existed within the compass of that man who appeared in Judaea; yes, and how the Wisdom of God can have entered into a woman's womb and have been born as a little child and uttered noises like those of crying children; and further, how it was that he was troubled, as we are told, in the hour of death, as he himself confesses when he says, "My soul is sorrowful even unto death" (Matt. 26:38); and how at the last he was led to that death which is considered by men to be the most shameful of all—even though on the third day he rose again.[82]

And as for apocalyptic and eschatological literature, which is "only a way of declaring God's control of history and his determination to manifest himself in history,"[83] it is Origen who preaches:

As we profess that God is incorporeal and omnipotent and invisible, so we confess with a sure and immovable doctrine that he cares about mortal affairs and that nothing happens in heaven or earth apart from his providence. . . . For providence is that by which he attends to and manages and makes provision for the things which happen.[84]

As this homily continues, Origen specifies one of the ways in which God's providential activity finds expression: "In accordance with this profession, therefore, that God is the provider and manager of all things, it follows that he makes known what he wishes or what is advantageous for men. For if he should not make these things known he will not be the provider for man nor will he be believed to care for mortal affairs."[85] Here Origen moves, as Hanson has done in the quote above, from God's providential action in history to his communicative action.

In light of examples such as these, it is clear that Hanson has distorted our picture of Origen's scriptural exegesis. There *were* occasions when he viewed history as Hanson would later advocate, as a "significant" event marked by God's direct self-disclosure, accessible to a literal interpretation.[86] Of course, Hanson could also point out—and rightly so—that not all history was an "event" for Origen. He did not see God's personal self-revelation in, for instance, the weaning of Isaac, or in the fact that the Hebrews marched through certain towns in the Sinai wilderness, or in the crucifixion of the king of Ai.[87] Not every episode recorded in the biblical narratives constituted an "event" for Origen, i.e., direct divine self-disclosure (recall Hanson's lofty account of history as event: "history is *par excellence* the field of God's revelation of himself").[88] But why this should be troublesome is not clear, especially since it does not appear that Hanson himself escapes this "problem." Would he see the aforementioned episodes as moments of God's self-revelation where "his will and purposes were made plain"? When he illustrates history as "event," he tellingly chooses situations (national crises), a figure (Jesus), or an institution (the church) that are described in biblical texts as illustrative of God's clear action in history. What about other, less theophanic, moments? Even for Hanson, one suspects, not all biblical history was an "event."

The first point, then, is this: that Origen was not so exclusively an allegorist that he failed to embrace, with Hanson, the "significance" of history as the field of God's self-revelation. The second issue concerns allegory itself. In those cases where Origen allegorized an episode that was admittedly *not* an event, Hanson invites his readers to conclude that it was merely a "parable." But if this conclusion is drawn, a damaging insinuation follows. In Hanson's schema, it is *only* history as event that is "significant," its importance conferred upon it because it alone is explicitly associated with divine revelation. By implication, then, in those cases where Origen did not allegorize an event, he allegorized a "parable," invariably described by Hanson as a past devoid of "significance" since it was not connected to divine revelation.[89] But does this follow? When Origen was not allegorizing an event, was he allegorizing a parabolic episode unrelated to divine revelation, and thus an episode without significance?

Here we encounter the main problem with Hanson's two-fold conception of history: it does not capture the complexity or scope of Origen's view of divine revelation. For Hanson, revelation is restrictive: it concerns God's disclosure of himself, in a direct manner, through a handful of historical events, figures and institutions. For Origen, revelation was far more expansive: it was not confined to God's self-revelation, but included a spectrum of teachings; it was not tied to a handful of momentous events, but included all the details of biblical history; it was, moreover, not simply found in history, but also in the narratives about this history—that is, even the Scriptures themselves were revelatory; and finally, God's communicative strategy in these writings was not restricted to the obvious, literal referent. It also included the allegorical.[90] For Origen, in other words, God's revelation was not confined to Hanson's "event." God's providential and revelatory action was expressed far more broadly, including through the Scriptures, the object of Origen's exegetical project. Thus, when he allegorized scriptural episodes that were not "events," it does not follow that they were "parables" as Hanson understood them, i.e., insignificant moments *devoid* of God's revelation. Quite the contrary, especially because these episodes were recorded in Scripture, they were also revelatory or significant.

Does Origen's exegetical project, allegory in particular, then, presuppose the view that "history could never be of any significance"? This claim is misguided in at least two ways. First, along with Hanson, Origen too acknowledged that history was the field of God's direct self-disclosure. Indeed, it is hardly clear that biblical history was more "eventful" for Hanson than it was for Origen. Second, Origen was willing to associate revelation, and thus significance, with far more than "events." In so doing, he actually had a much *wider* notion of history's significance than Hanson was willing to acknowledge. And this, I suspect, was Hanson's real (though unexpressed) grievance. Not that there was too little divine revelation in Origen's conception of the past, but too much.

## V. Conclusion

In this article I have sought to dispel some of the confusions that surround a persistent and often poorly nuanced critique of early Christian allegory: that it was not historical. As I have demonstrated, there are remarkably different ways in which this critique has been leveled against Origen. As I have also hoped to demonstrate, these criticisms have rarely hit their intended target, and when they have, they do not appear to be particularly troubling. The deficiencies in Origen's allegorical project must lie elsewhere.

*NOTES*

I would like to thank Ronald E. Heine and Paul Martens for their constructive comments on earlier drafts of this article. Abbreviations: ACW = Ancient Christian Writers; GCS = *Die Griechischen Christlichen Schriftsteller der ersten drei Jahrhunderte*; GK = *Origenes: Vier Bücher von den Prinzipien*, third edition, eds. H. Görgemanns and H. Karpp (Darmstadt: Wissenschaftliche Buchgesellschaft, 1992); FC = Fathers of the Church; SC = Sources Chrétiennes.

1 William Fairweather, *Origen and Greek Patristic Theology* (Edinburgh: T. & T. Clark, 1901), p. 79.

2 G. W. Butterworth, "Introduction," *Origen: On First Principles* (London: SPCK, 1936), p. lvii.

3 Joseph W. Trigg, *Origen: The Bible and Philosophy in the Third-century Church* (Atlanta, GA: John Knox Press, 1983), p. 179.

4 Bertrand de Margerie, *An Introduction to the History of Exegesis*, Vol. 1, *The Greek Fathers*, trans. L. Maluf (Petersham, MA: St. Bede's Publications, 1993), p. 197.

5 Pontifical Biblical Commission, *Letter to the Archbishops and Bishops of Italy* (August 20, 1941), in *The Scripture Documents: An Anthology of Official Catholic Teachings*, ed. and trans. Dean P. Béchard (Collegeville, MN: Liturgical Press, 2001), p. 214.

6 There are two additional history-related criticisms that I will not address: that Origen's allegory was not sensitive to progressive revelation, and that Origen was only interested in words, not their underlying events.

7 See esp. Eustathius of Antioch, *On the Belly-Myther, Against Origen*, p. 21; Epiphanius of Salamis, *Panarion*, 64.4.11; Theophilus of Alexandria, *Tractate on Isaiah* (*Theophilus of Alexandria*, trans. N. Russell [London: Routledge, 2007], pp. 160–161); Jerome, *Against John of Jerusalem* 7.

8 Jean-Marie Olivier, *Diodori Tarsensis commentarii in Psalmos*, Vol. 1, *Commentarius in Psalmos I–L*, CCSG 6 (Turnhout: Brepols, 1980), 7.125–130 (my translation). I have also consulted Diodore of Tarsus, *Commentary on Psalms 1–51*, trans. Robert C. Hill (Atlanta, GA: Society of Biblical Literature, 2005).

9 J.-M. Olivier, *Diodori Tarsensis*, 7.148–153.

10 J.-M. Olivier, *Diodori Tarsensis*, 8.154–160 (Hill modified).

11 J.-M. Olivier, *Diodori Tarsensis*, 7.130–133 (Hill modified). Diodore offers a similar definition of allegory later in his prologue to his *Comm. in Ps. 118*: "The Greeks call an allegory something that is understood in one way, but said in another [Ἕλληνες μὲν γὰρ ἀλληγορίαν ὀνομάζουσι πρᾶγμα ἄλλως μὲν νοούμενον, ἄλλως δὲ ἀγορευόμενον]" (L. Mariés, "Extraits du commentaire de Diodore de Tarse sur les Psaumes," *Recherches de Science Religieuse*, Vol. 9 [1919], 90.11–12).

12 Both examples are from the prologue to Diodore's *Comm. in Ps. 118* (L. Mariés, "Extraits du commentaire de Diodore de Tarse," 90.12–25; translation: K. Froehlich, *Biblical Interpretation in the Early Church* [Philadelphia, PA: Fortress Press, 1984], pp. 87–88).

13 Note as well the following fragment from an exegetical work on the Octateuch, in which Diodore famously writes: "We far prefer the historical to the allegorical sense [ὅτι τοῦ ἀλληγορικοῦ τὸ ἱστορικὸν πλεῖστον ὅσον προτιμῶμεν]" (J. Deconinck, *Essai sur la chaîne de l'Octateuque, avec une édition des commentaires de Diodore de Tarse qui s'y trouvent contenus* [Paris: Librairie Ancienne Honore Champion, 1912], frg. 57, lines 64–65).

14 J.-M. Olivier, *Diodori Tarsensis*, 7.133–135 (translation by Hill modified). A very similar defense of Paul can be found in the preface to Diodore's *Comm. in Ps. 118*.

15 J.-M. Olivier, *Diodori Tarsensis*, 7.139–140 (translation mine).

16 J.-M. Olivier, *Diodori Tarsensis*, 7.143–145 (Hill modified). The interpretation of the "abyss" (Gen. 1:2) is probably derived from Origen's *Commentary on Genesis* (*Die Kommentierung des Buches Genesis*, Origenes: Werke mit deutscher Übersetzung, 1/1, intro. and trans. Karin Metzler, [Berlin: DeGruyter, 2010]: C I 1). The interpretation of the "dragon" (Job 40:25; 26:13) also likely goes back to Origen (*Princ.* 1.5.5; 3.2.1). See as well Diodore's rejection of allegorizing the serpent (Gen. 3) as the devil in his commentary on Psalm 118.

17 Diodore did not explicitly identify his opponent(s) in the *Commentary on the Psalms*. While the literature has postulated a variety of sources that might have triggered his critique of allegory, scholars have not implausibly proposed that Origen ought to be considered one of these otherwise anonymous commentators criticized by Diodore. In addition to the previous footnote, consider (as we will see below), several passages in book four of *On First Principles* where Origen made statements about the authenticity of ostensibly historical narratives in Scripture, including the opening chapters of Genesis, that would certainly have appeared incriminating to Diodore. Note that Diodore's association of allegorical interpretation with Hellenism also suggests he had Origen in mind, since this association strongly echoed Porphyry's earlier critique of Origen's allegory: "But Origen, having been educated as a Greek in Greek literature, went over to the barbarian recklessness [i.e., Christianity]. . . . And he used the books of Chaeremon the Stoic, and of Cornutus. Becoming

acquainted through them with the figurative interpretation of the Grecian mysteries, he applied it to the Jewish Scriptures" (Eusebius, citing Porphyry, at *Ecclesiastical History* 6.19.5-8/GCS 9.2, 558.23-560.17).

Finally, as I will point out below, Diodore's pupil, Theodore, directs both of these criticisms (that allegory denies historicity and was improperly indebted to Plato) against Origen. For a survey of the attempts to identify the motives and opponents for Diodore's critique of allegory, see F. Thome, *Historia contra Mythos: Die Schriftauslegung Diodors von Tarsus und Theodors von Mopsuestia im Widerstreit zu Kaiser Julians und Salustius' allegorischem Mythenverständnis* (Bonn: Borengässer, 2004), pp. 3–14.

18    This tractate forms the preface to Theodore's interpretation of Psalm 118 and only survives in a Syriac translation, transmitted in a single manuscript that was published (with a French translation) by Lucas van Rompay, *Théodore de Mopsueste: Fragments syriaque du Commentaire des Psalmes (Psaume 118 et Psaumes 138–148)*, CSCO 189–190 (Louvain: Peeters, 1982). For an English translation, see F. G. McLeod, *Theodore of Mopsuestia* (London: Routledge, 2009), pp. 75–79. Note that several ancient bibliographic reports attribute to Theodore a distinct book against the allegorists (see Van Rompay, *Théodore*, preface, p. xlvii).

19    The *Commentary on Galatians* survives in a Latin translation (with scattered Greek fragments). H. B. Swete, *Theodori Episcopi Mopsuesteni in epistolas B. Pauli commentarii*, vol. 1, *Introduction. Galatians-Colossians* (Cambridge: Cambridge University Press, 1880). The best English translation of Theodore's interpretation of Gal. 4:22–31 is in K. Froehlich, *Biblical Interpretation in the Early Church*, pp. 95–103.

20    H. B. Swete, *Theodori Episcopi*, 73.26–74.3 (translation mine).

21    H. B. Swete, *Theodori Episcopi*, 74.6–75.2 (Froehlich slightly modified).

22    H. B. Swete, *Theodori Episcopi*, 79.5–7.

23    Pamphilus, along with Eusebius, wrote the first five books of this work ca. 307–310 (after Pamphilus' death in 310, Eusebius added a sixth). Only the first book survives in Rufinus' Latin translation (ca. 397). In section 122 Pamphilus writes: "It remains to respond to the slanderous accusation that Origen transforms all Scripture into allegory. We will show from those very books on which his detractors especially base their charges against him . . . that Origen does not deny the things that are reported in the Scriptures as having also been accomplished literally" (*Apology for Origen with the letter of Rufinus on the Falsification of the books of Origen*, trans. T. P. Scheck, FC 120 [Washington, DC: Catholic University of America Press, 2010], p. 95). Pamphilus cites at length from two passages in Origen's writings where he clearly announces his belief in the historicity of the people, events and places narrated in Scripture (sections 123 and 125). "The things that have been said," Pamphilus concludes in section 126, ". . . suffice to show the nature of his views regarding the historical record itself of the Scriptures" (Scheck modified). Pamphilus never identifies Origen's "detractors," but scholars widely regard Methodius (†311) as one of the opponents. His treatise, *On the Resurrection*, was explicitly written against Origen (see *Apology for Origen*, sections 18–19; L. G. Patterson, *Methodius of Olympus: Divine Sovereignty, Human Freedom, and Life in Christ* [Washington, DC: Catholic University of America Press, 1997], p. 16).

24    *Princ.* 4.3.1/GK 730, 323.5–732, 324.4 (Butterworth modified).

25    See *Princ.* 4.3.1. For other passages where Origen denies the historicity of biblical pericopes, see *Princ.* 4.2.9; 4.3.10, as well as the divergent discussions by H. de Lubac, *History and Spirit: The Understanding of Scripture according to Origen*, trans. A. E. Nash and J. Merriell (San Francisco, CA: Ignatius Press, 2007), pp. 111–116 and R. P. C. Hanson, *Allegory and Event: A Study of the Sources and Significance of Origen's Interpretation of Scripture* (Richmond, VA: John Knox Press, 1959), pp. 264–277. This tendency to deny historicity is especially pronounced in Origen's interpretation of the opening chapters of Genesis. See my forthcoming article, "Origen's Doctrine of Pre-Existence and the Opening Chapters of Genesis" in *Zeitschrift für Antikes Christentum*.

26    *Princ.* 4.3.1/GK 734, 325.1–4 (Butterworth).

27    *Princ.* 4.3.4/ GK 740, 328.11–15 (Butterworth). This argument betrays Origen's philological training. Late antique literary criticism—into which he had not only been initiated, but which he also taught—repeatedly wrestled with the historical plausibility of the literary narratives it sought to interpret. Critics employed a variety of criteria to help them determine whether these stories were factual or fictitious. As the above reflections from *On First Principles* indicate, Origen applied the same training he used to interpret the traditional

Greek literature to the biblical text (see esp. *Cels.* 1.42 and *Comm. in Jo.* 10.14–20). On this approach to narratives in late antiquity, see esp. R. M. Grant, *The Letter and the Spirit* (London: SPCK, 1957), pp. 99–102, and *The Earliest Lives of Jesus* (New York, NY: Harper, 1961), pp. 40–49; 50–78.

28  *Princ* 4.3.4/GK 742, 329.1–13 (Butterworth emended).

29  *Princ.* 4.3.5/GK 746, 331.3–6 (Butterworth).

30  *Hom. in Ez.* 1.3.6/SC 352, 52.74–77 (Origen, *Homilies 1–14 on Ezekiel*, ACW 62, trans. T. P. Scheck [New York, NY: Newman Press, 2010], p. 31).

31  *Hom. in Gen.* 2.1/SC 7 bis, 76.1–8 (Origen, *Homilies on Genesis and Exodus*, FC 71, trans. R. Heine [Washington, DC: Catholic University of America Press, 1982], p. 72).

32  This point is now widely recognized in the scholarship. For dossiers of passages where Origen asserts the historicity of biblical narratives, see J. Daniélou, *Origen*, trans. W. Mitchell (New York, NY: Sheed and Ward, 1955), pp. 139–199; H. de Lubac, *History and Spirit*, pp. 106–111, 131–134; R. P. C. Hanson, *Allegory and Event*, pp. 262–264.

33  For illustrations, see the detailed discussion in Bernard Neuschäfer, *Origenes als Philologe* (Basel: Friedrich Reinhardt, 1987), pp. 164–188. On Origen's meteorological, astronomical, astrological, mineralogical, zoological and medicinal remarks, see pp. 188–202.

34  For example, see *Hom. in Gen.* 2.1–2 (on Noah's ark); *Hom. in Josh.* 11.1 (sun and moon standing still); *Hom. 1 Sam.* 5 (Samuel's soul raised from the dead); *Cels.* 1.42–48 (God's presence at Jesus' baptism).

35  On the diverse ways in which this distinction has been construed, see Peter W. Martens, "Revisiting the Allegory/Typology Distinction: The Case of Origen," *Journal of Early Christian Studies*, Vol. 16 (2008), pp. 285–296.

36  See the distinction between an allegory and a type in Salomo Glassius' *Philologia Sacra* (Jena: Steinmann, 1623), where the former points to a "mystery of spiritual doctrine" and the latter to "events" in the New Testament (L. Goppelt, *Typos: The Typological Interpretation of the Old Testament in the New*, trans. D. H. Madvig [Grand Rapids, MI: Wm. B. Eerdmans Publishing Company, 1982], p. 6). Note also the fact/doctrine distinction in the lengthy entry, "Type," in *Cyclopedia of Biblical, Theological and Ecclesiastical Literature*, eds. J. McClintock and J. Strong, Vol. 10 (Grand Rapids, MI: Baker, 1881), III.3.

37  For variations of this definition, see: s.v. Ἀλληγορέω in H. Cremer, *Biblico-Theological Lexicon of New Testament Greek*, fourth edition, trans. W. Urwick (Edinburgh: T & T Clark, 1895), p. 97; J. Daniélou, "Qu'est-ce que la typologie?," in *L'Ancien Testament et les chrétiens*, ed. P. Auvray, et al. (Paris: Éditions du Cerf, 1951), p. 199; K. J. Woollcombe, "The Biblical Origins and Patristic Development of Typology," in *Essays on Typology*, eds. G. W. H. Lampe and K. J. Woollcombe (London: SCM Press, 1957), p. 39; A. T. Hanson, "Typology," in *The Oxford Companion to the Bible*, eds. B. M. Metzger and M. D. Coogan (New York, NY: Oxford University Press, 1993); H.-P. Mathys, "Typology," *The Encyclopedia of Christianity*, eds. E. Fahlbusch, et al., trans. G. W. Bromiley, Vol. 5 (Grand Rapids, MI: Wm. B. Eerdmans Publishing Company, 1999); s.v. "Types," in *Oxford Dictionary of Christian Church*, third edition, eds. F. L. Cross and E. A. Livingstone (Oxford: Oxford University Press, 2005).

38  E. Auerbach, *Mimesis: The Representation of Reality in Western Literature*, trans. W. R. Trask (Princeton, NJ: Princeton University Press, 1953), p. 73.

39  W. A. Bienert, *"Allegoria" und "Anagoge" bei Didymos dem Blinden von Alexandria* (Berlin: W. de Gruyter, 1972), p. 42; R. Greer and J. Kugel, *Early Biblical Interpretation* (Philadelphia, PA: Westminster Press, 1986), pp. 178–181; M. Simonetti, *Biblical Interpretation in the Early Church: An Historical Introduction to Patristic Exegesis*, transl. J. A. Hughes (Edinburgh: T & T Clark, 1994), p. 22.

40  W. Fairweather, *Origen and Greek Patristic Theology*, p. 71.

41  Erich Auerbach, "Figura," in *Scenes from the Drama of European Literature* (Minneapolis, MN: University of Minnesota Press, 1984), p. 53; C. H. Dodd, *The Interpretation of the Fourth Gospel* (Cambridge: Cambridge University Press, 1953), p. 142.

42  Luke Timothy Johnson, *The Writings of the New Testament*, third edition (Minneapolis, MN: Fortress Press, 2010), p. 32. This is a traditional position in New Testament scholarship: see H. Cremer, *Biblico-Theological Lexicon*, p. 97; F. Büchsel, ἀλληγορέω, *Theological Dictionary of the New Testament*, ed. G. Kittel, transl. G. W. Bromiley, Vol. 1 (Grand Rapids, MI: Wm. B. Eerdmans Publishing Company, 1964), p. 263; G. R. Osborne, "Type, Typology," in *Evangelical Dictionary of Theology*, ed. W. A. Elwell, second edition (Grand Rapids, MI: Baker

Academic, 2001). J. Daniélou applies this conception of the "non-Christian" allegorical referent to Origen (*From Shadows to Reality: Studies in the Biblical Typology of the Fathers*, trans. W. Hibberd (Westminster, MD: Newman Press, 1960), pp. vii-viii, 4; idem, *Origen*, pp. 174–199.

43  S.v. "Allegory," *Cyclopedia of Biblical, Theological and Ecclesiastical Literature*, eds. J. McClintock and J. Strong, Vol. 1 (Grand Rapids: Baker, 1867).

44  S.v. "Types," in *Oxford Dictionary of Christian Church*, third edition, eds. F. L. Cross and E. A. Livingstone (Oxford: Oxford University Press, 2005).

45  Carol A. Newsom, "Interpretation: Christian Interpretation in the Premodern Era," in *The New Oxford Annotated Bible with the Apocrypha*, third edition, eds. M. D. Coogan, M. Z. Brettler, C. A. Newsom (Oxford: Oxford University Press, 2007), p. 485.

46  For example, R. P. C. Hanson, *Allegory and Event*, refers to the "non-historical truths" of which historical events were parabolic enactments (p. 277), and a little later to "anti-historical" allegories of history (p. 280).

47  For dossiers illustrating Origen's figurative approach to the Old Testament, see J. Daniélou, *Origen*, pp. 139–173, 174–199; H. de Lubac, *History and Spirit*, pp. 103–128; 190–204; R. P. C. Hanson, *Allegory and Event*, pp. 277–281.

48  P. W. Martens, "Revisiting the Allegory/Typology Distinction," pp. 296–310.

49  See esp. *Princ.* 1.preface.3–10; 4.2.2; 4.2.7–9. When Origen summarized the teaching of Scripture, he did so in the following ways: in terms of its ethical and doctrinal instruction, the list of articles in the church's rule of faith, the motif of the soul's journey to God, and the figure of Jesus Christ. For a more detailed account of how Origen understood the scriptural message, see Peter W. Martens, *Origen and Scripture: the Contours of the Exegetical Life* (Oxford: Oxford University Press, 2012), pp. 201–221.

50  S.v. ἱστορία, *A Greek-English Lexicon*, ninth edition, eds. H. G. Liddell, et al. (Oxford: Clarendon, 1996). See as well, F. Young, *Biblical Exegesis and the Formation of Christian Culture* (Cambridge: Cambridge University Press, 1997), pp. 79–80; J. W. Trigg, "Introduction," *Allegory and Event*, p. xii.

51  In addition to the examples provided below, see: *Hom. in Jer.* 4.1.2; 9.1.4; 10.4.2; 14.12.4; 20.7.5; *Comm. in Jo.* 10.14–19; 10.159–160; *Princ.* 4.3.1; 4.3.4; *Hom. in Gen.* 2.1; 10.4; *Hom. in Ex.* 5.1; *Hom. in Ez.* 1.3.6; 1.5.1; etc.

52  *Hom. in Jer.* 19.14.3/SC 238, 232.32–34.

53  *Comm. in Jo.* 2.4/GCS 4, 52.18–20.

54  *Hom. in Gen.* 1.17/SC 7 bis, 70.7 ff (Heine slightly modified).

55  *Comm. in Jo.* 2.175/GCS 4, 85.28–34 (*Origen: Commentary on the Gospel according to John, Books 1–10*, trans. R. E. Heine, FC 80 [Washington, DC: Catholic University of America Press, 1989], p. 142).

56  *Hom. in Gen.* 7.1/SC 7 bis, 194.11–16 (Heine).

57  *Hom. in Ex.* 7.3/SC 321, 212.9–10 (Heine). Or again, of Jeremiah prophesying: "What, then," Origen asks, "does this history [αὕτη ἡ ἱστορία] mean for me" (*Hom. in Jer.* 1.2/SC 232, 198.7–8)? For similar statements where the simple record of events does not provide nourishment, but simply information, and thus needs to be transcended in search of an edifying doctrine, see: *Hom. in Gen.* 2.2–3; 10.2; 10.4; 15.1; *Hom. in Ex.* 1.5; *Hom. in Lev.* 5.5.1; *Hom. in Num.* 1.1.2–3; 25.3.1; 27.1–2, esp. 27.6.1; *Hom. in Josh.* 8.6; 9.8 *Hom. in Song* 1.4; *Hom. in Is.* 4.3; *Hom. in Ez.* 1.4; *Hom. in Lk.* 37.1; *Princ.* 4.2.7. Sometimes, the historical record conveys information that actually damages the faith: *Hom. in Josh* 12.3; *Comm. in Jo.* 20.67 (for more on this theme, see H. de Lubac, *History and Spirit*, pp. 118–128).

58  Note that Origen will sometimes assert that the ἱστορίαι have an edifying meaning at the level of the letter. See, for instance, *Hom. in Lev.* 3.2.1–6; 3.6.3; *Hom. in Num.* 11.1; 20.1.5; 22.2.1; *Hom. in Jd.* 5.2; *Hom. in Jer.* 5.15.1; *Princ.* 4.2.4–6; *Cels.* 4.47. But more often than not, they do not, and thus they require a figurative interpretation to extract a doctrine that is suitable for his audience.

59  A point already grasped by P. D. Huet in his *Origeniana* (Rouen: Bertholini, 1668)—see H. de Lubac, *History and Spirit*, pp. 133–134 and J. Daniélou, *Origen*, pp. 163–164. For a longer discussion of the authorial intent of Scripture's writers, see P. W. Martens, *Origen and Scripture*, pp. 194–200.

60  *Princ.* 4.2.4/GK 710, 313.1–4. It is in the light of the foregoing discussion that the following passage is to be heard: "For we must not suppose that historical things are types of historical

things, and corporeal of corporeal. Quite the contrary: corporeal things are types of spiritual things, and historical of intellectual." (οὐ γὰρ νομιστέον τὰ ἱστορικὰ ἱστορικῶν εἶναι τύπους καὶ τὰ σωματικὰ σωματικῶν, ἀλλὰ τὰ σωματικὰ πνευματικῶν καὶ τὰ ἱστορικὰ νοητῶν) (*Comm. in Jo.* 10.110/GCS 4, 189.27–29).

61  On the leading themes of the scriptural message, see *Princ.* 1.preface.3–10 and 4.2.7 (and ftn. 49 above).

62  See esp. B. de Margerie, who repeatedly associates Origen's allegory with both the denial of history (pp. 98, 111, 197) and his Platonic worldview (*Introduction to the History of Exegesis*, pp. 100–101, esp. p. 111). For an incisive account of Origen's relationship to Plato, see Mark J. Edwards, *Origen against Plato* (Aldershot: Ashgate, 2002).

63  Note Origen's unambiguous denial of Platonic forms, which he takes to be a world "that exists solely in the mind's fancy or the unsubstantial region of thought" (*Princ.* 2.3.6), as well as his insistence that there is not a plurality of *parallel* worlds, but that these are sequential (*Princ.* 3.5.3; 3.6.8–9).

64  See esp. the quote at ftn. 45 above.

65  So also, s.v. "allegory," *The Westminster Dictionary of New Testament and Early Christian Literature and Rhetoric*, ed. D. Aune (Louisville, KY: Westminster/John Knox Press, 2003), p. 31.

66  "For it is this Trinity alone which exceeds all comprehension, not only of temporal but even of eternal intelligence. The rest of things, however, which are external to the Trinity must be measured by ages and periods of time" (*Princ.* 4.4.1/GK 788, 350.23–26 [Butterworth]). On the time- and place-lessness of the Father and Son, see *Princ.* 4.4.1–2.

67  Thus, in broad agreement with J. Daniélou, who writes: "The thing that prevents him [i.e., Origen] from being a mere philosopher is that in his view Christianity is essentially history" (*Origen*, p. 153).

68  *Allegory and Event*, p. 7. At stake for Hanson with this question is the future direction of Anglican theology: "Anglican scholars in particular have always claimed that their appeal is to the Bible as interpreted by the early Fathers. But if the interpretation of the Bible by one of the greatest of these early Fathers is radically different from the interpretation which we would give of it today, and diverges so drastically in its assumptions, what is left of this appeal to the early Fathers" (p. 365)?

69  For Hanson's earlier attempt to deal with the deficiency of Origen's allegory, see "History and Allegory," *Theology*, Vol. 59 (1956), pp. 498–503.

70  Hanson, *Allegory and Event*, pp. 362; 368.

71  *Ibid.*, p. 363.

72  *Ibid.*

73  *Ibid.*, p. 364. Most of the chapter entitled "Historicity" investigates the passages where Origen denies and affirms historicity (pp. 259–277).

74  *Ibid.*, p. 364.

75  *Ibid.*

76  *Ibid.*, p. 276.

77  *Ibid.*, p. 365.

78  *Ibid.*, pp. 63, 126, on the sufficiency of the literal meaning of Scripture.

79  *Ibid.*, p. 363.

80  *Hom. in Ez.* 1.1.1/SC 352, 36.1–16 (Scheck).

81  Hanson, *Allegory and Event*, p. 364.

82  *Princ.* 2.6.2/GK 358, 140.25–141.5 (Butterworth emended).

83  Hanson, *Allegory and Event*, pp. 363–364.

84  *Hom. in Gen.* 3.2/SC 7 bis, 114.18–116.8 (Heine). Not only do we find this theme of providence repeatedly expressed in Origen's writings, he often uses the noun πρόνοια (providence) as a synonym for "God" (see *Princ.* 1.4.3; 2.1.1–3; *Comm. in Jo.* 2.31; on "providence" as an alternative for "God": *Princ.* 4.1.7; *Phil.* 10.2). Indeed, since Hal Koch's important study on this topic (*Pronoia et Paideusis: Studien über Origenes und sein Verhältnis zum Platonismus* [Berlin: W. de Gruyter, 1932]), many scholars consider divine providence not simply *a* theme, but an organizing principle in Origen's thought.

85  *Hom. in Gen.* 3.2/SC 7 bis, 116.11–15 (Heine).

86  It is also important to note that even when Origen allegorized, he did not necessarily deny history as "event." Hanson strongly suggests that "event" and "parable" are mutually

exclusive views of the past, but there are significant counter examples that indicate how Origen allegorized historical episodes that he *also* thought were events. For instance, while God's direct self-communication took place during the Babylonian captivity, this captivity was also "a sign of something else" (*Hom. in Ez.* 1.3.6 [cited above at ftn. 30]). Or again, while God's self-revelation transpired pre-eminently in the incarnation, "[t]he truth of the events recorded to have happened to Jesus cannot be fully seen in the mere text and historical narrative; for each event to those who read the Bible more intelligently is clearly a symbol of something as well" (*Cels.* 2.69/SC 132, 446.3–7 [*Origen: Contra Celsum*, trans. Henry Chadwick [Cambridge: Cambridge University Press, 1953], p. 118]). "Events" were far more compatible with allegory than Hanson suggests.

87   *Hom. in Gen.* 7.1; *Hom. in Ex.* 7.3; *Hom. in Josh.* 8.6, respectively. See as well the texts listed at ftn. 57 above.

88   Though it is important to re-iterate that just because an event was not an instance of direct, divine self-revelation, it does not follow for Origen that God was not providentially active in this case, or, as I will note below, that this event was not revelatory in some other way.

89   Hanson does not associate "history as parable" with revelation, only "history as event." For example: "To the biblical writers, history is not a parable, it is the field in which God most unmistakably acts" ("History and Allegory," p. 502). Also see the quote above at ftn. 76.

90   See esp. *Princ.* 1.pref.3–9; 4.1.1–4.3.5.

# 4

# "THIS IS THE DAY WHICH THE LORD HAS MADE": SCRIPTURE, MANUMISSION, AND THE HEAVENLY FUTURE IN SAINT GREGORY OF NYSSA

## HANS BOERSMA

One of the most common objections to pre-modern exegesis is that it does not do justice to the historical, earthly character of the biblical text. In their desire to allegorize and spiritualize, pre-modern theologians are often thought to neglect earthly and bodily concerns in favour of heavenly and spiritual realities. Put sharply, many are inclined to think that theologians such as St. Gregory of Nyssa were too heavenly minded to be of any earthly good. This article will reflect on this objection, and I will suggest that for Gregory, heaven and earth are not realities that we can separate as if they had little or nothing to do with each other. Instead, I will argue, it is precisely Gregory's spiritual interpretation and his anagogical or heavenly desire that motivates his concern for historical, embodied existence—including the matter of slavery.[1] So, I will link Gregory's interest in spiritual exegesis to his opposition to slavery. I will argue that the consequence of his theological approach to Scripture is not disinterested otherworldliness but a genuine concern to bring heaven to earth. For Gregory, social concern makes sense precisely in the context of his thoroughly heavenly-minded or anagogical approach to theology.

The mystical bent and the anagogical orientation of St. Gregory do not, therefore, leave him indifferent to social injustice, as he encounters it in his context particularly in the oppression of slavery and in the hardships caused

*Heaven on Earth?: Theological Interpretation in Ecumenical Dialogue*, First Edition.
Edited by Hans Boersma and Matthew Levering.
© 2013 Blackwell Publishing Ltd. Book compilation © 2013 Blackwell Publishing Ltd.

by poverty, leprosy, and usury.[2] Social concerns are an integral aspect of Gregory's overall thought. To be sure, Nyssen never regards temporal and material conditions as ultimate concerns. But the distinction between temporal (penultimate) and eternal (ultimate) significance cuts two ways. It may be true that social and economic suffering is not, in and of itself, a matter of ultimate significance (since on Gregory's view all suffering will be overcome in the eschaton). But it is also true that people who own human beings as if they were mere bodies *do* treat pleasure and material well-being as their ultimate ends, and it is this selfish focus on the present that Gregory wants to expose. This means that anagogical and eschatological concerns remain of paramount importance to Nyssen, also when it comes to the issue of slavery.

As I discuss St. Gregory's rationale for his opposition to slavery, I will address specifically the apparent discrepancy between his earthly interest in the bodily matter of slavery and his anagogical or heavenly concern for the soul elsewhere in his writings. For Gregory, these are not two profoundly dissimilar issues; rather, there is an underlying cohesion when he deals with matters of both body and soul, of heaven and earth. It seems to me that Gregory is always, first and foremost, an anagogical theologian, whose deepest interest lies in the heavenly well-being of the soul. But this in no way implies that he ignores the body. After all, his invectives against the social evil of slavery would be inexplicable if the body were of no account. Instead, I will argue, these denunciations only make sense in the light of Nyssen's deeply held anagogical convictions. In particular, I will argue that his opposition to slavery is grounded squarely in theological convictions, so that it is his anagogical approach that renders his social concern intelligible. Precisely because for St. Gregory slavery is not just a matter of "enslaved bodies," he feels compelled to express his outrage. The levelling of relationships that manumission implies is, for Nyssen, a proleptic implementation of heavenly, eschatological equality and, as such, is part and parcel of his ascetic and anagogical theology.

## Manumission in Annisa

There is a great deal of disagreement on how to interpret St. Gregory's opposition to slavery. A number of authors have minimized his rejection of slavery. Some maintain that Gregory, like his brother Basil, must have owned slaves himself.[3] Nyssen, so it is argued, never alludes to a practical solution for the emancipation of slaves and certainly does not directly confront the public social system on which slavery depended, in particular the *paterfamilias* system, which included slaves in its households.[4] Gregory's alleged omission of overt or practical demands that owners emancipate their slaves is also adduced as evidence that his position on slavery is less than forthright.[5] Faced with Gregory's sharp denunciations of slavery, these readers sometimes explain them as rhetorical *topoi* that should not be taken at face value.[6] By contrast, others have high praise for what they see as Nyssen's prophetic opposition to slavery.[7]

Fortunately, it seems to me that we can gain considerable clarity on Gregory's position, in part by avoiding some of the more common pitfalls. For example, while Gregory's most lengthy passage on slavery is clearly his denunciation in the fourth homily on Ecclesiastes, some of those who uphold the prophetic character of Gregory's views fail to take his other writings into account. Such investigation would, however, lend considerable strength to their conclusions.[8] Also, while we have no evidence of Gregory lobbying for changes in the empire's legal structures, and while his denunciations of slavery consistently take the form of sermonic appeals to slave owners to recognize the theological incongruity of their ownership and/or treatment of slaves, the social stature of the Bishop of Nyssa means that we ought not to underestimate the significance of these appeals. Furthermore, as we will see, the charge that Gregory does not present any overt pleas for emancipation simply does not stand up to scrutiny.[9]

The question whether or not St. Gregory himself owned slaves is difficult to answer with absolute certainty. It is clear that there were slaves in Gregory's family background. St. Basil, despite his obvious concern about the way slaves were treated, likely owned slaves.[10] Accordingly, in *De spiritu sancto*, he puts up a defence of slavery.[11] This is something Gregory never does. The family's move from their rich urban life in Neocaesarea to the country household of Annisa appears to have impacted Gregory deeply. While the family apparently moved away from the city in the late 340s, around 356 a much more radical change occurred. Gregory highlights the manumission that Macrina enacted in her monastic household, as she persuaded her mother Emmelia to "put herself in her mind on the same level (ὁμότιμον) with the many, and to share a common way of life with the virgins, making sisters and equals (ὁμοτίμους) of the slave girls and domestics who were with her."[12] Leading her mother down "to her own standard of humility (ταπεινοφροσύνης)," she showed her mother "how to live in equality (ὁμότιμον) with the whole body of virgins, that is, by sharing with them the same one table, the same kind of bed, and all the necessities of life on an equal basis (κατὰ τὸ ἴσον), with every distinction of rank removed from their life."[13] Anna Silvas explains the changes as follows: "First there was the emancipation of slaves, then in *c.* 356 the abrogation of social rank with Emmelia's adoption of the common life. By about 365 Annisa had emerged as a fully fledged cenobitic community, with an ordered place for ascetic men, women, and children."[14] To be sure, Gregory's positive appraisal of Macrina's actions does not in and of itself imply that he did not own any slaves. Still, seeing that his theological evaluation of slavery is, unlike Basil's, unambiguously negative, there is no reason to assume that Gregory's actions were inconsistent with his theological judgement. There is simply no positive evidence of Gregory owning slaves, and to have owned them would have made it difficult for his congregation to take his sermons on slavery seriously.[15]

Nyssen's attitude toward slavery is very much in line with his appreciation of the ascetic teachings of Eustathius (*c.* 300–379), with whom the Annasi household enjoyed a lengthy and close relationship, and whose radical asceticism was extremely influential on Gregory and his family.[16] For Macrina and Gregory, two issues were at stake in connection with slavery. First, manumission itself was required because of the inherent evil of enslaving other human beings. I will discuss Gregory's theological argumentation in this regard momentarily. Second, however, manumission did not just serve the social and economic improvement of the freed slaves. To be sure, freeing household slaves would likely involve a degree of upward mobility, even if the freed slaves would choose to remain as freed members of the same household. But Gregory also describes a downward mobility on the part of the former slave owners. He speaks of Emmelia "humiliating" (ταπεινοφροσύνης) herself to the level of slave girls, a humiliation that, as we have already seen, involved the equality (ὁμότιμον) of the "same one table" and the "same kind of bed."[17] The change in life was one in which Emmelia voluntarily gave up the "ostentatious manner and the services of domestics" to which she had been accustomed.[18] Similarly, Gregory's second eldest brother, Naucratius, entered upon a solitary life of "voluntary poverty."[19] The renunciation of slavery was part and parcel of a "philosophical and material way of life" that was "divorced from all earthly vanities and attuned to the imitation of the angelic life."[20] In short, life in the Annisa landholding was characterized as much by downward mobility on the part of Emmelia and Macrina as it was by upward mobility on the part of the slaves. This is not to deny that manumission of slaves was connected to Macrina's and Gregory's views of the human person. I simply want to observe that anthropological considerations were closely connected to ascetic concerns—that earthly matters of social concern were linked to the well-being of eternal, heavenly life. This meant for Gregory that rejection of slavery was not just the result of a concern for improvement in the lives of slaves—though it included that— but also implied the requirement on the part of the slave owner to lead a life of renunciation and poverty. Ironically, therefore, the decision to humble oneself by a downward movement to the life of a slave was at the same time an upward (anagogical) move: a proleptic implementation of the eschatological equality of heavenly existence.

Macrina's manumission of her slaves was not entirely unusual. Slavery appears to have been on the decrease in the empire in the fourth century, and Constantine had issued several edicts that gave the church a much larger say in how to deal with slaves, even if this legislation did not always assuage the situation of slaves in the empire.[21] In his edicts of 316 and 323, the emperor had legalized *manumissio in ecclesia*, allowing churches to free slaves in their communities,[22] a practice that appears to have taken place particularly during the celebration of Easter. Perhaps this is the process that Macrina's monastic community followed as well, though it is perhaps more likely that she freed her slaves through the enactment of *manumissio inter amicos*, in which, as Elm puts it, a "master simply declared a slave to be his friend, expressing this either by letter (*per epistulam*) or by inviting him to dine at the same table (*per mensam*)."[23]

The radical asceticism of Eustathius and his followers took the practice of ecclesial manumission to a new level. Their ascetic insistence on equality became such a concern to the ecclesial authorities that they issued a number of sharp condemnations at the Council of Gangra (340/1), with its third canon directly addressing the issue of slavery: "If anyone teaches a slave, under pretext of piety, to despise his master, to withdraw from his service and not to serve him with goodwill and all respect, let him be anathema."[24] Gregory, deeply influenced by Eustathius's teaching, can hardly have been impressed with the Council's promulgation.[25] To be sure, St. Gregory's sermons mostly addressed slaveholders rather than slaves, and so he never directly encouraged slaves to flee or to despise their masters. Still, his unequivocal condemnations of slavery can hardly be said to fit the spirit of the Council of Gangra.

None of this is to suggest that Nyssen was an activist or a lobbyist with secular authorities for the abolition of slavery or that he was entirely immune from an aristocratic sense of superiority toward slaves. We have no indication that Gregory went beyond denunciation of slavery in his sermons and other writings, and on occasion he did speak in derogatory terms about slaves. For example, one of the sermons that calls for manumission, *In sanctum Pascha*, also mentions final judgement, which will not escape "the worthless slave who pretended to have the rank of his Master,"[26] and contains the illustration of "wicked slaves who have spent all their master's money."[27] Elsewhere, Gregory depicts the followers of the anti-Nicene theologian Eunomius as "unrehearsed in theological doctrine, perhaps some slaves and worthless fellows and fugitives from menial service."[28] Thus, Gregory does seem willing to use the occasional negative stereotype of slaves to denounce his opponents. He may not quite measure up to today's attitudes toward slavery. Nonetheless, as we move to Gregory's views on the topic, it will become evident that they must have been exceptionally dynamic in their own context.

### Slavery and the Image of God

St. Gregory brings to the fore numerous arguments against slavery. Two clusters of arguments, however, predominate—anthropological and eschatological ones—and we will see that in both cases Nyssen links the slavery question closely to his anagogical approach to biblical interpretation. Gregory mentions his anthropological concerns particularly in his exegesis of the Lord's Prayer, of the Beatitudes, and of Ecclesiastes. Most extensive by far are the comments in his fourth homily on Ecclesiastes, though Gregory adduces a number of the same anthropological arguments in his fifth sermon on the Lord's Prayer.

The core of his logic here is centred on his belief that all human beings— slaves as well as masters—are made in the image of God. Regardless of what biblical passage Gregory deals with, he takes this theological conviction as his presupposition. To understand St. Gregory's attacks on slavery, we need to explore his understanding of the image of God in somewhat greater detail. First, the notion of freedom from necessity—which Gregory describes as free will (αὐτεξούσια)—constitutes for him the very core of what it means to be a human being. Thus, after mentioning man's rule over the animals in *De oratione dominica*, Nyssen comments: "But man He has adorned with the gift of free will (αὐτεξουσίῳ). Therefore he who is subject to you by custom and law is yet equal to you in dignity of nature. He is neither made by you, nor does he live through you, nor has he received from you his qualities of body and soul."[29] Reflecting on Solomon's dangerous boast in Ecclesiastes 2:7, "I acquired male and female slaves," St. Gregory comments indignantly: "What do you mean? You condemn men to slavery, when his nature is free (ἐλευθέρα) and possesses free will (αὐτεξούσιος), and you legislate in competition with God, overturning his law for the human species."[30] On most other occasions, Gregory distinguishes rather sharply between freedom (ἐλευθερία) that is opposed to slavery (whether physical or spiritual) and freedom (αὐτεξούσια) that consists of self-determination, that is, the human ability to choose either virtue or vice.[31] In this passage, however, Nyssen links the two, suggesting that slavery, as an attack on human freedom (ἐλευθερία) is at the same time an assault on free will (αὐτεξούσια). He does not explicitly state how it is that enslavement is also an attack on free will, and one might well object to Gregory that the external imposition of slavery cannot possibly obliterate a slave's free will. No doubt, Nyssen is aware of this. His point, however, is not that the slave owner is actually able to remove αὐτεξούσια. Rather, what is at stake is the master's attempt to reduce a human being to the level of an animal. His attack on another human being's dignity (through the removal of ἐλευθερία) does violence to that which makes him human and as such denies that person's αὐτεξούσια.

Second, Gregory links the image of God also with the human rule over creation. This link is clear not only in passages treating of slavery, but also in *De hominis opificio*, where Gregory describes man as the ruler (ἄρχων) who has dominion (ἀρχή) or rule (ἡγεμονία) over creation,[32] and where he explains that God

> made our nature as it were a formation fit for the exercise of royalty, preparing it at once by the superior advantages of soul, and by the very form of the body, to be such as to be adapted for royalty: for the soul immediately shows its royal and exalted character, far removed as it is

from the lowliness of private station, in that it owns no lord, and is self-governed, swayed autocratically by its own will; for to whom else does this belong than to a king? And further, besides these facts, the fact that it is the image of that Nature which rules over all means nothing else than this, that our nature was created to be royal from the first.[33]

Gregory unambiguously states that for human beings to be created in the image and likeness of God means that they have royalty and as such rule as kings over the created order (Gen. 1:26).[34] What is more, since a king does not have a master, Gregory goes back to his notion of free will by insisting that the soul is without master (ἀδέσποτον) and is self-governed (αὐτεξούσιον).[35] While at this point Nyssen does not spell out the implications for slavery, we will see that he does do so in his sermons on the Lord's Prayer and on Ecclesiastes. For St. Gregory, slavery is incompatible with human kingship over creation and, as such, contradicts the confession of human beings as made in the image of God.

To subject fellow human beings to slavery is, for Nyssen, a violation of the human person as ruler made in the image of God. Immediately before he mentions free will in *De oratione dominica*, Gregory comments:

You do not consider, when you are burning with anger against your servant (οἰκέτην), that it is not nature, but power that has divided mankind into servants (δουλείαν) and masters (κυριότητα). For the Lord (οἰκονόμος) of the universe has ordained that only the irrational nature should serve (δουλεύειν) man, as the Prophet says: *Thou hast subjected all things under his feet, all sheep and oxen, the birds and the beasts and the fishes* [Ps. 8:7–9 (6–8)]. He even calls them slaves (δοῦλα), as is stated in the Prophet's words elsewhere: *Who giveth to beasts their food, and herbs for the service* (δουλείᾳ) *of men* [Ps. 146 (147):9]. But man He has adorned with the gift of free will (αὐτεξουσίῳ).[36]

Gregory here places animals in the position of slavery vis-à-vis human beings, whose free will (αὐτεξούσια) does not brook slavery; again, to treat human beings as slaves is to treat them as animals. Nyssen makes the same argument in *In Ecclesiasten homilae*:

You have forgotten the limits of your authority, and that your rule is confined to control over things without reason. For it says *Let them rule over* winged creatures and fishes and four-footed things and creeping things (Gen, 1,26). Why do you go beyond what is subject to you and raise yourself up against the very species which is free, counting your own kind on a level with four-footed things and even footless things? *You have subjected all things* to man, declares the word through the prophecy, and in the text it lists the things subject, *cattle* and *oxen* and *sheep* (Ps 8,7–8). Surely human beings have not been produced from your cattle? Surely cows have not conceived human stock? Irrational beasts are the only slaves of mankind. But to you these things are of small account. *Raising fodder for the cattle, and green plants for the slaves of men*, it says (Ps 104/103,14). But by dividing the human species in two with "slavery" and "ownership" you have caused it to be enslaved to itself, and to be the owner of itself.[37]

In this passage, too, St. Gregory describes animals as being in slavery to human beings, this time explicitly referring to Genesis 1:26. The image of God in human beings is visible in their rule over the animals. One can justify slavery only by first reducing rational human beings to the level of irrational animals. Hence Nyssen's rhetorical questions, "Surely human beings have not been produced from your cattle? Surely cows have not conceived human stock?" Defenders of slavery, Gregory charges, fail to take note of the radical distinction between humans and animals.

Third, Gregory links the notion of the image of God to the unity of humanity. In *De hominis opificio* Gregory distinguishes between the first creation— God's foreknowledge of the fullness (πλήρωμα) of humanity—and the second creation—the creation of human beings, gendered as male and female. For Gregory, the former constitutes the image of God.[38] This unity of humanity is for Gregory ultimately the eschatological unity of all human beings in Christ, since it is Christ who constitutes the πλήρωμα of God.[39] This means that it is also Christ who is the actual image of God and whose humanity renders our humanity meaningful. Nyssen expresses this same fullness by speaking of the whole lump (φύραμα) of humanity (cf. Rom. 11:16; 1 Cor. 5:6–7).[40] This Christological and eschatological unity of humanity has obvious social implications. Gregory, we saw, maintains in one of his sermons on the Lord's Prayer that "it is not nature, but power that has divided mankind into servants and masters";[41] and in a nearly identical passage in his fourth sermon on Ecclesiastes, he states that "by dividing the human species in two with 'slavery' and 'ownership' you have caused it to be enslaved to itself, and to the owner of itself."[42] David Hart rightly points out the significance of St. Gregory's objection to any "division" of human beings between slave and master:

> Gregory's rhetoric . . . presses well beyond the issue of mere manumission and adumbrates that of abolition; the logic seems as irresistible as it does anachronistic—and therein lies its mystery. If any part of Gregory's sermon [on Ecclesiastes] perhaps provides a clue to the deeper currents of his thought, and to the stridency with which he expresses himself, it is this last phrase: "You have divided human nature. . . ."[43]

Gregory, Hart rightly maintains, regards slavery as a sin against God's own ultimate purpose, which is the unity of the entire πλήρωμα of humanity.

Whereas the word "fullness" (πλήρωμα) has primarily an eschatological referent, the expression "of the same race" (ὁμόφυλος) refers more unambiguously to the common "make-up" of humanity. Gregory uses it four times in his fourth homily on Ecclesiastes, three times in explicitly objecting to the arrogance in claiming ownership over someone who is "of the same race,"[44] and once in insisting on the absurdity of regarding someone "of the same race" as being on the level of animals.[45] Gregory expounds on this basic "sameness" of human beings when he challenges the slave owner to prove his superiority:

> What do you have to sustain your title as owner? I see no superiority over the subordinate accruing to you from the title other than the mere title. What does this power contribute to you as a person?—not longevity, nor beauty, nor good health, nor superiority in virtue. Your origin is of the same ancestors, your life is of the same kind, sufferings of soul and body prevail alike over you who own him and over the one who is subject to your ownership—pains and pleasures, merriment and distress, sorrows and delight, rages and terrors, sickness and death. Is there any difference in these things between the slave and his owner? Do they not draw in the same air as they breathe? Do they not see the sun in the same way? Do they not alike sustain their being by consuming food? Is not the arrangement of their guts the same? Are not the two one dust after death? Is there not one judgment for them?—a common Kingdom, and a common Gehenna?[46]

The basic "sameness" of human beings, based in their being "of the same race" (ὁμόφυλος) implies a radical equality with obvious social implications. In his sermon on Jesus' blessing of the "poor in spirit," Nyssen warns those who have attained high office and power against the danger of pride and conceit. They "stay no longer within the bounds of human nature," insists Gregory,[47] and instead "assume divine power and authority" by considering themselves masters (κύριοι) over the life and death of others.[48] St. Gregory questions this arrogance: "How then can he be sovereign (κύριος) over a life which does not belong to him, when his own does not belong to him? Even that person, therefore, if he becomes poor in spirit, looking to the one who willingly became poor because of us, and observing the equal respect (ὁμότιμον) we owe to members of our own race, will not inflict injury on those who share his origin as a result of that mistaken masquerade of government. . . ."[49] Ownership of other human beings violates, on Gregory's understanding, the equality of human beings that is grounded in a basic kinship and similarity among all who are made in the image of God.

## Slavery and the Resurrection

Considering Gregory's anthropology, it does not come as a surprise that he regards slavery as incompatible with the resurrection. He brings to the fore the intimate nature of the link between the doctrine of the resurrection and the abolition of slavery much more clearly in a sermon that he likely preached on 21 April 379.[50] Easter, Gregory makes clear in this sermon, represents the dawn of the resurrection life, and as such implies the presence of the heavenly eschaton—to which the Psalmist alludes as he sings in Psalm 117 (118) of "the day which the Lord has made" (Ps. 117 (118):24).[51] This great eschatological day is present, according to Nyssen, in congregational worship— and, we may add, through congregational worship in the social structures of family life. The overlapping meanings of "the day which the Lord has made"—referring at one and the same time to the historical day on which Christ rose from the dead; to the annually repeated feast of Easter; and to the final day of judgement[52]—are the result of a typological interpretation, in which the chronological dimension of time is transcended. The "day" of Christ's resurrection coincides with the annual celebration of Easter, as well as with the final resurrection day. It is this anagogical exegesis, in which Gregory takes the listener from "the day which the Lord has made" in Psalm 117 (118) to the eschatological reality of heaven itself, that allows Nyssen to make eschatological demands on his congregation. Put differently, he regards the newness of the coming heavenly reality as fundamentally at odds with the earthly institution of slavery.

The result is that Nyssen presents here his most daring denunciation of slavery. He does not just denounce the institution as such—something he does in numerous places—but he actually calls on the slave owners in his congregation to free their slaves:

> Now is the prisoner freed, the debtor forgiven, the slave liberated by the good and kindly (φιλανθρώπῳ) proclamation of the church, not being rudely struck on the cheek and released from beatings with a beating, nor being exhibited to the mob on a stand as though it were a show, getting insult and indignity as the beginning of his freedom, but released and acknowledged with equal decency.[53]

Gregory bases his appeal for manumission squarely on the resurrection of the final day, as he adds: "For through the resurrection hope come zeal for virtue and hatred for vice, since, if we take away the resurrection, one saying will prevail with everyone: 'Let us eat and drink, for tomorrow we die (1 Cor. 15,32).'"[54] The heavenly realities of the resurrection must take shape in the earthly life of the church.

Marguerite Harl points out that in his sermon St. Gregory compares the freedom that manumission gives with the freedom that results from resurrection, as he addresses the slave owners: "You masters have heard; mark my saying as a sound one; do not slander me to your slaves as praising the day with false rhetoric, take away the pain from oppressed souls as the Lord does the deadness from bodies; transform their disgrace into honour, their oppression into joy, their fear of speaking into openness; bring out the prostrate from their corner as if from their graves, let the beauty of the feast blossom like a flower upon everyone. If a royal birthday or victory celebration opens a prison, shall not Christ's rising relieve those in affliction?"[55] Gregory's plea to "bring out the prostrate from their corner as if from their graves" and his comparison between a royal birthday or victory celebration and the resurrection posit an unmistakable theological connection between manumission and Easter. Harl rightly comments: "Freeing slaves from disgrace . . . prefigures the resurrection from the dead."[56]

Gregory appeals to the Joseph narrative of the cupbearer and the baker in Genesis 40 to reinforce this link between redemption from slavery at Easter and redemption from sin on the day of resurrection: "Even the one who remains in slavery benefits," says Gregory. "Though his offences be many and serious and surpassing mitigation and pardon, the master is moved by the peacefulness of the day and accepts with kindness (φιλάνθρωπον) the one rejected and regarded as in disgrace, as Pharaoh did the cupbearer from prison. For he knows that at the appointed resurrection, in likeness of which we honour this day, he needs also the indulgence (ἀνεξικακίας) and generosity (ἀγαθότητος) of his master; lending mercy now he awaits the repayment in due time." [57] The theme of judgement and forgiveness is present not only in the Joseph narrative, but also in the release of slaves at Easter and in God's mercy on the last day. Again, Gregory's typological exegesis allows him to overcome the limitations of a purely chronological understanding of time: the same judgement and forgiveness are present in the Joseph narrative, in Gregory's own congregation, and on the final day. The Joseph narrative itself already contains the depth dimension of the resurrection of Easter and of the last day. In each of these instances, there is a release of some kind, whether from prison (Joseph narrative), slavery (Gregory's social context), or the grave (final resurrection).[58]

It is true, of course, that Gregory envisions the possibility of some remaining in slavery. He comments, "Even the one who remains in slavery benefits." While Gregory's comment is somewhat ambiguous, I suspect that he does not have in mind an unchanged continuation of slavery. After all, he immediately follows up with the example of the cupbearer from Genesis 40. In that account, the cupbearer was forgiven and released from prison, only to return to Pharaoh's service. Gregory may well have in mind, therefore, the kind of manumission that was practiced by Macrina's household: while the slaves were released and henceforth treated as equals, they remained in the service of the household, though from now on in a voluntary capacity. Gregory, therefore, comments that also those who continue in slavery benefit: like the cupbearer, they experience their masters' kindness and forgiveness, and like the cupbearer, they are received back into their masters' service. At the very least, the new condition is unlike the old. Since they have been treated with kindness and mercy, the master-slave relationship cannot but be affected.

For Gregory, at stake in manumission is not only the slave's freedom but also the slave owner's own ability to imitate and participate in God's character. On the final day of resurrection, the slave owner himself "needs also the indulgence (ἀνεξικακίας) and generosity (ἀγαθότητος) of his master." All of us, including the slave owner, hope that God, the master of all human beings, will one day show his indulgence and goodness. It stands to reason, therefore, that the human slave owner should display a similar indulgence and goodness toward his slaves by letting them share tangibly in the freedom of Easter. Furthermore, Gregory intimates, by so imitating the character of God, the human master may expect repayment in due time—no doubt alluding to the day of resurrection. The slave owner may be assured of his ultimate redemption at the end of time if in anticipation he redeems his own slaves today. Thus, it is the slave owner's heavenly concern that ought to make him interested in social justice on earth.

Several times in his sermon, Gregory appeals to the slave owner's φιλανθρωπία, a term akin to our words "generosity," "benevolence," "kindness," or "largesse." The concept was common in late antiquity, describing a virtue that was demanded from all, but particularly from gods and kings.[59] The term came into prominence especially through Stoic philosophy, and Emperor Julian strongly encouraged the pursuit of φιλανθρωπία in the Roman Empire in an attempt to offset the gains of the Christians, whose generosity was obvious to all.[60] Nyssen, too, encourages φιλανθρωπία throughout his writings; the examples from *In sanctum Pascha* are illustrative of the high regard that he displays for this virtue throughout his writings. St. Gregory consistently regards it as a divine virtue *par excellence*, and he maintains its importance particularly over against Eunomius, for whom φιλανθρωπία implies weakness—which means for him that it can be applied only to the Son, not to the Father.[61] For Eunomius, the Incarnation, as the Son's display of φιλανθρωπία, indicates his inferiority. Gregory, in response, insists that we properly describe God's nature as φιλανθρωπία, since we dare not "exclude the Father from a share in the thanksgiving for things restored."[62] When Gregory, therefore, appeals to slave owners' φιλανθρωπία, he is really asking them to reflect the love of God's self-condescension in the Incarnation.

### Conclusion

We may conclude that Nyssen's objections to slavery fit squarely within the overall anagogical or heavenly drive of his theology. Slavery, for Gregory, treats a fellow human being—created in the image of God and thus meant for resurrection freedom—as a mere object to be counted among one's earthly possessions. Throughout his exegetical works, Gregory finds occasion to reflect on the theological problems connected to slavery. Gregory's eschatology, especially, cannot tolerate an objectification of the human body. *On the Holy Pascha* makes clear that by freeing his slaves, the owner gives them a foretaste of the heavenly reality of the ultimate Easter redemption. It is of particular significance that this heavenly or anagogical orientation of Gregory's theology also motivates his exegesis. In Nyssen's biblical interpretation, the chronological strictures of time are overcome as a result of the arrival of the eschaton. The day which the Lord has made is not only the resurrection day that is to come, but it is also the day of Christ's own resurrection as well as the annual Easter celebration. God's judgement and forgiveness are present not only in the final day of resurrection but also in the Joseph narrative and in the social context of Gregory's congregation. Put differently, because of Christ's resurrection, both biblical history and the life of the believers participate already in the final resurrection day which the Lord has made. It is, therefore, Nyssen's spiritual exegesis that allows him to posit the heavenly reality as already present and thus as making moral demands on embodied social existence. Gregory's spiritual exegesis does not cause him to ignore concerns of embodied, social existence. Quite the contrary, in fact: it is Gregory's typological exegesis that, at least in part, drives his opposition to slavery.

This is not to say that the condition of the slave is Gregory's only (or even his ultimate) concern. His description of the practice of manumission in Annisa indicates that he believes it benefits not just the slave but the owner as well: the enactment of radical equality is a deliberately anagogical step through which the owner comes to share in the resurrection life of heaven: "This is the day which the Lord has made." For Gregory, then, manumission does not just represent a concern with the body—though it does that, to be sure—but in and through compassion for the material well-being of the body, Gregory displays his even greater desire that the souls of slave owner and slave alike might secure the future day of resurrection joy. Gregory is certainly interested in bringing heaven to earth; this desire for social justice is hardly out of line with his penchant for spiritual interpretation and with the anagogical, otherworldly bent of his theology. Rather, we could say, for Gregory social justice becomes a sacramental practice, in which we may discern already today something of the heavenly reality that is to come. God's desire to bring heaven to earth gets its impetus—and, I would argue, its continuing power and relevance—from the absolute priority that the heavenly future holds in Gregory's theology.

NOTES

I want to thank Ron Dart, Jim Fodor, Susan Holman, Mariam Kamell, and Matthew Levering for their kind assistance at various stages of my research on this essay.

1  Throughout this essay, I use the term "anagogy" in the way that Gregory himself often uses it, namely, as referring to the upward or heavenly direction of the Christian life and of biblical exegesis. The common, more restrictive use of the term "anagogy" as referring to the eschaton is a later development that goes back to Pseudo-Dionysius in the East and Cassian in the West. See Charles Kannengiesser, *Handbook of Patristic Exegesis: The Bible in Ancient Christianity*, The Bible in Ancient Christianity, Vol. 1 (Leiden: Brill, 2006), 257.

2  This article only deals with slavery. Gregory's writings on poverty, leprosy, and usury are theologically consistent with his attitude toward slavery, as I hope to make clear in a

forthcoming book, *Embodiment and Virtue in Gregory of Nyssa: An Anagogical Approach* (Oxford: Oxford University Press, 2013).

3   Susanna Elm, *"Virgins of God": The Making of Asceticism in Late Antiquity* (Oxford: Clarendon Press, 1994), p. 103, n. 87; Richard Klein, "Gibt es eine Sklavenethik bei Gregor von Nyssa? Anmerkungen zu David R. Stains, 'Gregory of Nyssa's Ethic of Slavery and Emancipation'," in Hubertus R. Drobner and Albert Viciano (eds.), *Gregory of Nyssa: Homilies on the Beatitudes: An English Version with Supporting Studies: Proceedings of the Eighth International Colloquium on Gregory of Nyssa (Paderborn, 14–18 September 1998)*, Supplements to Vigiliae Christianae, Vol. 52 (Leiden: Brill, 2000), pp. 593–604, at p. 597.

4   Lionel Wickham, "Homily IV," in Stuart George Hall (ed.), *Gregory of Nyssa: Homilies on Ecclesiastes: An English Version with Supporting Studies: Proceedings of the Seventh International Colloquium on Gregory of Nyssa (St Andrews, 5–10 September 1990)* (Berlin: de Gruyter, 1993), pp. 177–184, at p. 179; Klein, "Gibt es eine Sklavenethik," pp. 598–599, 602; idem, *Die Haltung der kappadokischen Bischöfe Basilius von Caesarea, Gregor von Nazianz und Gregor von Nyssa zur Sklaverei*, Forschungen zur antiken Sklaverei, Vol. 32 (Stuttgart: Steiner, 2000), pp. 213–214.

5   Rachel Moriarty, "Human Owners, Human Slaves: Gregory of Nyssa, *Hom. Eccl.* 4," *Studia Patristica*, Vol. 27 (1993), pp. 62–69.

6   *Ibid.*, p. 68. Faced with the apparent rejection of slavery in *Vita s. Macrinae* and *De anima et resurrectione*, Klein comments "daß in diesen spätantiken Preisreden sehr viel Topik enthalten ist, wobei der Bescheidenheitstopos an erster Stelle steht ("Gibt es eine Sklavenethik," pp. 508–509).

7   Trevor Dennis, "The Relationship between Gregory of Nyssa's Attack on Slavery in His Fourth Homily on Ecclesiastes and His Treatise *De hominis opificio*," *Studia Patristica*, Vol.17 (1982), pp. 1065–1072; idem, "Man beyond Price: Gregory of Nyssa and Slavery," in Andrew Linzey and Peter J. Wexler (eds.), *Heaven and Earth: Essex Essays in Theology and Ethics* (Worthing: Churchman, 1986), pp. 129–145; Maria Mercedès Bergadá, "La Condamnation de l'esclavage dans l'Homélie IV," in Hall (ed.), *Gregory of Nyssa: Homilies on Ecclesiastes* (Berlin: de Gruyter, 1993), pp. 185–197; David R. Stains, "Gregory of Nyssa's Ethic of Slavery and Emancipation" (Ph.D. diss., University of Pittsburgh, 1994); Daniel F. Stramara, "Gregory of Nyssa: An Ardent Abolitionist?" *St Vladimir's Theological Quarterly*, Vol. 41 (1997), pp. 37–60; D. Bentley Hart, "The 'Whole Humanity': Gregory of Nyssa's Critique of Slavery in Light of His Eschatology," *Scottish Journal of Theology*, Vol. 54 (2001), pp. 51–69; J. Kameron Carter, "Theology, Exegesis, and the Just Society: Gregory of Nyssa as Abolitionist Intellectual," *Ex Auditu*, Vol. 22 (2006), pp. 181–212.

8   This is most clearly the case when Trevor Dennis wrongly maintains that "there is no other attack on slavery to be found anywhere else in his [i.e., Gregory's] writings" ("Man beyond Price," p. 142; cf. *ibid.*, p. 139).

9   It seems to me that Klein's harsh denunciation of Stains' dissertation is particularly problematic considering the generally solid character of the dissertation and the limited nature of Klein's own discussions.

10   Basil of Caesarea, "Letter XXXVII," in *Saint Basil: The Letters*, trans. Roy J. Deferrari, Loeb Classical Library, Vol. 190 (1926, repr.; Cambridge, MA: Harvard University Press, 1972), pp. 194–195. Cf. Stains, "Gregory of Nyssa's Ethic of Slavery," pp. 187, 213–224.

11   St Basil the Great, *On the Holy Spirit*, trans. Stephen Hildebrand, Popular Patristics Series, Vol. 42 (Crestwood, NY: St. Vladimir's Seminary Press, 2011), pp. 87–88 (Chapter 20).

12   *Vita s. Macrinae* (hereafter *Macr*), in *Gregorii Nysseni Opera* (hereafter *GNO*) VIII/1, ed. Virginia Woods Callahan, (Leiden: Brill, 1963), p. 378. ET: Anna M. Silvas, *Macrina the Younger, Philosopher of God*, Medieval Women: Texts and Contexts, Vol. 22 (Turnhout: Brepols, 2008) (hereafter Silvas), p. 118.

13   *Macr*, p. 381 (Silvas, p. 121).

14   Silvas, p. 43.

15   Elm essentially charges Gregory with hypocrisy (*"Virgins of God,"* p. 103, n. 87).

16   Cf. J. Gribomont, "Le Monachisme au IV$^e$ s. en Asie Mineure: de Gangres au Messalianisme," *Studia Patristica*, Vol. 2 (1957), pp. 400–415; idem, "Saint Basile et le monachisme enthousiaste," *Irénikon*, Vol. 53 (1980), pp. 123–144; P. Huybrechts, "Le 'Traité de la virginité' de Grégoire de Nysse: Idéal de vie monastique ou idéal de vie chrétienne?" *Nouvelle Revue Théologique*, Vol. 115 (1993), pp. 227–242; Elm, *"Virgins of God,"* pp. 106–111; Philip Rousseau,

*Basil of Caesarea* (Berkeley, CA: University of California Press, 1994), pp. 73–76; Jason M. Scarborough, "Asceticism as Ideology: Gregory of Nyssa's *De virginitate,"* *Union Seminary Quarterly Review*, Vol. 57 (2003), pp. 131–150; Anna M. Silvas, *The Asketikon of St Basil the Great* (Oxford: Oxford University Press, 2005), pp. 56–60; idem, *Macrina the Younger*, pp. 22–28; Terrence G. Kardong, "Who Was Basil's Mentor?," *American Benedictine Review*, Vol. 60 (2009), pp. 183–201, 299–309, at pp.191–201.

17   *Macr*, p. 381 (Silvas, p. 121).
18   *Macr*, pp. 377–378 (Silvas, p. 118).
19   *Macr*, p. 378 (Silvas, p. 118).
20   *Macr*, p. 382 (Silvas, p. 121). For discussion of the use of the term "philosophy" among the Cappadocians as denoting ascetic discipline, see Jaroslav Pelikan, *Christianity and Classical Culture: The Metamorphosis of Natural Theology in the Christian Encounter with Hellenism* (New Haven, CT: Yale University Press, 1993), pp. 181–182.
21   Stains, "Gregory of Nyssa's Ethic of Slavery," pp. 56–78.
22   William L. Westermann, *The Slave Systems of Greek and Roman Antiquity*, Memoirs of the American Philosophical Society, Vol. 40 (Philadelphia, PA: American Philosophical Society, 1955), pp. 154–155; Elm, *"Virgins of God,"* p. 85.
23   Elm, *"Virgins of God,"* p. 85.
24   Silvas, *Asketikon*, p. 490. Cf. Stains, "Gregory of Nyssa's Ethic of Slavery," pp. 154–156.
25   Cf. Kardong, "Who Was Basil's Mentor?," p. 196.
26   *In sanctum Pascha* (hereafter *Sanct Pasch*), in *GNO* IX, ed. Ernestus Gebhardt (Leiden: Brill, 1967), p. 246; ET: "Discourse on the Holy Pascha," trans. S. G. Hall, in *The Easter Sermons of Gregory of Nyssa: Translation and Commentary: Proceedings of the Fourth International Collo-quium on Gregory of Nyssa; Cambridge, England: 11–15 September, 1978*, ed. Andreas Spira and Christoph Klock, Patristic Monograph Series, Vol. 9 (Cambridge, MA: Philadelphia Patristic Foundation, 1981), pp. 5–23. I have adjusted the translation slightly in a few places. Cf. Stains, "Gregory of Nyssa's Ethic of Slavery," p. 344.
27   *Sanct Pasch*, p. 264. Cf. Stains, "Gregory of Nyssa's Ethic of Slavery," p. 344.
28   *De deitate Filii et Spiritus Sancti* (hereafter *Deit fil*), in *GNO* X/2, ed. Ernestus Rhein (Leiden: Brill, 1996), pp. 120–121; translation by Stains ("Gregory of Nyssa's Ethic of Slavery," p. 207) adjusted. In debate with Eunomius, Gregory insists that "to allege that the Lord exists in the form of a slave before he comes in the flesh is the same as alleging that we say the stars are black, the sun murky, the sky flat on the ground, water dry, and all that kind of thing" (*Contra Eunomium* (hereafter *Eun*) III, in *GNO* II, ed. Wernerus Jaeger (Leiden: Brill, 1960); ET by Stuart Hall available on-line: http://theo.kuleuven.be/page/translations III.iii.55). Neither of these two passages advocates lashing of run-away slaves (as claimed by Klein, "Gibt es eine Sklavenethik," p. 597). The mere use of the term "worthless fellows" (μαστιγίαι) hardly justifies such an assertion. In fact, one could argue that the passage from *Eun* III presents a negative picture of slavery rather than of slaves.
29   *De oratione dominica* (hereafter *Or dom*), in *GNO* VII/2, ed. Johannes F. Callahan (Leiden: Brill, 1992), p. 71; ET: "The Lord's Prayer," in *The Lord's Prayer, The Beatitudes*, ed. and trans. Hilda C. Graef, Ancient Christian Writers, Vol. 18 (New York, NY: Paulist Press, 1954) (hereafter *Graef*), p. 81.
30   *In Ecclesiasten homilae* (hereafter *Eccl*), in *GNO* V, ed. Paulus Alexander (Leiden: Brill, 1962), p. 335; ET: "Gregory, Bishop of Nyssa: Homilies on Ecclesiastes," trans. Stuart George Hall and Rachel Moriarty, in *Gregory of Nyssa: Homilies on Ecclesiastes: An English Version with Supporting Studies: Proceedings of the Seventh International Colloquium on Gregory of Nyssa (St Andrews, 5–10 September 1990)*, ed. Stuart George Hall, (Berlin: de Gruyter, 1993).
31   Cf. Bergadá, "Condamnation de l'esclavage," pp. 188, 191–192.
32   *De hominis opificio* (hereafter *Op hom*); ET: *On the Making of Man*, in *Nicene and Post-Nicene Fathers* II/5, ed. and trans. H. A. Wilson (New York, NY: Christian Literature Company, 1893), II.1 (*PG* 44.132D); *Op hom* III.1 (*PG* 44.133D).
33   *Op hom* IV.1 (*PG* 44.136B-C). Gregory goes on to explain that humanity's likeness to the king showed itself not in a purple robe but in virtue, not in a sceptre but in immortality, and not in a royal diadem but in a crown of righteousness (*Op hom* IV.1 (*PG* 44.136C)).
34   Cf. Dennis, "Man beyond Price," p. 140.
35   Cf. the very similar passage in *Oratio catechetic magna* (hereafter *Or cat*), in *GNO* III/4, ed. Ekkehardus Mühlenberg (Leiden: Brill, 1996), p. 75; ET: *The Catechetical Oration of St. Gregory*

*of Nyssa*, ed. and trans. J. H. Srawley, Early Church Classics (London: Society for Promoting Christian Knowledge, 1917) (hereafter Srawley), p. 90.

36  *Or dom* 70–71 (Graef, p. 81).
37  *Eccl* 335–336.
38  *Op hom* XVI.8 (*PG* 44.181B).
39  Cf. Johannes Zachhuber, *"Plêrôma,"* in *Brill Dictionary of Gregory of Nyssa* (Leiden: Brill, 2010) (hereafter *BDGN*).
40  Cf. Johannes Zachhuber, *"Phyrama,"* in *BDGN*.
41  *Or dom* 70 (Graef, p. 81).
42  *Eccl* 336.
43  Hart, " 'Whole Humanity'," p. 53.
44  *Eccl* 334, 349, 351.
45  *Eccl* 335. Cf. Bergadá, "Condamnation de l'esclavage," pp. 186, 194.
46  *Eccl* 337–338. Moriarty helpfully highlights the similarity between Seneca's *Letter* 47 and the second part of this quotation from Gregory ("Human Owners," p. 65). Indeed, it seems clear that Gregory's anti-slavery rhetoric builds on Stoic attempts to ameliorate the plight of slaves. He clearly saw in the Stoic insistence on a common humanity a point of contact with his own Christian convictions.
47  *De beatitudinibus* (hereafter *Beat*), in *GNO* VII/2, ed. Johannes F. Callahan (Leiden: Brill, 1992), p. 87; ET: "On the Beatitudes," trans. Stuart George Hall, in *Gregory of Nyssa: Homilies on the Beatitudes: An English Version with Supporting Studies: Proceedings of the Eighth International Colloquium on Gregory of Nyssa (Paderborn, 14–18 September 1998)*, ed. Hubertus R. Drobner and Albert Viciano, Supplements to Vigiliae Christianae, Vol. 52 (Leiden: Brill, 2000). Cf. Gregory's warning: "You have forgotten the limits (ὅρων) of your authority . . . " (*Eccl* 335).
48  *Beat* 88.
49  *Beat* 88. Cf. *Or dom* 71 (Graef, p. 81).
50  Jean Daniélou, "La Chronologie des sermons de Grégoire de Nysse," *Recherches de science religieuse*, Vol. 29 (1955), pp. 346–372, at pp. 350–351.
51  Gregory also reflects on this Psalm in two other Easter sermons: (1) *De tridui spatio* (*GNO* IX), p. 279; ET: "On the Three-day Period of the Resurrection of Our Lord Jesus Christ," trans. S. G. Hall, in Spira and Klock (eds.), *Easter Sermons*; (2) *In sanctum et salutare Pascha* (*GNO* IX), p. 310; ET: "The Holy and Saving Pascha," trans. S. G. Hall, in Spira and Klock (eds.), *Easter Sermons*.
52  Thus rightly Marguerite Harl, "L'Éloge de la fête de Pâques dans le Prologue du Sermon In Sanctum Pascha de Grégoire de Nysse (In Sanctum Pascha p. 245, 4–253, 18)," in Spira and Klock (eds.), *Easter Sermons*, pp. 81–100, at pp. 92–93.
53  *Sanct Pasch*, p.250.
54  *Sanct Pasch*, p. 251.
55  *Sanct Pasch*, p. 251.
56  Harl, "Éloge de la fête," p. 91.
57  *Sanct Pasch*, pp. 250–251.
58  Cf. Harl, "Éloge de la fête," p. 92.
59  See Glanville Downey, "Philanthropia in Religion and Statecraft in the Fourth Century after Christ," *Historia: Zeitschrift für alte Geschichte*, Vol. 4 (1955), pp. 199–208; Demetrios J. Constantelos, *Byzantine Philanthropy and Social Welfare* (New Brunswick, NJ: Rutgers University Press, 1968), pp. 3–16, 43–61; Brian E. Daley, "Building a New City: The Cappadocian Fathers and the Rhetoric of Philanthropy," *Journal of Early Christian Studies*, Vol. 7 (1999), pp. 431–461, at pp. 434–437.
60  Downey, "Philanthropia," pp. 203–204; Daley, "Building a New City," pp. 436–437.
61  *Eun* III.x.36. For the connection between Gregory's anti-Eunomian doctrine of the Trinity and his insistence on divine φιλανθρωπία, see Giulio Maspero, *"Philanthrôpia,"* in *BDGN*. For Gregory's use of the term in the *Oratio catechetica magna*, see Downey, "Philanthropia," p. 204.
62  *Eun* III.x.37.

# Part II

# Reading Scripture

# 5

# IMPERIAL LOVER: THE UNVEILING OF JESUS CHRIST IN REVELATION

## PETER J. LEITHART

Like the moral philosophers in Alasdair MacIntyre's parable, biblical scholars have for several centuries fumbled about with fragments of what was
once a unified interpretive framework. Medieval theologians worked within
the system known as the quadriga. The senses of Scripture (literal, allegorical,
tropological, anagogical) formed a four-wheeled chariot of contemplative
reading that, like the four-faced cherubic chariot of Ezekiel, formed a vehicle
of ascent to the God of heaven.[1] With the Reformation and even more after
the rise of biblical criticism, this system fractured into far more than four
pieces. Much modern biblical scholarship sticks close to the literal sense,
using the tools of philology, archeology, textual criticism, and close literary
analysis to establish the history of the text, its original meaning, the history of
Israelite religion, or the *actual* historical events to which biblical writers give
theological shape. Dozens of subordinate tools have developed. Meanwhile,
the churches that are most serious about the Bible have focused on the
tropological work of teasing out edifying applications of Scripture to believers and their communities, with only passing and mostly negative references
to "higher criticism." Catholics never abandoned allegory, but it quickly fell
out of favor among Protestants, though the disfavor was more often theoretical than practical.[2] At least everyone knows, or thinks they know, what
allegory is. The term "anagogical" has all but disappeared from Christian
discourse. Mention anagogy in mixed company, and you will almost certainly
be greeted with a bewildered, "Don't you mean an*a*logy?"

Recent advocacy of "theological" or "spiritual" interpretation represents
an unsurprising reaction to this disarray and an effort to return to the more
holistic readings of the past. Theological reading pushes beyond the literal to

*Heaven on Earth?: Theological Interpretation in Ecumenical Dialogue*, First Edition.
Edited by Hans Boersma and Matthew Levering.
© 2013 Blackwell Publishing Ltd. Book compilation © 2013 Blackwell Publishing Ltd.

the theological and specifically Christological meaning of a text. Theological interpretation is also specifically, and explicitly, a reaction to the dominant grammatical-historical paradigm of biblical studies that tries to escape the constraints of Christian dogma. In his Series Preface to the Brazos Theological Commentary, editor R. R. Reno cites Benjamin Jowett's claim that biblical scholars aim to discover the "pure" meaning of the uncluttered text by setting aside theological precommitments and argues that this ambition still animates much biblical scholarship. Even after downing a draught of post-modern suspicion, many continue to share the modern assumption that humans have a natural aptitude for reading and thus have no need for liberating and healing disciplines of Christian practice.[3]

I find this reaction heartening, as theologians are encouraged to read Scripture and Bible scholars are exhorted to consider the theological import of the text. Yet I have two reservations. I recognize that "theological interpre-tation" means something different to nearly every theological interpreter, but I think my reservations apply widely enough to hit some real targets. First, I worry that some of the considerable gains of modern biblical scholarship will be ignored. I say this as a Neanderthal who finds many of the primary "achievements" of modern scholarship useless and absurd: JEDP tells us nothing about the history of the Pentateuch but instead gives methodological primacy to what John Milbank calls the "liberal Protestant metanarrative"; biblical scholars place far too much confidence in the sketchy findings of archeology and speculative reconstructions of ancient history; Q never existed, and is a completely unnecessary hypothesis; the modern dating of the gospels is nonsensical, for why would Jews wait for decades to write about the events they had awaited since Yahweh called Abram from Ur? Yet modern biblical scholarship has made undeniable contributions to our knowledge of the Bible and its world: anthropological perspectives have decoded the logic of Israel's purity and sacrificial systems; comparative mythology has clarified the historical and theological significance of Israel's stories of creation, fall, and flood; careful literary analyses of biblical narrative and Pauline echoes have enhanced our appreciation of both the beauty and theological power of Scripture; recent studies of the political hothouse of first-century Israel illuminates the teaching of Jesus and Paul. Even wrong-headed modernist projects have yielded important fruit. I have basic theo-logical objections to the "quest of the historical Jesus"; purely as a matter of historical method, it does not seem wise to begin with such thoroughgoing skepticism about the value of one's primary sources. Yet without the quest, would anyone have arrived at Schweitzer's essentially correct conclusion that Jesus came to Israel as an eschatological prophet? Apart from the quest, would we know as much about the setting of first-century Judaism as we now do?

We know far, far more about the ancient world than any medieval monk. Essential as monkish interpreters are, there ought to be no yearning to return to a supposed age of innocence, and the best interpreters of the past would not have wanted us to return. Allegorist though he was, Origen studied philology, botany, zoology, and whatever else might elucidate the literal sense of Scripture; in *de doctrina Christiana*, Augustine laid out a complete program of liberal and scientific study whose main design was to support biblical exegesis. Origen would have been delighted at the ways that, say, modern scholars use numismatic evidence to understand the operation and spread of Roman power in Palestine. To the extent that theological and spiritual interpreters overlook the densities of the literal sense that are the gift of modern scholarship, to that extent they remain bound to the modern fascination with novelty. To the extent that theological interpreters skim past the thorns of critical scholarship, to that extent theological interpretation will fail in one of its main purposes: the breach between theology and biblical studies cannot be bridged if theologians ignore or belittle what biblical scholars do.

Even more is at stake on this point, however. If spiritual interpretation is unconcerned with history and philology, it runs the risk of turning the Bible into a compendium of ideas rather than a record and theological interpretation of history. To anticipate the discussion below, if a "spiritual" commentary on Revelation ignores issues of dating, authorship, and historical setting, it will fail theologically as well as historically. The point of Revelation is what it says, in and through its vivid symbols, about an actual series of events. Because God is a God of habit, those actual events figure similar events at different times and places. But Revelation is not a mere pattern of symbols with no specific referent. Were spiritual interpretation to overlook issues of "introduction," it would become as much a species of Gnosticism as modern critical scholarship.

My second main worry is that theological interpretation has remained too much at the level of hermeneutical theory. Admittedly, several series of commentaries on the Bible are currently under production. Still, much of the effort of the past two decades has been expended on theory.[4] Theory is best formulated *after* practice has had time to grope its way along. Theory should drink from a cask of *aged* practice. If theological interpretation becomes dependent on *a priori* hermeneutical theories, it at once risks repeating errors it hopes to escape. The goal of theological interpretation, as I see it, is to hear the living word of the living God, but a theory of theological interpretation can muzzle that word just as surely as the theories of biblical scholarship. Theological interpreters are more aware that their methods are theologically laden than modern biblical scholars have generally been, yet I still worry that theological interpretation might become a slave of method. What is needed is not more theoretical reflection. If I were king of the world, I would declare a moratorium on the production of hermeneutics textbooks. What is needed is more exemplary practice.

The remainder of this article is a modest effort to deflect these two worries about the future of theological interpretation. To address my first worry, I offer a reading of a small portion of the Apocalypse that assumes that the instinct of modern biblical scholarship to give careful attention to the literal sense is theologically sound. Attention to the literal sense does not block spiritual interpretation but, as Thomas said, *proliferates into* the spiritual senses. Accordingly, my interpretation addresses questions concerning Revelation's literary structure, John's redeployment of Old Testament texts, the historical and chronological setting of the Apocalypse, and recent political readings of Revelation. To address my second worry, I offer a reading rather than a theory of interpretation. More broadly, without explicitly following the quadriga (which is hard to use on New Testament texts in any case), I offer an interpretation that is simultaneously literal-literary, tropological-political, mystical-spiritual, Christological and ecclesiological, and, being an interpretation of the Apocalypse, inevitably anagogical. I hope it illustrates what interpretation might look like on the other side of modern fragmentation.

## I. "In the Spirit"

The consensus among contemporary scholars is that these visions took place and/or the book was written during the reign of Domitian in the last decade of the first century. During the nineteenth century, however, the majority of scholars concluded that the book appeared several decades earlier, during the reign of Nero.[5] A great deal rests on the interpretive decision about this issue. If the book appeared at the end of the first century, it primarily describes conflicts between Christians and Roman persecutors and figures conflicts between church and empire, and scholars have recently been hard pressed to find much evidence of persecution.[6] On this reading, "Babylon" signifies Rome, and by extension all tyrants throughout the ages. Rome has a prominent role in the book even if the book is dated in the 60s; Rome is the beast that rises from the sea to make war on the saints (Revelation 13). But the earlier date leaves open the possibility that "Babylon" is a figure for Jerusalem, the religious capital of the ancient world in the Jewish mind. On such a reading, the conflict of the book is centrally Jews *v.* Christians, like the conflicts in the gospels and Acts. I cannot lay out the arguments for my position here, but I am convinced of the earlier date and convinced that the harlot city burned and devoured by her former lovers is Jerusalem.[7] Revelation describes not the fall of Rome, but the destruction of the old Jerusalem-centric order by the Romans in 70 A.D.

Revelation is a series of four visions, each of which begins with the phrase "in the Spirit" (εν πνευματι).[8] After an opening greeting and benediction, John introduces himself as a "brother" and "fellow partaker in the tribulation and kingdom and perseverance" of Jesus. Then he says, "I was in the Spirit on the Lord's day" (1:10), before he recounts the book's initial Christophany during which Jesus commissions him to write to seven churches of Asia. The commissioned messages follow in the next two chapters. This is the Patmos section of the book. In 4:3, εν πνευματι appears again, and this opens the second and longest section. In Spirit, John sees an open door in the sky and enters to witness the heavenly liturgy, the conferral of a book to the Lamb who opens seven seals, the blowing of seven trumpets, and the outpouring of seven bowls onto the harlot city. Next John is "in Spirit" in the wilderness to see the harlot city destroyed (17:3) and finally he views the Bride descending from heaven as he stands on a mountain "in Spirit" (21:9–10). The visions move from Patmos to heaven to the wilderness to the mountain, the last two visions recapitulating Israel's movement from Egypt to Sinai.

Though the four visions form a geographic sequence, they are also grouped in two sets of two. The first two uses of εν πνευματι occur in the statement "I was in the Spirit," but in the last two visions, the Spirit is not an environment but a power, a wind-storm, that bears John to a new location ("he carried me away εν πνευματι"; 17:3; 21:10).[9] Further, the first two visions focus on Jesus. In chapter 1, Jesus stands unveiled before John, while in chapter 5 Jesus appears as the slain Lamb opening the seals. The final two visions are feminine, first the civic whore and then the purified bridal city of gold. In Spirit, John's view moves from the male Christ to the feminine Church, progressing like the creation account that moves from the formation of Adam from the dust to the building of Eve from Adam's bleeding side (Genesis 2:15–24). Noting this trajectory is important for grasping the political theology of Revelation.

In chapter 1, John is in Spirit on the Lord's day. A voice like a trumpet calls him from behind (1:10). When he turns, he first sees lampstands (1:12), then the clothing of the "one like a son of man" (1:13), and finally the person himself in the midst of the lampstands (1:14–16). The inward movement resembles the progress of a high priest through the veils into the inner sanctuary to see the glory of the Lord. Here Jesus embodies the glory.[10] As seen by John, the glorified Jesus is a mosaic constructed from overlapping and interlocking biblical fragments. As a human figure among the lampstands (1:12), Jesus is both a priest and a new Adam among the golden trees of a glorified garden.[11] Like a priest too, he wears a robe girded across the middle with a golden belt (1:13). To John's gaze, Jesus is also a vertical human temple (vv. 14–16).[12] His head is white with glory like the cloud of Yahweh's presence in the Most Holy Place; his right hand is in the location of the *menorah* and holds stars like the lamps of the lampstand; his feet are glowing bronze like the bronze altar of the temple court. Jesus is also a cosmic figure with a face like the sun and stars in his hand. The Song of Songs and several visions of Daniel form the major part of the background of John's description.[13]

## II. Jesus the Lover

Twice in the Song of Songs, Solomon sings an ecstatic head-to-toe hymn of praise to the bride using a form that, because of its resemblance to Arabic love poetry, biblical scholars have come to call a *wasf* (4:1–6; 7:1–9).[14] Between these, the bride describes the attractions of her man to the daughters of Jerusalem in a similar style (5:10–16). While she desperately searches the streets for her absent lover, her companions ask, "what kind of beloved is your beloved?" (5:9). Her description begins with his head of gold, moves down over his face to his hands, abs, and legs before moving back upward to his mouth full of sweetness. Like the lover's description of the bride, this *wasf* of the male lover draws heavily on natural imagery. His hair is like "clusters of dates" and is "black as a raven"; his eyes are like doves, his lips like lilies; his overall appearance as impressive as a cedar of Lebanon. He is a garden of delights to the bride as much as she is to him. Intertwining the natural similes is a thread of cultural and specifically architectural imagery. The lover's head is gold; his hands are rods of gold set with beryl, and his abs are like ivory inlaid with sapphires; his legs are alabaster pillars set on pedestals of gold. He is not only a garden, but a human temple or palace.[15] In any case, the bride's description convinces her companions. Though initially skeptical that any man is worth the trouble, they join in her quest (6:1).

In its poetic shape, John's description of Jesus resembles the *wasf* of Song of Songs 5. John begins with Jesus' head and hair, moves to his eyes, down to his feet, and then back up to his hand, mouth, and face. This formal parallel is sufficient of itself for us to surmise that the first unveiling of Jesus is the unveiling of a Lover. That is as it should be, since, as noted, the book is moving toward the unveiling of a Bride who joins with her Lover in an eternal marriage supper.

The connection with the Song is strengthened by several details of John's description. According to the Massoretic text of Song of Songs 1:2, the "lovings" (דֹּדֶיךָ) of the bridegroom are better than wine. For unexplained reasons, the Septuagint rendered "lovings" as μαστοι, "breasts" and in this the Septuagint was followed by the Vulgate (*quia meliora sunt ubera tua vino*). The Son of Man John sees is girded across his "breasts" (μαστοι) with a golden girdle (1:13). Jesus is feminized, like Moses the "nursing father" (Numbers 11:12; Heb. אֶת־הַיֹּנֵק יִשָּׂא הָאֹמֵן כִּי מִן), like Paul the apostolic wet nurse (1 Thessalonians 2:7; Gr. ως αν τροφος θαλπη τα εαυτης τεκνα). Jesus is the maternal Word who gives the milk of the word to the children of his Father. Perhaps too μαστοι is a startling gloss on the Johannine announcement that the "Word was made flesh." The eternal Word so identifies himself with the Bride he comes to save that, though male, he can in vision appear in female flesh. Whatever the Christological import of the passage, the literary effect of μαστοι is to connect John's vision with the initial description of the Lover of the Song, whose kisses intoxicate like wine.[16]

Another detail later in the passage is drawn from the Song as well. When he first sees Jesus in his glory, John falls at His feet as a dead man, but Jesus raises him up and reassures him: "I was dead, and behold, I am alive forevermore, and I have the keys of death and Hades" (1:18). The combination of θανατος and αδης occurs a number of times in the LXX (Job 33:22; Psalm 6:6; 48:15; Proverbs 2:18; 5:5; Isaiah 28:18), but it occurs prominently in the theme verses of the Song of Songs: "love is strong as death, zeal as jealous as Hades" (8:6; LXX, κραταια ως θανατος αγαπη σκληρος ως αδης ζηλος). Jesus is the living Love of the Father, the Love that many waters cannot quench, the Fire of Yah stronger than death.

The conclusion of the seven letters to the churches confirms that the Song of Songs has shaped John's description of the initial unveiling of Jesus. The clearest allusion to the Song comes at the very end of the letter to the Laodiceans: "Behold, I stand at the door and knock; if anyone hears My voice and opens the door, I will come in to Him, and will dine with him, and he with Me" (Revelation 3:20; Gr. ιδου εστηκα επι την θυραν και κρουω). The promise to dine with the receptive members of the Laodicean church antici-pates the marriage supper of the Lamb at the end of Revelation (19:9), and the Eucharistic overtones are clear. The scene strongly recalls Song of Songs 5:2, where the bride wakes to the sound of her lover's knocking on her door (LXX, κρουει επι την θυραν) and the sound of his voice (LXX, φωνη). In the Song, the lover wants to make love, and the immediately preceding verse describes the love-making as a feast: "I have eaten my honeycomb and my honey; I have drunk my wine and my milk. Eat friends; drink and imbibe deeply, O lovers" (5:1). The lover seeks entry to feast on his beloved, and the allusion to this scene in Revelation 3:20 lends an erotic overtone to Jesus' invitation to the Laodiceans. Jesus wants to enter to enjoy a feast of love with the few remain-ing in the Laodicean church who are still passionate members of his Bride.

Because the Laodiceans are neither hot nor cold, Jesus threatens to spew them out of his mouth (Revelation 3:15–16), and in this we have another link with the Song. The image of vomiting (εμεσαι) is derived in part from Torah, where the land spews out people that worship idols and practice sexual perversions (Leviticus 18:25, 28; 20:22). In Revelation, Jesus is the "land" of the Christian church, their source of abundant life. The imagery of Revelation 3:15–16 also links to that of the Song. As just noted, the scene at the door in Song of Songs 5:2 is immediately preceded by a love feast, where the lovers devour one another (4:16–5:1). When Jesus knocks at the door of the Laod-icean church, he too has been eating, and his mouth has been full of Laod-iceans. He desires to "eat" them into his body, so that by eating him the church might become what she receives. But he finds them distasteful. The Laodiceans should be producing fruit and food that burns with the flame of Yah (cf. Song of Songs 8:6–7), hot in the mouth of the lover, Jesus; or, they should provide a drink of wine and milk to cool his tongue. They do neither. Their works are like warmed-over leftovers, and Jesus abhors the fare. He will not swallow much less feast on a church so tasteless to his palate.[17]

The first vision of Revelation (1:9–3:22), then, begins with a description of Jesus that mimics the Song of Songs in form and in several particulars, and it ends with a scene drawn very explicitly from the Song.[18] Within this frame,

Jesus commissions John to write the messages he hears from Jesus to the seven churches of Asia. Jesus the Lover sends a sevenfold love letter to his sevenfold Asian Bride. For those familiar with the contents of the seven letters, this seems a jarring description. "I have this against you" and "Repent" and "I will make war" and "I will cast you on a bed of sickness" and "you have a name that you are alive but you are dead" and "you are neither cold nor hot"—these hardly seem the endearments of a lover. But they are. As Jesus says at the climax of the series, "Those whom I love (φιλεω), I reprove and discipline" (3:19; cf. 1:5; 2:4, 19; 3:9, all of which use some form of αγαπ-). Jesus rebukes lukewarmness because he seeks a passionate Bride, whose responding love is, like his own, stronger than death and fiercer than Sheol.

The Song helps structure not only the first vision of Revelation, but the book as a whole. John's first vision begins with an unveiling of Jesus the lover, and the book ends with an impassioned plea from the bride and the Spirit for Jesus the lover to return: "The Spirit and bride say, 'Come' . . . Yes, come quickly . . . Come, Lord Jesus" (Revelation 22:17, 20). Despite the fact that the bride has descended from heaven and the marriage supper has begun (Revelation 19:1–10), the Apocalypse ends unended, with an eschato-logical reserve yet to come, an anagogical excess that arouses the Spirit-filled bride to expectancy. So too in the Song. The lovers appear to consummate their love (Song of Songs 4:16–5:1), and the lover views his beloved's naked body unveiled (7:1–7). She is a tree, and he has already climbed her to drink juice from the clusters that are her breasts (7:8). Despite this union and intimacy, the Song ends with the lovers separated, and with the bride longing for *dodi*, "my beloved," to return: "Hurry, my beloved, and be like a gazelle or a young stag, on the mountains of spices" (8:14). The passionate lovers of the Song figure the life of Jesus the bridegroom with the women who follow him, and both anticipate the glorified lover of the Apocalypse, the Lamb whose marriage supper begins with the bride's descent.

These intertextual linkages are given another layer by parallels between the Apocalypse and the gospel of John.[19] John's gospel too echoes the Song at various points. Jesus performs his first sign at a wedding, during which he takes the role of the bridegroom by providing an abundance of superb wine (John 2:1–11). John responds to questions about Jesus by calling him the bridegroom whose voice calls the bride to himself. John decreases because he is only "best man," preparing the bride for the bridegroom's coming and announcing the joy of the wedding (3:27–30). Jesus has wedding wine and is the bridegroom, but where is the bride? John 4 records Jesus' encounter with the Samaritan woman who has been used and cast aside by one man after another. In Jesus, she finds a true husband. At the end of John's gospel, Jesus is again the bridegroom of the Song as he appears to Mary in the garden of his resurrection (20:11–18). In each of these instances, Jesus the bridegroom encounters potential brides, then departs. He specifically tells Mary Magdalene to stop clinging to him, since he has to ascend to his Father

(20:17). John's gospel thus leaves the bridal figures longing for the full coming of the bridegroom to pitch his nuptial tent and begin a feast of love. Only at the end of Revelation does a bride appear who is suitable for Jesus the bridegroom, and even then the bride still yearns for his final arrival, still sings the Song of the beloved: "Let him kiss me with the kisses of his mouth, for his love is better than wine."

So much for Jesus as Lover. But *Imperial* Lover?

## III. Son of Man and Ancient of Days

Even before Jesus reveals himself to John, the trajectory of the Apocalypse has been set by a quotation from Daniel 7:13: "Behold, he is coming with the clouds" (Revelation 1:7). In Daniel, the Son of Man appears after the prophet has seen a series of beasts arising from a storm-stirred sea, beasts later explained as symbols of "kings who will arise from the earth" (Daniel 7:17). While Daniel watches, thrones are set up, a court is assembled, the Ancient of Days takes his seat, books are opened, and the court renders its decision to remove dominion from the beasts (v. 12). Then Daniel sees "One like a Son of Man" ascending to the Ancient of Days on the clouds of heaven, and this figure is given "dominion, glory, and a kingdom" that once belonged to the beasts (vv. 13–14). Daniel learns from the interpreting angel that not only the individual Son of Man but also the "saints of the Highest One" receive sovereignty, dominion, and the greatness of all kingdoms (vv. 18. 21–22). The shared kingdom of the Son of Man and the saints is "His kingdom" (v. 27), the kingdom of God.

John reinforces the link with Daniel 7 when he describes Jesus as "one like a Son of Man" (1:13; ομοιον υιον ανθρωπου; the LXX of Daniel 7:13 has ως υιος ανθρωπου). As John's gaze penetrates past Jesus' clothing to his person, he sees that Jesus resembles not the Son of Man but the Ancient of Days. According to Daniel, the Ancient of Days wears a "vesture like white snow" and has a head of hair "like pure wool" (Daniel 7:9; το τριχωμα της κεφαλης ωσει εριον λευκον καθαρον), and at the beginning of his *wasf* John sees a Jesus with "head and hair . . . white like white wool, like snow" (Revelation 1:14; η δε κεφαλη αυτου και αι τριχες λευκαι ως εριον λευκον, ως χιων). Jesus is the Son of Man, but in glory he has "aged" into the Ancient of Days. In the light of Daniel 7, that means that Jesus is not only the recipient but a giver of kingdoms. Thus, this conflation of characters from Daniel 7 antici- pates Revelation 20. After the dragon is sealed up like the beasts of Daniel, thrones are set up, "they" sit on them, and judgment is passed in favor of the saints (v. 4). At the end of Revelation 20, God sits on his great white throne and opens his books to render judgment on the "small and great" that gather before him (vv. 11–14). By the end of the book, the saints and martyr- witnesses of the Highest One are given dominion that once belonged to the dragon and his bestial associates. Jesus already rules the kings of the earth at the outset (1:5), but his holy ones do not yet share his rule. Through the events of the Apocalypse the βασιλειαι of this world have become the βασιλειαι of the Lord and of his Anointed One, the Son of Man (Revelation 11). Revelation dramatizes the delivery of the kingdoms of this world to the victors who overcome by faithful witness to death, the victors who follow Jesus the Victor to victory.

That Jesus has feet like burnished bronze not only links him with the gold-and-ivory lover of the Song of Songs but also with the various metal men of Israelite prophecy. In Daniel 2, Nebuchadnezzar dreams of a metal statue that Daniel later interprets as a preview of the succession of empires that will follow Babylon: after the Babylonian head of gold comes the Persian torso of silver, the Greek thighs of bronze, and the Roman legs of iron.[20] The bronze figure that Daniel himself sees in 10:5–6 resembles the glorified Jesus even more closely:

> I lifted my eyes and looked, and behold, there was a certain man dressed in linen, whose waist was girded with pure gold of Uphaz. His body also was like beryl, his face had the appearance of lightning, his eyes were like flaming torches, his arms and feet like the gleam of polished bronze, and the sound of his words like the sound of a tumult.

Daniel, like John later, falls before the metal man in a deep sleep until the man touches him and instructs him to record his words (Daniel 10:17–21). The parallels with Revelation 1 are evident.[21]

When we see how Daniel 2 and 10 join together, and then see that both are given a Christological interpretation in Revelation 1, we conclude that the figure John sees before him is the embodiment of empire, the *imperium*-in-Himself that is Jesus, the living version of Nebuchadnezzar's metal statue. As Son of Man, Jesus receives the kingdoms of the earth; as Ancient of Days, he confers the kingdoms on his disciples; as the metal man, Jesus incorporates the empires of late antiquity as the heir of all their glory and dominion. All of the treasures of the nations have become members of the body of Jesus.

That Jesus is revealed as the heir of the glory and authority of ancient empires provides another lens through which to read the "letters" that make up the bulk of the Patmos section of Revelation. Though the messages to the churches are often described as epistles, that is a generic oversimplification. True, they exhibit epistolary features: each begins by mentioning an addressee and a description of the sender, and each ends with a promise that might be taken as a closing benediction. Yet, the messages do not entirely follow normal epistolary form, and commentators have sought sources in other genres. Each opens with the declaration Ταδε λεγει, which is used over two hundred times in the LXX to introduce prophetic messages. By John's time, the phrase was already archaic, a Greek equivalent of the Authorized Version's "Thus saith" and a neat rhetorical device to reinforce the venerable authority of the prophetic messages of Jesus, the Ancient of Days.[22]

David Aune has argued, further, that the messages to the churches resemble imperial edicts in various details. Edicts typically began with a reference of the emperor, followed by a "he says" or "they say" introduction. Frequently, the emperor claims to "know" the situation into which he is speaking. Edicts declare the emperor's decisions, and this disposition is followed by a sanction, an exhortation or promise or threat, praise or blame, to secure obedience to the edict. Imperial edicts were often directed to local concerns, not applicable to every province. Aune concludes, "The author's use of the royal/imperial edict form is part of his strategy to polarize God/Jesus and the Roman emperor."[23] The Roman emperor issues his edicts from the capital to the provincial governors, and Jesus, as heavenly Emperor, issues edicts to the "angels"[24] who preside over the provincial capitals of his alternative imperial system, commending the faithful, correcting abuses, warning of his approaching Parousia. The messages to the churches are love letters, but letters from an Imperial Lover.

## IV. Conclusion: The Political Theology of Revelation

Much recent New Testament scholarship has discussed the "counter-imperial" thrust of the gospel. In important respects, this is a healthy recovery of the political dimension of the New Testament, but too often these interpretations ignore or neutralize contrary evidence, often using the tools of historical criticism to do so. For Elisabeth Schussler Fiorenza,[25] the problem with anti-imperial readings is that they are *insufficiently* critical of the New Testament. Anti-imperial interpreters like Richard Horsley are far too conservative for her tastes. They "have highlighted the interplay of religion and politics in the emperor cult, identified the imperial cross-cultural patronage system, and elaborated Paul's counterimperial gospel," but they fail to see that "even resistance literature will re-inscribe the structures of domination against which it seeks to argue."[26]

For feminist post-colonial critics, "the anti-imperial approach, like the 'new perspective,' still remains within the traditional Protestant paradigm, which uncritically accepts Paul's rhetorical self-construction and continues to celebrate Paul as an heroic individual and great the*logian [her asterisk], but now no longer constructs him over and against Judaism but over and against the political domination and religious paganism of the Roman Empire."[27] Schussler Fiorenza rightly chides anti-imperial readers for crossing out all the statements in Paul's letters that support rather than subvert empire: "anti-imperial biblical scholarship cannot grasp the imperial ideology at work in early Christian writings, such as in Paul's letters or the book of Revelation."[28] For her own part, Schussler Fiorenza takes "radical democracy" as her standard, and searches for "traces of a scriptural rhetoric that can inspire the resistance to empire." We cannot assume that Scripture is anti-imperial, but instead have to "identify the languages of empire and its death-dealing ideologies inscribed in scriptures" and also "identify biblical visions and values that would contribute to a radical democratic understanding of society and religion."[29]

In an intriguing discussion of the Apocalypse, Schussler Fiorenza claims that dualistic readings that set the bride and harlot in binary opposition are finally "imperial" readings, since binary oppositions are inherently conflictual and domineering. But she also realizes that imperial language disturbingly reasserts itself and does so positively: "The anti-language of Revelation asserts: empire does not belong to Rome but to the followers of the Lamb. They have been constituted as a *basileia*, as an empire in the redemption from the slavery of empire through Christ. Hence, they now have imperial rule over the earth (1:6; 5:10) and as citizens of the new Jerusalem, they will reign forever (22:5)."[30] Schussler Fiorenza worries that this "anti-language" might become internalized in such a way that it "determines the self-understanding of Christians today." If Christians were to embrace this "imperial self-understanding," they would project "evil onto the 'others' who do not follow Christ, the poor, the prostitutes, homosexuals, the feminists, and other powerful or objectified wo/men."[31]

My analysis of the imagery of the unveiling of Jesus above indicates that Schussler Fiorenza is correct in her fundamental claim about Revelation: the rhetoric of empire *is* embedded in the text and Revelation *does* promise that the people of God will be constituted "an empire."[32] Contrary to Schussler Fiorenza and other writers, this "anti-language" is not a sign of the church's unfortunate capitulation to the first-century Roman *Zeitgeist*. John views Jesus as the fulfillment of the hopes of Israel, including her political hopes. The political hope of Israel at least from the time of Daniel was not merely that the Roman imperial order would end, but that the power and glory and dominion of the imperial order would be given over to the saints of the Most High, the servants of the Son of Man. Revelation announces the fulfillment of that hope, and if I am correct about the date and historical setting of the book, Israel's longings are consummated, ironically, in the overthrow of a Jerusalem that has turned from her lover to ride the back of the Roman beast (Revelation 17). Israel's political yearnings were fulfilled in a new Jerusalem whose descent from heaven marked the beginning of the Lamb's wedding feast. On this reading, the Lamb's wedding gift was given to the bride long ago, yet the full realization of that gift remains future. The marriage supper of the Lamb has begun with the bride's appearance, but the bride and the Spirit want yet more. The Lamb has taken his throne, and has shared the Father's gift of authority over the nations with his bride, but the bride still longs for the nations to beat their swords into ploughs and refuse to learn war anymore.

In Revelation, this political hope is entwined with a form of erotic mysticism: the hope of Israel was that the Lover would again come bounding over the mountains of spices like a gazelle or a young stag to raise his Bride to her throne. Israel longs for her lover to arrive so that she can enjoy his love that is better than wine, but her yearning is also a passion for political consummation in a world made right. Revelation indicates that the pathway toward the fulfillment of this desire lies through martyrdom in its double sense— witness and faithful self-sacrifice. Early Christian martyrs died in the same hope: they looked to the time when headless martyrs and those who resisted Roman sword and fire would be not only vindicated but enthroned with Christ for a thousand years. This is the political message of Revelation: Jesus the Imperial Lover, the Son of Man glorified into the Ancient of Days, has conferred a kingdom upon his saints. He gives the nations with all their treasures to his bride as a wedding gift.[33]

*NOTES*

1  For the development of the quadriga in the early centuries, see Henri de Lubac, *Medieval Exegesis: The Four Senses of Scripture*, 3 Vols., translated by E. M. Macierowski, (Grand Rapids, MI: Wm. B. Eerdmans Publishing Company, 1998–2009). I have defended the logic of the quadriga explicitly in "The Quadriga or Something Like It: A Biblical and Pastoral Defense," in Mark Husbands and Jeffrey P. Greenman, eds., *Ancient Faith for the Church's Future* (Downers Grove, IL: IVP, 2008), pp. 110–125, and implicitly throughout my *Deep Exegesis: The Mystery of Reading Scripture* (Waco, TX: Baylor University Press, 2009).

2  Puritan interpretations of the Song of Songs, for instance, continued to use allegorical methods. See George L. Scheper, "Reformation Attitudes toward Allegory and the Song of Songs," *PMLA*, Vol.89 (1974), pp. 551–562. Reformed "redemptive-historical" interpretation also overlaps considerably with older modes of interpretation.

3  The Series Preface is found in each of the volumes. I happen to be looking at Robert Jenson, *Ezekiel* (Grand Rapids, MI: Brazos, 2009), pp. 10–11.

4  Those who doubt me may treat themselves to an Amazon.com search of "theological interpretation."

5  For a summary of the evidence, see David E. Aune, *Revelation 1–5*, Word Biblical Commentary Series, (Nashville, TN: Thomas Nelson Inc., 1997), pp. lvi–lxx. Recent advocates of an early date include Thomas Slater, "Dating the Apocalypse to John," *Biblica*, Vol. 84 (2003), pp. 252–258, and J. Christian Wilsdon, "The Problem of the Domitianic Date of Revelation," *New Testament Studies*, Vol. 39 no. 4 (1993), pp. 587–605. A slightly older essay defending the early date is Albert A. Bell, "Date of John's Apocalypse: The Evidence of Some Roman Historians Reconsidered," *New Testament Studies*, Vol. 25 no. 1 (1978), pp. 93–102. Adela Yarbro Collins, "Dating the Apocalypse of John," *Biblical Review*, Vol. 26 (1981), pp. 33–45, considers and rejects the earlier dating.

6  See Leonard L. Thompson, *The Book of Revelation: Apocalypse and Empire* (Oxford: Oxford University Press, 1997). Because the historical evidence does not match the view that the saints in Revelation are under intense persecution, many recent interpreters have concluded that the book is concerned with subtle forms of pressure to conform rather than with persecution. The blood and gore (e.g., in chapter 14) are not at all literal but vivid rhetorical symbols of the spiritual dangers of accommodation.

7  A few pieces of internal evidence might be cited: *Jerusalem* is the city that drinks prophetic, saintly blood (Matthew 23:34–39; Revelation 17:6). Under the law, a priest's daughter who becomes a whore is burned (Leviticus 21:9), and the harlot city Jerusalem is likewise burned (Revelation 21:16). "Babylon" is replaced not with a new Rome, but with a new Jerusalem that descends from heaven as a pure bride (Revelation 21:2). In the symbolic associations of the book, Bride is to Harlot as new Jerusalem is to X. The symmetry is preserved if X = old Jerusalem.

8  E. Michael Rusten, "The Structure of the Book of Revelation," unpublished paper presented at the Evangelical Theological Society Annual Meeting, Atlanta 2010. Several of the following paragraphs are taken from my *Between Beast and Babel: America and Empires in Biblical Perspective* (Eugene, OR: Wipf & Stock, 2012), used by permission of Wipf and Stock Publishers.

9   This might also be an exodus reference. Yahweh claims to have borne Israel on eagle's wings from Egypt, and describes himself protectively "hovering" (רָחַף Deuteronomy 32:11) over His people as the Spirit "hovered" over the waters in the creation (Genesis 1:2:רָחַף).
10  See John 1:14: The Word "tabernacled" among us, and we saw His glory.
11  The lampstands of the tabernacle are described as almond trees (Exodus 25:33–34; 37:19–20).
12  The original priestly garments already echoed the tabernacle and its furnishings. See Meredith Kline, *Images of the Spirit* (Eugene, OR: Wipf & Stock, 1999).
13  The description in verses 14–16 is organized chiastically, moving from head to feet and then back, with Jesus' voice at the structural center:
   A. Head and hair white like wool and snow
     B. Eyes are flame of fire
       C. Feet like burnished bronze
         D. Voice
       C'. In hand, seven stars
     B'. Sword coming from his mouth
   A'. Face like sun shining
14  For simplicity's sake, I call the male speaker "Solomon" or "the Lover" and the female the "bride" or the "beloved." For the purposes of this article, I leave the question of authorship to the side.
15  Perhaps we should conclude not "Men are from Mars, women are from Venus" but rather "Men are buildings, women are gardens."
16  This passage and Christological readings of the Song were sources for the theme of "Jesus as Mother" explored in Carol W. Bynum, *Jesus as Mother: Studies in the Spirituality of the High Middle Ages* (Berkeley, CA: University of California Press, 1984). Though John uses no natural imagery in his description of Jesus, the mineral and metallic imagery alludes to the *wasf* of the lover in Song of Songs 5. The lover's head is gold, his torso is ivory and precious jewels, his legs alabaster on pedestals of gold. Similarly, Jesus has feet like burnished bronze and a sword is coming from His mouth.
17  Many commentators interpret the hot, cold, and lukewarm temperatures as references to the water from hot springs that is assumed to have been carried by the aqueduct found at Laodicea (see Aune, *Revelation*, p. 357). The text says nothing about water, and given the festal imagery of 3:20 it seems likely that the message is about food throughout. Besides, it is difficult to make sense of Jesus wanting either hot or cold, but not lukewarm water. Spicy or cooling food makes more sense.
18  John works through the Song in reverse order. He begins the vision with a *wasf* like that of Song of Songs (5:10–16) and moves back to the opening verses of Song of Songs 5, the lover's knocking (5:2), and finally to the feast (5:1). Revelation's first vision thus chiastically inverts the Song:
   A. Feast of love, Song 5:1
     B. Lover knocking, Song 5:2
       C. *Wasf* of lover, Song 5:10–16
       C'. *Wasf* of Jesus, Revelation 1:14–16
     B'. Jesus knocking, Revelation 3:22a
   A'. Jesus wants to dine, Revelation 3:22b
19  The dislodging of the Apocalypse from John is one of the *unfortunate* results of modern scholarship. Virtually no commentator today accepts the traditional view that the John of Revelation is the Beloved Disciple of the gospel. I think they are one and the same. Even if that is not correct, however, the textual linkages between John and Revelation are deep and pervasive. In addition to the points I make in the text, I would add this: John's prologue famously describes the incarnation as the Word "tabernacling" (εσκηνωσεν, from σκηνοω) among us (1:14). The verb is used nowhere else in the New Testament, except in Revelation, where it appears four times: The enthroned Father "tents" among the saints (7:15), some creatures tent in the sky (12:12) and they are the object of the beast's attacks (13:6). This theme comes to a climax with the descent of the bride (21:2), which is greeted by a loud voice announcing that "the tabernacle of God is among men and he will tabernacle with them" (σκηνωσει μετ' αυτων; 21:3). In short, John begins with a divine Word tabernacling among men; the Apocalypse ends with the Lord tabernacling among men in the holy city, Jerusalem, the bride of the Lamb. The inclusion can hardly be accidental. Warren Gates of

Knox Theological Seminary has worked out the parallel structures of John and Revelation in great detail, and argued plausibly that the books form a single two-volume chiasm. His work is partially available at http://imaginingavainthing.wordpress.com/, accessed February 15, 2012.

20  For simplicity's sake, I leave out the iron-and-clay feet.
21  The connection between Daniel 10 and Revelation 1 is a commonplace observation among commentators. See Aune, *Revelation*, pp. 95, 99.
22  Pointed out by David E. Aune, "The Form and Function of the Proclamations to the Seven Churches (Revelation 2–3)," *New Testament Studies*, Vol.36 (1990), pp. 182–204.
23  Aune, "Form and Function"; Aune, *Revelation*, pp. 126–129.
24  I take αγγελος as a reference to human messengers or leaders in the church, essentially the presiding bishop of the church in each city of Asia. The simplest argument for this interpretation is the commonsensical one offered by James Jordan: if Jesus addressed spiritual angels, why would He write through a human amanuensis?
25  Elisabeth Schussler Fiorenza, *The Power of the Word: Scripture and the Rhetoric of Empire* (Minneapolis, MN: Fortress Press, 2007), pp. 2–7.
26  Stephen Moore likewise complains about the "reinscription" of imperial attitudes into the Apocalypse, noting that there is direct continuity from Revelation to Constantine. See Stephen Moore, *Empire and Apocalypse: Postcolonialism and the New Testament* (Sheffield: Sheffield Phoenix Press, 2006), p. 97.
27  Fiorenza, *The Power of the Word*, p. 5.
28  *Ibid.*
29  *Ibid.*, pp. 9–10.
30  *Ibid.*, p. 143.
31  *Ibid.*
32  I have explored this theme throughout the Bible in my *Between Babel and Beast* (Eugene, OR: Wipf & Stock, 2012).
33  On this theme, see Allan J. McNicol, *The Conversion of the Nations in Revelation*, Library of New Testament Studies, (London: T&T Clark, 2011). Richard Bauckham is correct that the "theme is the transfer of the sovereignty of the whole world to God from the dragon and the beast" (*The Climax of Prophecy: Studies in the Book of Revelation* [London: T&T Clark, 1993], p. 242), but it is equally the case that the sovereignty of the whole world is shared out from God and the Lamb to the saints who shed their blood as witnesses. In fact, the latter theme is the more crucial one. Jesus himself is king at the beginning of Revelation; what happens in the book is the elevation of a queen to share his throne.

# 6

# TRANSLATION AND TRANSCENDENCE: THE FRAGILE FUTURE OF SPIRITUAL INTERPRETATION

## DAVID LYLE JEFFREY

Perhaps just because this is so secular an age, there has been a spike of interest among theologians in spiritual interpretation. On the whole this has been a positive development, restoring balance. The benefits, however, may be largely confined to those who can read the scriptures in their original languages and the commentary tradition in Latin. The laity, who in a secular age are arguably most in need of a recovery of spiritual sense and theological vision, are largely bypassed, shut out of the conversation. Their deprivation will continue, I suggest, just so long as contemporary English translations of the Bible and the liturgy are themselves impoverished and even misconstrued by a prevalent reduction of sacred language to its merely material affect or technical register. In this article I want a) to illustrate the extreme gravity of materialistic translation in a preponderance of English translations of the Bible appearing since the 1960s, more than fifty of which have already been published and marketed vigorously (with more on the way); b) to show how the net effect of many of these efforts can be a tacit desacralization of Holy Scripture; and c) to argue that pursuant to any translation which would aspire to the theological power and enduring memorability of the four-hundred year old KJV, theologians who care about spiritual interpretation will perforce have to refurbish many key terms and titles in Scripture in a way which habituates their proper spiritual meaning. It will be obvious in what follows that I presume a view of scripture as revelation, and with that its corollary, namely that it not

*Heaven on Earth?: Theological Interpretation in Ecumenical Dialogue*, First Edition.
Edited by Hans Boersma and Matthew Levering.
© 2013 Blackwell Publishing Ltd. Book compilation © 2013 Blackwell Publishing Ltd.

to be expected that the God of Holy Scripture will always talk just as we talk.

## Translation and Motive

No one familiar with the history of Bible translation is unaware that particular pagan cultures invariably present particular impediments to accurate translation. This is more evident when inaugural translations are attempted among "unreached people groups" (to use a locution of the SIL/Wycliffe translators). Examples adduced to highlight this problem, or to justify quite problematic, if creative solutions, can seem quaint to non-specialists. But that doesn't mean that in the context of the target language the impediments are trivial; the sheep/shepherd imagery of Psalm 23 and the parables of Jesus can present a real problem for translators working to re-present the text of Scripture in a culture (e.g., Inuit) in which such analogies and figures of speech, in some ways critical for spiritual understanding, are inherently without apropos for the people in such cultures. A far more serious impediment, however, may exist amongst Bible readers closer to home. It is increasingly apparent that in western, comparatively well-educated and urbanized cultures, a more acute insensitivity to biblical language now exists, namely, a tone-deafness to figurative locutions and spiritual resonance per se. One way that many recent modern translators of Scripture into English have tried to deal with what C. L. Wrenn has called a "spiritual contraction [since the seventeenth century] which renders the symbolic language properly necessary to religious material no longer receivable"[1] is by acceding to the perceived current state of the language in much the same fashion as have editors of school texts and popular news media. This has meant rendering the Greek and Hebrew of the text "accessibly," that is by transposition of what the translator thinks is the essential meaning of a passage into current, colloquial American idiom at a low-vocabulary level. In far too many cases, as I have suggested elsewhere, this choice to privilege a low common denominator discourse has come at a grievous cost to both literal and spiritual meaning in the text as we have received it.[2]

Some of the worst instances of loss occur in pseudo "translations"—actually paraphrases—which offer themselves as attempts to render clear for the contemporary reader what in older translations is thought to have by now become obscure. That accommodation of this sort is appealing in the religious marketplace of our time is evident, but hardly unproblematic. An apparently innocuous (but in fact not at all innocuous) instance of what populist transposition to mere colloquial idiom may do to understanding of a text explicitly devoted to spiritual interpretation can be seen in Hebrews 11:1. Here, for the familiar "Faith is the substance of things hoped for, the evidence of things unseen" (KJV), *The Message* offers, "the fundamental fact of existence is that this trust in God, this faith, is the firm foundation *under everything that makes life worth living*. It is our handle on what we can't see." At first glance this sounds pretty much like a garden variety evangelical application, which of course is the point. Verse 2 in this rendition goes on to add, "The act of faith is what distinguished our ancestors, *set them above the crowd*" (italics mine). Surely this, too, is colloquial American English of our era, and it falls on the ear of some listeners quite comfortably. But that is a problem: in the original, the text was carefully wrought to aim in another direction. Moreover, paraphrase or not, it is not helpful to the original meaning that *The Message* is here prolix in a way which so effectively obscures the purport of that original: "everything that makes life worth living" evokes temporal rather than spiritual benefits of faith, and that at the head of a passage which intends throughout to speak of an *agon*, a running *through* worldly trials toward an explicitly spiritual goal, a city prepared by God (vv. 13–16), a "tabernacle not made with hands" (Heb. 9:11). Being "set above the crowd," likewise a colloquialism with overtones, can too easily be read as implicitly an appeal to another possible motivation in the reader quite contrary to what the writer clearly has in mind, namely desire for earthly social distinction and recognition. At best this sort of locution affords an impoverished analogy to the original sense.

The New Life Version, not a paraphrase, translates the sentence in this way: "Now faith is being sure we will get what we hope for. It is being sure of what we cannot see." Here again the effect on a first-time reader is likely to be reductive of the richer sense of the original, since it is colored by a "name it and claim it" aura of association; "get what we hope for" subtly shifts focus to un-named desires of the individual believer. While more accurate lexically than the paraphrase, this version also carries a tacitly materialist overtone.

The Greek is clearly more spiritual in intent than either rendition: "Ἔστιν δὲ πίστις ἐλπιζομένων ὑπόστασις, πραγμάτων ἔλεγχος οὐ βλεπομένων." In a recent review article, Robert Pogue Harrison has commented aptly on the way in which the KJV translators improved upon both Tyndale's and the Geneva translation of our verse in this respect.[3] Where Tyndale had, "Faith is the sure confidence of things, which are hoped for, & a certainty of things which are not seen," the Geneva translators put "Now faith is the ground of things, which are hoped for, and the evidence of things which are not seen." The 1611 King James translators, more succinctly and, in the light of ὑπόστασις more accurately, have "Now faith is the substance of things hoped for, the evidence of things not seen." The advantage is not merely a greater elegance in diction. As Harrison points out,

> Tyndale's "sure confidence" is a very loose translation of the Greek hypostasis, which means literally "standing under" (*hypo*, under + *histhastai*, stand, middle voice of *histannai*, cause to stand). The Geneva version's "ground" is a much closer approximation, yet the KJB's choice of "substance" is brilliant. Not only does "substance" mean literally

"standing under," it also comes with a host of religious associations and connotations. . . .[4]

Among these connotations, both in the Greek of the original and the Latin of Jerome's Vulgate translation, is the conviction that faith is not to be understood as something we rise up to, the effect of positive thinking, or even a premise in the ordinary sense. Least of all is it self-confidence. Rather, faith is a gift of God by which we assent to his authority (*ex ousia,* i.e., God's "being" —*ousia*—or his "substance"); his Being becomes an authority so internalized that in a very "real" spiritual sense we "stand under" it reflexively. It is thus "substantial" in the spiritual way Aquinas, and not John Locke and his successors, understood the term: "substance" here refers exclusively to Being (things unseen), and not to materiality (cf. OED). Aquinas, who interestingly renders "evidence" as *argumentum* in his commentary on Hebrews (11:1), grasps the point at issue squarely when he writes: "If someone wishes to reduce these words to due form, he can say that faith is the habit of mind by which eternal life is begun in us . . . since by the *divine authority* the intellect is convinced to assent to things it does not see."[5] He adds, "And when we say that faith is of things to be hoped for, it is distinguished from faith as it is commonly taken, which is not ordered to beatitude."[6] This spiritual understanding of faith, of substance, of evidentiality, not to say of the goal of beatitude to which they are ordered, is not in the original to be confused with "be-happy attitudes" or "the power of positive thinking." But some of our popular translations—and much popular exposition—make confusion for many readers on this and similar points almost inevitable. Phrases such as "getting what we hope for" and "everything that makes life worth living" are neither translations nor adequate approximations of what the text says. When a reader takes them to be what "the Bible says", wittingly or not, these "translations" actually undermine the original text.

   Part of the motive for new translation is evidently a desire for contemporary currency; the typically announced purpose is to render the text of Scripture not only accessible but comfortable for contemporary readers. Another, and on the evidence arguably more powerful, motive for the extreme proliferation of recent translations is clearly profit for the translators and especially the publishers. A great deal of material reward is in the offing. These motives conspire. The more "cool" and "easy" or "uncomplicated" the translation sounds, the better people like it. The new text apparently needs no interpreter, because God and the translators do us the favor of bringing their message down to our level. After all, that was the whole point of koiné Greek from the beginning—wasn't it?

   Well, maybe not. It is fairly obvious to a reader of the New Testament in Greek that, while the basic language is demotic, the diction and usage one finds, e.g., in much of Luke, many passages in Paul, and in Hebrews, is far from commonplace. Rather, it is notably a species of what Longinus, in his

*Peri Hypsous,* called "elevated style."[7] This characteristic is consistent with the diction of speeches in the divine voice in the prophets (e.g., Isa. 40–43) and Job (e.g., ch. 38 ff). In each case elevated, poetic language is associated with the divine voice, and the literary form accords. This is hardly surprising. The God of the Old Testament is reported in Isaiah as having reminded his chosen people, ". . . my thoughts are not your thoughts, neither are your ways my ways . . . for, as the heavens are higher than the earth, so are my ways higher than your ways, and my thoughts higher than your thoughts" (Isa. 55:8–9, KJV). This particular text, moreover, connects the warning about misrepresentation with words about God's word going forth into the world (v. 11). In Matthew 13:10–16, Jesus famously rejects the disciples' concern that he teaches too much in figurative language, which many in his audience cannot apparently follow, and he makes it clear that the purpose of his figurative speech is not only to instruct the willing but to exclude those who are not "given . . . to know the mysteries of the kingdom of heaven" (v. 11). The word "mysteries" is here indicative. Spiritual interpretation is required of an inherently spiritual language, most especially where the divine voice is involved; neither here nor anywhere else does the divine voice in Scripture promise to make everything perspicuous to everyone. Should the contemporary translator or the one who paraphrases then presume to try to render everything in Scripture *apparently* perspicuous to the reading level of a public which perhaps in more than one sense has "ears dull of hearing" (v. 15)? Especially at the risk of making the text appear to say something less difficult, or which may comfort readers in their dullness, assuring them that they 'get it' when they probably don't? Obviously there are many facets to these questions, and translators' difficulties are far from the only ones to worry about, but it seems that contemporary translators should take them more seriously.

*Sacral Language and Divine Names*

I have remarked elsewhere on comparable reductions of meaning in translations of passages in the Old Testament.[8] When *chokma-lev* in Exodus (31:6; 35:25; 36:2) is translated wisely by the KJV translators dead literally as "wise-hearted," it preserves both relation to *chokma*, wisdom, and a pertinent distinction from it. *Chokma-lev,* a species of creative imagination and discernment concerning beauty found in Bezalel and his cohort, from the divine point of view suits them uniquely to preparing the art of the tabernacle. It is distinguished here from wisdom per se in that it is regarded less as something to be pursued, imitated and studied (e.g., *chokma* in Proverbs) than a distinctive gift of God. Those chosen to create the art of the tabernacle are deemed worthy not because they are already known to be crafty, but just because they are revealed to Moses as having been Spirit-filled, gifted by God himself for artistic work fitted to the beauty of holiness. Now let us consider what happens to *chokma-lev* in representative modern translations. NIV, NAB, and NASB render *chokma-lev* as "skill," the ESV has "ability," the New Living Translation has "expertise," *The Message* has "aptitude for crafts." In all these cases, what has been lost in translation is not less than the main point—the sacral, sacramental element of divine giftedness, which in this passage is presented as intrinsically necessary to a holy work and worship. Any reduction of *chokma-lev* to a term of mere material affect muffles the spiritual significance of this holy artistry in a particularly dismal way. If we may shift to Greek to say so, what we have left on the page of most modern translations is all *techné* and no *logos*.[9]

Readers of contemporary translations of similar New Testament passages–that is, passages in which the language is about spiritual as distinct from material gifts—may encounter many such attempts to 'explain in contemporary terms,' rephrasing the words of Jesus, even, in which the result undermines the original simply by attempting to provide a contemporary and *material* analogue for what has been offered as a timeless and spiritual truth. In John 8:12, for example, where the ESV sensibly resembles RSV and KJV, the text reads: "Again Jesus spoke to them, saying, 'I am the light of the world. Whoever follows me will not walk in darkness, but will have the light of life.'" This translation follows the Greek closely in a metaphorical language familiar to John's contemporaries as poetic philosophical discourse about ultimate reality; what is at issue is spiritual rather than physical passage or enlightenment. When *The Message* gives "Jesus once again addressed them: 'I am the world's Light. No one who follows me stumbles around in the darkness. I provide plenty of light to live in,'" the effect of the attempt is to literalize the metaphor, to temporize it. It may give the reader a graphic mental image, but at best a subjective and perhaps even trivializing deflection from the evident point of the passage, which immediately ensues in a debate with the Pharisees about the nature of truth and what counts as verification.

Normative early Christian exegesis, such as that of Augustine in his tractates on John, immediately sought to show that in these words Christ is clearly not speaking literalistically, as the Manicheans would have it, referring to himself as the sun. Nor, as Augustine is at pains to say, is this saying of Jesus an attempt to borrow Graeco-Roman myths of Phoebus-Apollo to himself. Rather, Augustine says, he is declaring a higher spiritual reality, namely that "there is a light which made the light of the sun."[10] The Light of the eternal uncreated Wisdom was here speaking in his normatively poetic fashion, which Augustine sensibly sees as requiring a spiritual interpretation. He responds to Jesus' figurative locution by appealing to comparable light metaphors from elsewhere in Scripture that likewise refer to divine illumination in a spiritual way.

Comparatively, what was perhaps moderately challenging for Augustine's audience, namely, understanding the spiritual register intended in a biblical rather than Graeco-Roman way, may be far exceeded in difficulty for a modern exegete when his audience largely lacks any mythopoetic imagination whatsoever. In this case the resonance of the spiritual sense of "light" can have been flattened by a mundane, temporizing narrowing of the term. At least as damaging may be the contemporary English reader's loss of another implicit hierarchical overtone in the saying—lost because the reader lacks familiarity with characteristically regal expressions. It is obvious that most modern republican, democratic societies have in one way or another abolished the concept of royal decree;[11] unfortunately, deafness to the regal voice can be a hindrance even in the visual arts, e.g., to the viewer of an artistic representation of such a saying of Jesus as is found in John 8:12. Thus, at S. Maria Maggiore in Rome, when in centuries past a worshipper coming in through the portal (the *basilike stoa* deliberately recalls the triumphal arches of the Roman emperors), looked up to see not Caesar, not the Sol Invictus, but rather a mosaic of Christ enthroned in the New Jerusalem with the Scriptures opened to "*Ego sum lux mundi, qui . . .*" (John 8:12) a profound imaginative juxtaposition unavoidably would have occurred. Not only does the balance of the saying invited by the *qui*—"he that follows me"—flood into such a Christian mind, but also a recollection that the basilica, once the tribunal chambers of an earthly emperor, was now a sanctuary in which one might encounter the real presence of a far higher king, the *melech ha 'olam, basileî ton aionon, rex caelum,* "King of kings and Lord of lords." A host of related passages from Scripture would inevitably flood into the mind of one who had heard the word read so often in the liturgy: "the entrance of thy word giveth Light" (Ps. 119:130); "in thy Light we see Light" (Ps. 36:9), etc. "Light," in such a light, is a trope, polysemous and spiritual, and it indubitably requires just such a spiritual interpretation as Augustine and a host of other commentators gave it. One may doubt whether a contemporary tourist would reflexively think in this way. So too for contemporary Bible readers lacking an informed guide; whereas readers from apostolic through early modern times would have understood this saying of the Lord in a context where the transcendent, regal, and eschatological register of the saying was paramount, translators wrestling with a leveled, democratized, and prosaic culture can too easily obscure the crucial point by attempting to make the language 'accessible' through a species of accommodation to the preoccupations of such a culture, thus in a mundane, literal-minded way.

## Piety Without Poetry

Clearly, modern translators operate at a disadvantage. Their intended readers lack poetry. They also lack respect for authority. But Holy Scripture so frequently expresses divine authority in poetic speech that these lacunae erect a huge barrier for readers who are likely to associate whatever diminished notion of authority they retain with prosaic and propositional language, and who often regard poetic language as ephemeral or needlessly obscure. We can thus sympathize with the contemporary translator who feels compelled to overcome the limits of both vocabulary and worldview in his audience by prosaic and explanatory interposition.[12] What this misguided effort can produce, however, and sadly, is an impression in the reader that God's thoughts are pretty much our thoughts, his language our language. It need hardly be added that this misprision is theologically dangerous. There is some truth to the remark of Joseph Joubert, that "with God it is necessary to be neither a scholar nor a philosopher, but child, slave, pupil, and above all, a poet."[13] If there is one general technical limitation evident in most contemporary English translations of the Bible, it is that too few contemporary translators are poets, or even practiced readers of poetry.

In evangelical contexts especially, poetry can arouse ambivalence; it is a Reformation habit of mind to assert, but in a different fashion than had Aquinas and Nicholas Lyra much earlier, the primacy of the literal sense. For Aquinas, there was more to the "literal" sense than there is for most descendents of the Reformation, in that he did not view the literal as merely the archeological or one-dimensional historical sense. One way of describing his view is simply to say that for Aquinas the resonance of terms in Scripture is rich with multi-dimensional significance, that in his view, as in that of Augustine and others before him, the words of the Bible were very often inherently figurative, or polysemous.[14] The spiritual senses of the medieval exegete are those "based upon the literal sense and presuppose it";[15] they certainly do not deny it. Such an exegete had, however, a less impoverished understanding of language. In practice, this medieval expectation of a surplus of meaning in a term was to produce a more poetic appreciation of the literal sense, in which even when what is at first glance "literal" might also be understood "spiritually." Theologians are entirely familiar with this reflexively, and so, typically, are other readers whose familiarity with the language of the Bible is habitual. There is nothing particularly medieval or Catholic about this; it is inherent in biblical language, and to pre-modern readers a commonplace. Thus, when the great Jesuit exegete Cornelius Lapide (1567–1637), commenting on Matthew 13:44, says that the proper literal meaning of the treasure hidden in the field is "the Gospel, its teaching, its faith",[16] he is not saying anything that Calvin the Reformer would have found inherently objectionable.[17] Both understood that Christ taught *semper in figura loquens*, in poetic language, and that such language axiomatically invited a spiritual interpretation. But their shared literary appreciation, namely that in Scripture the literal sense can be itself already figural, seems much less reflexive in many of their descendents among recent translators.

Spiritual interpreters of Scripture respect the poetry of Scripture—its inherent polyvalence as well as indirection—because they regard the words of Scripture as vehicles for mysteries that are, to common speech, ultimately unspeakable. Their own stance before the text must accordingly be as tentative as it is reverential; they are compelled to use the subjunctive and optative voice rather than the imperative and indicative in their commentary; they are obliged by the figural language of Scripture especially to venture of a term, "this is something it 'may' or 'would seem to' portend," rather than, apodeictically, "this is what it means." Such are the reflexes of readers of poetry. Bonaventure, in his *Breviloquium*, captures the spirit of their enquiry in this way:

> Beneath the rind of the open letter lies hidden a mystical and profound meaning; and this for the confounding of our pride, so that by these supreme depths lying hidden beneath the lowliness of the letter both the proud may be humbled, the unclean repelled, the unjust turned away, and the negligent aroused to an understanding of the mysteries. And since they that listen to this teaching are not of one class but of every class—for indeed all who would be saved must know something of this teaching, it therefore has a manifold understanding that so it may take captive every understanding and at the same time adapt itself to every understanding, may exceed all understanding, and yet may enlighten and alike enkindle by its varied ray every understanding that diligently applies itself to it. (*Breviloquium* Proem 5)

"Enkindle" is a seminal verb here. This stance and expectation leaves the text more open to interpretation, to new canonical connections, subsequent recognition and deeper and nuanced understanding. But what happens when a translation or paraphrase preemptively narrows the potential for interpretation by an incorporated material application? Many contemporary translators, perhaps naturally enough in their circumstances, are, by contrast with earlier translators, more comfortable when they can "nail down" a literal meaning even at the cost of reducing a spiritual term to its material affect.

Literal-mindedness is thus as often a quagmire as is literal rendition a path to firm footing where translation is concerned. Here too the caution of St. Paul applies: the shared task of translators and interpreters is to be "sufficient as ministers of the new covenant, not of the letter but of the Spirit, for the letter kills, but the Spirit gives life" (2 Cor. 3:6). Where literal rendition preserves an intended spiritual sense it is obviously a good thing; it vivifies. Equally, where literalizing "explanation" or reduction of a word merely to its material affect obscures or occludes an intended spiritual sense, it is most certainly not a good thing; it preempts natural access to the spiritual sense. Further, there are far too many instances where a supposed attempt at literal accuracy, pressed into the service of some agenda of "new historicism," kills more than poetic diction.

*The Common English Bible*, an ecumenical effort of about 120 translators (twelve of whom are Catholics), seemed at first promising, and there are clearly some virtuous passages in this version.[18] But sadly, here too the dominance of the language of social construction has led to slanted (politically corrected) colloquialisms which narrow the meaning: "alien" becomes "immigrant," "angels" become "messengers" (pleasing, perhaps, to those who wish to add an Islamic overture, but nonetheless a literal equivalent which kills a crucial spiritual distinction in the original). In this version neither John the Baptist or Jesus call on people to "repent," but rather less judgmentally, to "change your heart." Generic language such as the inclusive use of "man" or "mankind" is studiously avoided; new-created Adam becomes simply "the human"—even though, predictably, Eve is still "a woman." The translators retain "son of Adam" in the genealogy of Christ as it is found in Luke chapter 3, but the CEB reader may have lost the linkage with the name as it traditionally first appears in Genesis, where pre-fallen "Adam" has been erased (though "Adam" is used after the Fall he isn't named until Gen. 4). Far more seriously, Messianic titles for Jesus are also obscured; Jesus is no longer "the Son of Man," but "the Human One." At this point theological misrepresentation disqualifies the translation for those who regard "Son of Man" as a messianic title. Even for those who don't, the locution has the odd effect of making Jesus seem like a character in an episode of *Star Trek*, with the narrator sounding like a Klingon, or at least someone from another galaxy: "the Human One must suffer many things and be rejected" (Lk. 9:22), "the Human One is Lord of the Sabbath"(Lk. 6:5), and "As it was in the days of Noah, so it will be in the days of the Human One" (Lk. 17:26). Meanwhile, the translators have no trouble with retaining "Be'ezalel" (Lk. 11:19) and "Satan" (Lk. 10:18). The risk to the ordinary reader in this tacit erasure of the messianic title can be a kind of philologically induced Arianism.

*Translation and Worldview*

Having ears to hear, yet not hearing, is in the Scriptures themselves represented as a function of what we might now perhaps think of as a disjunction or contradiction in categories—not an incapacity to grasp the denotative lexical meaning of words and the grammar of sentences, but rather an obtuseness to intention in the speaker. Such obtuseness can obviously be either willed or unwilled. In the same fashion, translators may miss the intention in a passage—or its possibility of polyvocity—not because of a desire to mislead or to impose an alien worldview upon the text (though contemporary translations include examples of that), but perhaps simply because they do not themselves live habitually within the discourse they are attempting to capture, or have become by an alien cultural *habitus* desensitized to it at a philological if not theological level. Yet the task of the translator remains, no less than that of the expositor, to permit the reader and worshipper to consider spiritual things in a spiritual way.

In a critical review of the controversial *Today's New International Version* (2005), now the most popular of English versions, Leroy Huizenga discerns "an evangelicalism married to modernity."[19] While he commends revisions in which this version sticks closer to the Greek than its predecessor, Huizenga laments (justifiably, in my view) problems resulting from "the rise of lively language at the expense of fidelity to the form of the original." He also notes a defect which owes to the translators' evident desire to produce an effect which (regarding a different translation of the Old Testament) Edward L. Greenstein has called "flawless, native-looking veneer,"[20] and thus to repress such features as verbal repetition in the original text in favor of employing a wide range of possible synonyms. This effort is an expression of contemporary western stylistic values, however, in particular a modern desire for elaborating novelties of expression. But such a predilection is contradictory to the stylistics or poetics of the original, which often requires repetition of the radical in a term to develop both theme and extended resonance. Huizinga points to numerous examples in Mark and Matthew in which both thematic development and narrative irony is lost to synonyms. He also cites NIV interpolations in the service of contemporary concern for gender issues, some of which obscure the Christological portent of the quotation, such as that in Hebrews 2:6–8 of Psalm 8:4–6. The announced commitment of the recent NIV edition to linguistic descriptivism, the position that language is always changing and that any concept of correct usage must be based on the culture of the host language, Huizinga duly finds problematic. It will by now be clear that I share his opinion, especially concerning the overweighting of contemporary idiom, and most especially in passages where it entails a tacit bias away from the primacy of the original text. Linguistically, this theoretical stance courts theological misrepresentation.

No one has been more influential in modern evangelical and Protestant translation than the late Eugene Nida, with his emphasis on "functional" and "dynamic" equivalence as the proper object of translators. His shadow still looms large in the twentieth-century history of such important organizations as SIL/Wycliffe translators.[21] But the effect of his influence has been to tilt translation heavily in the direction of literalizing expression within the colloquial argot of the receptor cultures, sometimes referred to as the "target language," but now, more amiably, as the "host language." Recently there has been considerable pushback on the privilege accorded to dynamic equivalence.[22] This is understandable, not least because it has become apparent that some minority language translations have been so overly conscious of the host-language culture that the translations ran the risk of sounding more like that culture than like the countercultural message—for all cultures—of the gospel itself.[23] Worse, when looked at from an anthropological perspective, some translations have seemed to reflect an intermediary Americanized cultural grid or screen.

Catholic Bible translators have in particular wrestled with these issues, and, both in English translations of the liturgy and of Scripture itself, it must be acknowledged, the position of the Church has often been uncertain or conflicted.[24] That said, in the paradigm established by the *Liturgiam Authenticam* of 2001, helpful directives for future translations have more recently emerged. In the words of Emil Wcela, *Liturgiam Authenticam* expresses a desire for translations "marked by sound doctrine, exact wording, free from ideological influence, and in a language worthy of the sacred mysteries and worship."[25] All translations are to be from the original texts (following the decree of Pope Pius XII and the reiteration of Pope John Paul II); the translation will seek "formal equivalence" (i.e., literal rendition) rather than "functional equivalence," and translations should be "in a language which is easily understandable, yet which at the same time preserves the dignity, beauty, and doctrinal precision [of the original text]."[26] Though referred in the first instance to liturgy, these principles have now been widely understood to pertain to biblical translation as well. These principles, it seems to me, are rightly ordered from a theological perspective, however challenging they may be to translators in some situations and for some passages.

It is clear, moreover, that just as with the proponents of "dynamic equivalence" and "linguistic descriptivism," the position of the *LA* proceeds from a particular worldview. Though engaged with the same primary text and its transmission, these two ("dynamic equivalence" and "linguistic descriptivism") and "formal equivalence" do not reflect the same worldview. It is clear that George Steiner was right to observe that the work of the translator inevitably proceeds from an underlying philosophy of the translator.[27] Greenstein's refraction of this observation is to say not only that "different styles of translation manifest different theories of translation," but that "the merit of any translation rests not only on the skill of the translator, but even more fundamentally on the philosophy that underpins it."[28] What must be said about the disposition of many contemporary translations is that they tend— much more than is warranted by the text itself—to reduce theological mysteries to mundane analogies. Once normalized in translation, a barrier to spiritual understanding is erected at the linguistic level by inadequate comparisons. We may not think of such inadequacies as proceeding from an undergirding philosophy of translation, but in fact they usually do. The worldview of modernity, privileging present consciousness and cultural preoccupations as normative, makes it harder—not easier—to "hear" what Scripture is saying spiritually.

What also must be reckoned with in our own context is that our present English culture typically privileges content over form in translation to a degree disabling of the poetics of the Bible itself. We think of translation and the translator's task in a markedly prosaic way. But this is to miss the performance context of much of the Scripture itself, which even in the New Testament did not focus on the individual reader but on the community, and on the text as something to be *heard in community*. The form of the text was expressed by a rhetorical style, a poetic, suited for reading aloud in liturgical settings.[29] The first translators into English, in the era of Bede and Caedmon, recognized this as a pertinent analogue to the community reception and participation in a story held in common, normatively received and heard by the community assembled together for an oral/aural event. The undergirding philosophy of these earlier English translators privileged oral reception of Scripture likewise as a means of hearing together. Happily, this understanding placed them closer to the experience of Scripture in the early Church than we are ourselves. One does not have to read long in the *Ecclesiastical History* of Bede or the Anglo-Saxon saints' lives to see that they understood, in the same way as the authors and hearers of the gospel in Palestine, that "faith comes by hearing" (*ex akoes*) and hearing by "the word of God." Sadly, among non-liturgical Christians in our culture today, it is all too possible to attend public worship and not hear the Scriptures read aloud, or if cited in a sermon, to hear only disconnected extracts, occluding the poetics and elevated diction of the whole. Among liturgical Christians, it must be said, it is still normative to hear the Scripture read in a liturgical setting, but not always read well because the reader is not practiced, or because the translation used was not prepared with public reading in mind. But this deficiency too is a matter of a shift in worldview from the worldview of both the text and that of many intervening centuries of translation. The translators of the KJV worked consciously to capture the style of the original Hebrew and Greek, which they also saw as an oral poetic, reading aloud each pericope to each other to be sure that the text could be heard by the congregation in ways which did not separate form from content in the passage.[30] Although their achievement in creating an oratorical English was not generally understood as in itself a characteristic feature of faithful translation at the time, by the eighteenth century it had become clear that in carefully preserving such features as Hebrew parallelism, the KJV translators were presenting an elevated poetic form as part of the meaning of the Scriptures; tone, mood, and a sense of the beauty of holiness itself (Ps. 29:2) were by their efforts conveyed remarkably well in our English tongue.[31] It is no accident that the KJV—and similarly conceived translations such as the NKJV, RSV, and ESV—read much better aloud than most other modern translations.[32] It is likewise no accident that in Christian communities (largely evangelical) that have opted for translations accommodated to consumer-oriented, individualistic, and media-saturated 'worship', the public reading of Scripture in worship has declined. What are the implications? And what are the implications for situations in which Scripture still is read, though in an impoverished translation, and with a resulting loss of tone, mood, elevated style, and in many cases any hint of the beauty of holiness itself? Will this create a situation fruitful for spiritual interpretation?

When SIL/Wycliffe translators work for years to produce a translation of the New Testament in some polysynthetic or agglutinative language on the margins of our own world, it is normative for translation, often while still in process, to be received and first used orally, then revised. To take an example from a work in progress, Steve Watters, translating in Dzongkha, a

Sino-Tibetan language, rendered the Lord's Prayer in eight-syllable couplets, the poetic form used by that people for their most treasured ancient tales; it was immediately adopted by the Dzongkha speakers and used liturgically, long before the translation project was completed. Watters' contemporary translator's choice mirrors that of the earliest English translators, and indeed that of the translators of the King James Version. They too used a slightly archaic and elevated form of their language, borrowing both an aura of ancient authority, so rendering the Bible in what Alister McGrath has called "the language of the court."[33] Majesty of expression, or elevated diction in all of these cases has communicated the first and foundational element of spiritual understanding, which is to recognize that what is being heard when Scripture is read is not the evanescent and politically accommodated words of men, but the eternal Word of God.

It is the performance context of Holy Scripture that modern translators seem most of all to have forgotten. Yet this context is part of the meaning and message of the text. Accordingly, I suggest, translators should lift their eyes from the narrowest considerations of semiotic range and technical conveyance to the orality and communal reception of the text as intrinsically a part of what a faithful translation needs to convey. As folklorist Richard Bauman has put it, performance couples elevated language and authority naturally; it "usually suggests an aesthetically marked and heightened mode of communication, framed in a special way and put on display for an audience."[34] Even today, when we hear such language, we recognize that it compels our attention distinctively. This is precisely the intention of the language of Scripture itself, and translations which sacrifice that to achieving a "down to earth" colloquialism, *ipso facto* yield up, in their flight from the poetry of it, something essential to the spiritual authority of the text as Word of God. In general a wise translator should resist the impulse to literalistic explanation in the midst of translating, and always leave the poetry alone.

*Translation and Spiritual Interpretation*

In the conference that gave birth to these articles it was suggested by one of our Reformed colleagues that a revived focus on spiritual interpretation could have little prospect of longstanding interest in the Protestant churches. In this article I have endeavored to suggest that popularizing English translations and the leveling colloquialism they encourage are surely part of the reason his judgment may be borne out. It is difficult, however, to accede indifferently to the prospect of Protestant rejection of the contributions of the spiritual interpretation movement. It seems more evident now than ever that if theologians and preachers are to build upon the "sure foundation" and the "living stones of the prophets and the holy apostles", then spiritual interpretation is not optional; it is a necessity, enjoined by the text of Holy Scripture itself. Yet attempts to communicate such understanding for a laity in any tradition whose sense of biblical language has been flattened and disfigured by ineffectual translation will be severely hampered.

In recent historical perspective, it is rather easy to see how selective editing of what all Christians regard as in some sense divinely authorized text can be done by translators for the sake of redefining critical biblical concepts and, in the process, occluding the transcendent to immanent polarity of Scripture as the revealed Word of God.[35] More often, however, we should regard instances of mistranslation as probably unconscious, reflexive symptoms of a systemic modernist predisposition to elide the vertical or transcendent axis. These efforts, even if they leave the canon intact, are nonetheless a species of immanentizing, in the name of "humanizing," biblical language, effectively making the reader the primary locus of meaning rather than Scripture itself. Charles Taylor's "Immanent Frame" certainly applies. I think Taylor is warranted in saying that in general postmoderns of all sorts tend to operate in a "discourse derived from Protestantism"; but also that this discourse is not less evident now in Catholic environments. In the language of biblical translation, both Protestant and Catholic, we may readily trace that contemporary secularist reflex which has tacitly assumed that, in Taylor's phrase, "the human good is in its very essence sensual, earthly."[36] The spin-drift of religious aspiration back downward to earth has actually been going on for some time: Hans Boersma reiterates Taylor's observation pertinently when he says that "the Protestant Reformation was part of a shift that had been in the making for centuries, and of which the de-sacramentalizing of the cosmos was the most significant feature."[37] Sadly, the reach of this de-sacramentalizing impulse into the very language of the Church has recently accelerated; however counter-intuitively, too much contemporary biblical translation is fully implicated in a more general and fundamental drift away from transcendence.

My argument is that a faithful translator should discern when the literal sense of the words in a passage most likely intends a spiritual interpretation and not interfere with it. Discernment—philological, theological, and spiritual—seems to me to be necessary at every step. Some translations clearly labor to get the spiritual dimension right; others almost seem to ignore it. Mistranslation calculated to obscure transcendent reference has accordingly become a serious problem not only for basic doctrinal understanding in the laity generally, but also for spiritual interpretation specifically. Insistence that the language of Scripture be brought down to the language of the shopping mall is a symptom of deeper disorder in our culture. This is not a valid evangelical impulse, however construed as such. Its effects extend far beyond the cultic translations of fringe groups, or even the gender-inclusive issues that have corrupted the sense and distorted the Christology of some translations.

We ought, I suggest, carefully to consider communally our choices of contemporary mainstream Scripture translation in the context of the possibility of renewed spiritual interpretation in the Church. If an immanen-tized understanding is locked into the translations of the Bible laypeople are reading, we should perhaps not wonder if some are attracted to secondary manifestations of a more generally immanentized worldview such as appears in some of the colorful but de-spiritualized marketing strategies of the "emergent church," the attempted disarming of the doctrine of the Trinity and divine authority in books such as *The Shack*, the abolition of hell in Rob Bell's *Love Wins* or, for that matter, the abolition of heaven in Timothy Jackson's *The Priority of Love*; all of these are consistent, immanentist phenom-ena.[38] Orthodox theological redress should begin, I suggest, at a much more fundamental level, namely in thoughtful attention to a widespread tendency in English-speaking Christian discourse to redefine the language of canonical Scripture itself, often in such a way as to undermine the spiritual character of critical theological concepts at their source. Translations should be chosen on the basis of the degree to which they remain true to the language of scripture and the form in which that language is expressed in the original languages. Although it is not my principal thesis in this article, it should be apparent that I regard stylistic distortion, whether in translation or in preacherly exegesis, as itself a dangerous species of misrepresentation. Failure to reflect genre, to translate everything in the same register despite the genre conventions and varied register of voice in the original, is a dangerous species of stylistic mis-representation. Accordingly, I would encourage translators to resist the form/content dichotomy in translation altogether where Holy Scripture is the text, and in particular to resist the overweighting of a one-dimensional target language at the expense of a polysemous original, which in the case of Scripture often depends heavily on form (style, repetition, rhythm, parallel-ism, trope, etc.) to deliver transcendent spiritual meaning.[39]

## A Final Note on Translation

What would be required for a translation to be as faithful as possible to the original and yet accessible to the English reader? Here I want to agree wholeheartedly with Leland Ryken: a good translation is one in which "the author's own words are reproduced, figurative language is retained rather than explained, and stylistic features and quirks of the author are allowed to stand as the author expressed them."[40] Translators, as well as interpreters and preachers can all too easily succumb to a kind of linguistic "Stockholm Syndrome," inadvertently yielding to the spirit of this present age which, to cite Taylor again, "identifies in a strongly transcendent version of Christian-ity a danger for the goods of the modern moral order."[41] When translators are captive more to the *zeitgeist* of the target language than to the spirit of the scriptural text, even the high purpose with which they began can soon be stifled.

Friedrich Schleiermacher, in his essay "On the Different Methods in Translation," observed the tension with which every translator must wrestle: "Either the translator leaves the author in peace, as much as possible" he writes, "and moves the reader towards him; or, he leaves the reader in peace, as much as possible, and moves the author towards him."[42] Much of recent Bible translation has veered too far in the direction of leaving our contemporary culture undisturbed. For readers of the Scriptures in English, I suggest, the future of spiritual interpretation—and even the role of theology for lay instruction itself—will depend on a careful use of translations which exhibit literary and philological excellence in the pursuit of formal equivalence, and which provide for oral experience in the worshiping community of the high diction of divine discourse. This will require that theologians, teachers and preachers recover and restore to community comprehension (and usage) the deeper meaning, the "poetry" of English words, formal equivalents, which, though now for some a distant melody, still need to be heard if Scripture in translation is to be represented not merely as the words of men, but as the eternal Word of God.

*NOTES*

1   C. L. Wrenn, *Word and Symbol: Studies in English Language* (London: Longmans, 1967), p. 11.
2   See my article in *Touchstone* (March/April, 2012), pp. 28–39.
3   Robert Pogue Harrison, *New York Review of Books*, Jan 20, 2012.
4   *Ibid.*
5   Italics mine.
6   *Commentary on the Epistle to the Hebrews*, trans. Chrysostom Baer, O. Praem (South Bend, IN: St. Augustine's Press, 2006), p. 231. Cf. *ST* 1, q1, art 10; also *Quaestiones de quodlibet*, 8, q6, a.1–3.
7   Longinus, *On the Sublime*, trans. W. Rhys Roberts (Cambridge: Cambridge University Press, 1899), secs. 8, 12, 39–40. New Testament scholars have long questioned the cliché: see here Nigel Turner, *Grammatical Insights into the New Testament* (Edinburgh: T&T Clark, 1965), pp. 183 ff; also Bruce Metzger, "The Language of the New Testament," in *The Interpreters Bible*, Vol. 7, ed. G. A. Buttrick *et al.* (Nashville, TN: Abingdon Press, 1951), p. 46. One of the reasons for elevated style in New Testament Greek is clearly the echoing of the Hebrew Bible in vocabulary, rhythm, syntax, and phrasing. See also Nigel Turner, "The Literary Character of New Testament Greek," *New Testament Studies*, Vol. 20 (1974), pp. 107–114.
8   *Touchstone*, op. cit.
9   Interestingly, the only other text in the Hebrew Scriptures that makes use of *chokma-lev* is 1 Kings 3:12, in which God honors Solomon's wise request for the gift of wisdom (*chokma*) by granting him something greater, a *lev chakam*, a wise heart. He, too, we should note, has been chosen to build a sanctuary for the Lord.
10  *On the Gospel of John*, 24.3.
11  Kierkegaard, from *For Self-Examination*, pr. in Thomas C. Oden, ed, *Parables of Kierkegaard* (Princeton, NJ: Princeton University Press, 1978), pp. 12–13.
12  Leland Ryken also expresses considerable sympathy for those he critiques, *inter alia*, in his *Understanding English Bible Translation: The Case for an Essentially Literal Approach* (Wheaton, IL: Crossway, 2009).
13  *Pensées* 1.93 (Paris: Perrin et Cie, 1923), p. 27.
14  As Henri de Lubac has shown in the first volume of his magisterial *Exégèse Médieval* (Paris: Aubier, 1957), translated by Marc Sebanc *et al.* (Grand Rapids, MI: Wm. B. Eerdmans Publishing Company, 1998), this view of scriptural language had been normative from the apostolic period forward.

15    *ST* 1, q1, art 10; also *Quaestiones de quodlibet*, 7, q 6. art 1–3. Recommended to non-specialists here is the helpful volume edited by Thomas Weinandy, OFM Cap., Daniel A. Keating, and John P. Yocum, *Aquinas on Scripture: An Introduction to His Bible Commentaries* (London and New York: T&T Clark, 2005), notably in this connection the introduction by Nicholas Healy and the essays by Weinandy and Matthew Levering.

16    *The Great Commentary*, 4 vols., trans. Thomas W. Mossman (London: John Hodge, 1903), Vol. 4, pp. 317–319.

17    *Calvin's Commentaries: A Harmony of the Gospels*, trans. T. H. L. Parker (Grand Rapids, MI: Wm. B. Eerdmans Publishing Company, 1972), Vol. 2, pp. 82–83; cf., re John 8:12, Vol. 4, p. 210.

18    *Common English Bible* (Nashville, TN: Abingdon Press, 2011). *The Holman Common Standard Bible*, now in preparation, does not at this point look like a probable answer to the need for a common standard English translation either—at least from the pages I have seen.

19    Leroy Huizenga, "The Collins Bank Bible," *First Things* (October, 2011), pp. 53–55.

20    Edward L. Greenstein, "Theories of modern Bible translation," *Prooftexts*, Vol. 3 no. 1 (January, 1983), pp. 9–39; at p. 17.

21    Nida won wide acceptance for his view that the priority of meaning over form means that "certain rather radical departures from the formal structure are not only legitimate but may even be highly desirable." Eugene A. Nida and Charles R. Taber, *The Theory and Practice of Translation* (Leiden: E. J. Brill, 1969), p. 13. See also Eugene A. Nida, *Towards a Science of Translating* (Leiden: E. J. Brill, 1964). In his *Bible Translation* (New York: American Bible Society, 1947), Nida articulates the view that "words are merely vehicles for ideas" (p. 12); this presupposes that the translator who thinks this way will invariably have the precise idea intended by the text. In practice, paraphrasing and revisioning too often suggest that the translator has assumed that he has had a better idea.

22    Ryken's *The Word of God in English* (2002) is a notable example from a Reformed perspective; Emil A. Wcela, "What is Catholic about a Catholic Translation of the Bible?" *Catholic Biblical Quarterly*, Vol. 71 (2009), pp. 247–263 expresses resistance from a Catholic perspective. See also Raymond van Leeuwen, "We Really Do Need Another Translation," *Christianity Today*, October 22, 2001, p. 30.

23    http://obit-mag.com/articles/-grim-reader-sept-2-2011-esther-gordy-edwards-eugene-nida-and-jeanette-ingberman

24    Wcela, "What is Catholic about a Catholic Translation of the Bible?", pp. 256–257.

25    *Ibid.*, p. 259; *LA*, sec. 3.

26    *Ibid.*; *LA*, sec. 25–27.

27    George Steiner, *After Babel: Aspects of Language and Translation* (New York: Oxford University Press, 1975), pp. 47 ff; p. 80.

28    Greenstein, "Theories of modern Bible translation," p. 10.

29    James A. Maxey, *From Orality to Orality: A New Paradigm for Contextual Translation of the Bible* (Eugene, OR: Cascade Books, 2009), p. 1. While I do not agree with several aspects of Maxey's argument, I strongly agree with his emphasis on the centrality of oral performance for the texts of the Bible both originally and historically.

30    "Appointed to be read aloud in churches," the KJV was heavily punctuated so as to guide public readers. See F. F. Bruce, *The English Bible: A History of Translations from the Earliest English Versions to the New English Bible* (New York: Oxford University Press, 1961), pp. 108–110. Adam Nicolson, *God's Secretaries: The Making of the King James Bible* (San Francisco, CA: HarperCollins Publishers, 2003) is among those who document the practice of the translator teams reading each pericope aloud several times as their work progressed (p. 209).

31    Robert Lowth, Professor of Poetry at Oxford from 1741 and Bishop of London from 1777–87, gave a series of lectures in Latin, later translated in 1787 as *Lectures on the Sacred Poetry of the Hebrews*. This work established both among biblical scholars and poets the poetic and liturgical character of much of the Bible. Recently, Robert Alter, in *Pen of Iron: American Prose and the King James Bible* (Princeton, NJ: Princeton University Press, 2010), has picked up these points in regard to secular oratory.

32    It is interesting that the Catholic Bishops of Australia have recently decided to move away from the NRSV and to use a slightly modified ESV in their lectionary. file://The%20Archdiocese%20of%20Canberra%20&%20Goulburn%20-%20News%20&%20Events.webarchive

33 See Alister McGrath, *In the Beginning: The Story of the King James Bible, and How it changed a Nation, a Language and a Culture* (New York: Anchor, 2011); also his essay in David Lyle Jeffrey, ed., *The King James Bible and the World it Made* (Waco, TX: Baylor University Press, 2011), pp. 11–28; and especially Laura Knoppers, "Translating Majesty," in Jeffrey, pp. 29–48.

34 "Performance," in *Folklore, Cultural Performances and Popular Entertainments* (New York: Oxford University Press, 1992), p. 41.

35 Another example of concern from a philologist is that by Ian Robinson, in his detailed negative review of the *Good News Bible*, which he found diminished by its word choices for divine transcendence. See his "The Word of God Now," *PN Review*, Vol. 6 no. 5 (1980), esp. pp. 26–27.

36 Charles Taylor, *A Secular Age* (Cambridge, MA: Harvard University Press, 2007), pp. 546–547.

37 Hans Boersma, *Heavenly Participation: The Weaving of a Sacramental Tapestry* (Grand Rapids, MI: Wm. B. Eerdmans Publishing Company, 2011), p. 11. Boersma's point anticipates the important new book by Brad S. Gregory, *The Unintended Reformation: How a Religious Revolution Secularized Society* (Cambridge, MA: Harvard University Press, 2012).

38 William P. Young, *The Shack* (New York: Hachette Book Group, 2007); Rob Bell, *Love Wins: A Book about Heaven, Hell, and the Fate of Every Person who Ever Lived* (New York: HarperOne, 2011); Timothy Jackson, *The Priority of Love: Christian Charity and Social Justice* (Princeton, NJ: Princeton University Press, 2002).

39 Dell Hymes, *Now I only Know So Far: Essays in Ethnopoetics* (Lincoln, NB: University of Nebraska Press, 2003), p. 48.

40 Leland Ryken, *The Word of God in English: Criteria for Excellence in Bible Translation*, p. 10. See also his *Understanding English Bible Translation: The Case for an Essentially Literal Approach*, and his *The ESV and the English Bible Legacy* (Wheaton, IL: Crossway, 2011), which provides useful insight into the consideration and care that went into the ESV translation.

41 Taylor, *A Secular Age*, p. 546.

42 Friedrich Schleiermacher, "On the Different Methods of Translation," trans. A. Lefevre, in Amos Leslie Wilson, ed., *German Romantic Criticism* (New York: Continuum, 1982), pp. 1–30; at p. 9.

# 7

# READINGS ON THE ROCK: TYPOLOGICAL EXEGESIS IN CONTEMPORARY SCHOLARSHIP

## MATTHEW LEVERING

In his *Essay on the Development of Christian Doctrine*, John Henry Newman argues that for the Fathers, typology (and the spiritual sense of Scripture) played a significant role in doctrinal formulation.[1] As examples of such biblical interpretation in the patristic defense of the divinity of the Son, he points to the following biblical texts: " 'My heart is inditing of a good matter,' or 'has burst forth with a good Word;' 'The Lord made' or 'possessed Me in the beginning of His ways;' 'I was with Him, in whom He delighted;' 'In Thy Light shall we see Light;' 'Who shall declare His generation?' 'She is the Breath of the Power of God;' and 'His Eternal Power and Godhead.' "[2] The Fathers considered these texts to speak of Christ. When the Old Testament is not read in this way, Newman holds, the fulfillment that Christ brings will not be apparent.[3] He adds that even the Council of Trent, whose arguments are often seen as strictly scholastic and as therefore having little place for typological reasoning, "appeals to the peace-offering spoken of in Malachi in proof of the Eucharistic Sacrifice; to the water and blood issuing from our Lord's side, and to the mention of 'waters' in the Apocalypse, in admonishing on the subject of the mixture of water with wine in the Oblation."[4]

Is Newman right that the use of typological reasoning is what we should expect of orthodox Christian faith? The answer to this question, I think, depends upon whether typological interpretation—both in Scripture and as a mode of the Church's exegesis—can instruct us about the persons and events of salvation history, that is, about the past.[5] I investigate this problem by surveying three contemporary Protestant approaches to typological exegesis, by Richard B. Hays, Peter Enns, and Peter Leithart respectively. As

*Heaven on Earth?: Theological Interpretation in Ecumenical Dialogue*, First Edition.
Edited by Hans Boersma and Matthew Levering.
© 2013 Blackwell Publishing Ltd. Book compilation © 2013 Blackwell Publishing Ltd.

we will see, Hays and Enns demonstrate the value of typological exegesis both for the New Testament authors and for addressing certain problems facing the Church today, including how to form believers as the people of God and how to read the Old Testament. In their view, however, typological reasoning—despite its omnipresence in the New Testament's theologies of Jesus Christ—does not instruct us about the past. For his part, Leithart holds that typological reasoning may attain to real insight about the past, because typology exposes the providential patterns of history. I agree with Leithart, although I think that his approach requires the Church's Magisterium.

*I. Richard B. Hays: Typological Imagination and the Church's Practices*

**Typology in Hays's *First Corinthians***
My first task is to provide a critical overview of Hays's approach to typology. I begin with Hays's treatment of 1 Corinthians 10 (especially verses 1–4) in his *First Corinthians*. Hays observes that in 1 Corinthians 10, "By speaking of Israel as 'our fathers' and by reading the wilderness narrative as a typological prefiguration of the church's experience, Paul blurs the boundary between past and present and invites his readers to reimagine their lives as belonging to that story."[6] In this reimagining, the Corinthians' claim to belong to the story of Israel depends upon their union with Israel's Messiah, as well as upon the corresponding claim that Israel has always been ordered eschatologically by God toward fulfillment in the Messiah and his community. The latter claim raises the question of whether or in what way Paul's blurring of "the boundary between past and present" is legitimate. Does the wilderness narrative (Exodus and Numbers) intrinsically possess a typological character, or has Paul added typology in a manner extrinsic to the event and/or the narrative? In other words, is there a basis in Israel's past for the typological connection with the Gentile converts of Corinth?

   With these issues in view, Hays examines 1 Corinthians 10:1–4. When Paul describes the Israelites on the exodus journey as being baptized and eating supernatural food, Hays says that biblical interpreters "should not make the mistake of supposing that the Old Testament itself interprets these events as sacramental symbols or that Jewish tradition before Paul had conceived of these events as figurative foreshadowings of future realities."[7] Rather, Paul is simply "thinking metaphorically, perceiving illuminating likenesses between dissimilar entities."[8] Paul's statements should not be used to claim that sacramental grace was at work in Israel. This would be anachronistic and would miss the point that in developing his typological metaphors, "Paul is reading Israel's story through the lens of the church's experience and discovering figurations of God's grace."[9] The "figurations" help to explain the Church's experience in Christ and the Holy Spirit, but do not describe the persons and events of Israel's Scriptures.

Hays points out that Paul's typological metaphors belong to a genre of scriptural interpretation common in his day. As Hays notes, Wisdom of Solomon 11:4 suggests that Wisdom arranged to give the journeying Israelites water "out of flinty rock, and slaking of thirst from hard stone" (cf. Exodus 17:6). In 1 Corinthians 1:30, Paul states that God made Christ "our wisdom." This may be the link by which Paul arrives at the view that "the Rock was Christ." Philo, too, identifies the rock with the wisdom of God. Hays concludes that Paul's statement should be taken as an evocative metaphor rather than as a claim about the past. Paul's goal is to issue a moral warning to the Corinthians, namely that if they continue to share in sacrificial meals offered to pagan gods, they will be judged and condemned to death for their idolatry, just as were most of the Israelites on the exodus journey.

For Hays, therefore, the key is not the particular types, which are metaphors, but rather the insistence that the Corinthians should make decisions today by locating themselves typologically within the scriptural narrative. In his view, typological reasoning of this kind should be practiced by all Christians. Typology helps us to inhabit the biblical stories and to be formed by them in our own individual and communal decision-making. Thus Hays encourages his fellow preachers "to let our metaphorical imagination work boldly as we seek to discover previously undiscerned correspondences between our world and the scriptural story."[10] The purpose of these metaphorical types is not to learn more about the biblical world itself, but to learn how to inhabit the biblical story ourselves and to be configured to its patterns. As Hays argues, "Thinking typologically is a necessary survival skill for adult Christians. . . . Rather than seeking to make the text relevant, Paul seeks to draw his readers *into* the text in such a way that its world reshapes the norms and decisions of the community in the present."[11] Typology encourages us to affirm that the people of God that we encounter in Scripture is the people of God that we are today, and to learn how to live as God's eschatological people by inhabiting the stories of God's people Israel.

If Paul means only to stimulate the metaphorical imagination of his congregation, however, why does he say that certain events *happened to Israel* as types? The answer, Hays thinks, is Paul's eschatological perspective. Paul holds that everything God accomplished within his people in the past was done in view of the eschatological fulfillment that has now occurred in Christ and the Holy Spirit. As Hays says, "From the privileged perspective of the new eschatological situation in Christ, Paul rereads the Old Testament stories and finds that they speak in direct and compelling ways about himself and his churches, and he concludes that God has ordered these past events 'for our instruction.'"[12] But could God have ordered the events of Israel's history so that these events actually were the types that Paul thinks they were?

In answering this question, it is instructive to compare Hays's reading of 1 Corinthians 9:9–10, where Paul claims that a Mosaic law about oxen "was written for our sake," with Hays's interpretation of 1 Corinthians 10:1–4.

With respect to 1 Corinthians 9:9–10, Hays comments that "a careful look at the context of Deuteronomy 25:4 lends some credence to Paul's claim about this particular text. The surrounding laws in Deuteronomy 24 and 25 (especially Deut. 24:6–7, 10–22; 25:1–3) almost all serve to promote dignity and justice for human beings; the one verse about the threshing ox sits oddly in this context."[13] This differs, Hays thinks, from Paul's typological reading of Exodus 17:6 (and the exodus journey) in 1 Corinthians 10:4, where Paul teaches that "the Rock was Christ." But it seems to me that Hays does not pay sufficient attention to Exodus 12–17, which contains the major "types" of Christian sacramental theology: the Passover lamb and Passover meal (Exodus 12), the crossing of the Red Sea (Exodus 14–15), the manna (Exodus 16), and the water from the rock (Exodus 17), as well as the pillars of cloud and fire (Exodus 13) that symbolize the Holy Spirit. So long as sacraments are understood analogously, Exodus 12–17 provides a context highly favorable to Paul's claim about Israel that "all ate the same supernatural food and all drank the same supernatural drink" (1 Cor. 10:4), despite Hays's warning against "supposing that the Old Testament itself interprets these events as sacramental symbols."[14] Why does Hays attend to the context of Deuteronomy 25:4 but not to that of Exodus 17:6?

The same chapter of 1 Corinthians includes the following sacramental text: "The cup of blessing which we bless, is it not a participation in the blood of Christ? The bread which we break, is it not a participation in the body of Christ? Because there is one bread, we who are many are one body, for we all partake of the one bread" (1 Cor. 10:16–17). Hays argues that Paul means that the participants in the meal "are brought into partnership or covenant (cf. 11:25) with Christ."[15] For Hays, Paul's words "have nothing to do with mysteriously ingesting Christ in the meal."[16] Paul has in view neither Jesus' real presence in the Eucharist, nor a sacramental eating of Jesus' body and blood that would configure us to Jesus. To emphasize this point, Hays states that "Paul is not thinking of some sort of mystical union effected through the meal—an idea foreign to the Old Testament."[17] Hays's conclusion here is arguably shaped by his view that Paul's sacramental types have no basis in Israel's history or in Israel's narrative. I would contend to the contrary that Paul's types do suggest "some sort of mystical union." If the Israelites in some sense "drank from the supernatural Rock" and ate "supernatural food," then one might suppose that the eschatological fulfillment of this supernatural nourishment (and supernatural presence) would indeed be a "mystical union" with Christ "effected through the meal."

In sum, comparison of Hays's discussion of Paul's typological reading of Deuteronomy 25:4 (1 Corinthians 9:9–10) with his discussion of Paul's typological reading of the Exodus narrative (1 Corinthians 10:1–4) suggests that Hays is more comfortable with typology when it has to do with the community's moral practices than when it bears upon sacramental doctrine. Paul's typological use of Exodus, with its sacramental overtones, raises issues for

Hays that do not arise when Paul uses Deuteronomy typologically for the purpose of shaping the community's treatment of those who preach the Gospel. Hays's assumption that Paul is not right about the "supernatural" or sacramental character of the manna and water can be challenged on the basis of Hays's more fully appreciative account of typological reasoning when applied to the moral practices of Israel and the Church. Why does Hays not allow that Paul's typological extension of Christian sacraments (baptism and the Eucharist) can uncover something true about Israel's past?

### Typology in Hays's *Echoes of the Scripture in the Letters of Paul*

Discussing 1 Corinthians 10:1–13 in *Echoes of the Scripture in the Letters of Paul*, Hays makes many of the same moves that we have seen in his commentary. He notes that Paul has in view "Israel's experiences in the wilderness."[18] Paul's interpretation of these experiences as "types" (1 Cor. 10:6) means, Hays thinks, that we should not read Paul's interpretation as descriptive of Israel's actual experiences in the wilderness. Rather, Paul's interpretation is a work of imagination whose aim is to interpret the present experiences of his Corinthian congregation. Hays states that "Paul fancifully explores the figurative possibilities inherent in the imaginative act of reading Exodus as metaphor for early Christian experience."[19] He grants that Paul's "fanciful analogies" have a "serious point," namely to exhort the Corinthians to take seriously their responsibility to avoid idolatry.[20]

Among the "fanciful analogies" are Paul's claims that the Israelites "were baptized into Moses in the cloud and in the sea" (1 Cor. 10:2), that the Israelites consumed "supernatural food" and "supernatural drink" (1 Cor. 10:3–4), and that a "supernatural Rock" (Christ) followed them (1 Cor. 10:4). These types transpose the Corinthians' present experiences of baptism, the Eucharist, and Christ's presence to the past journeying of the Israelites under Moses. According to Hays, these types instruct the Corinthians that "participation in spectacular spiritual experiences does not relieve the people of God from ethical responsibility."[21] By placing the Corinthians in the shoes of the Israelites who experienced such wondrous miracles but whose later rebellion against God prevented them from entering the promised land, Paul exhorts the Corinthians to live according to the moral of the scriptural story rather than continuing to live from within pagan narratives about food offered to idols. Paul aims to move the Corinthians by means of "explicit and startling figurative claims; the effect of the passage is achieved through an outpouring of explicit figurations."[22] We would be missing the point if we concluded that Moses "passed out baptismal certificates."[23]

Hays is concerned to show that Paul's typology in 1 Corinthians 10 does not efface historical Israel. Recognizing the problem caused by denying that the types have a basis in Israel's history/narrative, Hays asks: "If Israel's story is a metaphor for Christian experience, has Paul so usurped the meaning and claims of the precursor story that he has in effect annihilated it, deprived it of a right to independent existence? . . . Does the Pauline Israel/ church typology annihilate Israel and subordinate Scripture to Paul's own belated conceptions?"[24] In response, Hays emphasizes that "Paul thinks of the Corinthian Christians as Gentiles no longer; they have been incorporated into Israel."[25] The Scriptures of Israel directly address the Corinthian Christians as members of the one Israel. When Paul speaks in 1 Corinthians 10 of the consequences of Israel's unfaithfulness, he does so to show the Corinthians the moral path that they themselves are on, not to negate the "independent existence" of Israel's story of the exodus. Hays explains that this "is surely one reason for Paul's fanciful reading of Christ back into the exodus: if Christ was present to Israel in grace and judgment just as he is now present to the church, the Corinthians have no remaining ground for supposing themselves to possess an immunity from judgment that Israel did not possess."[26] This does not detract from the significance of the events of Israel's actual history. As Hays says, "The church discovers its true identity only in relation to the sacred story of Israel, and the sacred story of Israel discovers its full significance—so Paul passionately believed—only in relation to God's unfolding design for salvation of the Gentiles in the church."[27]

The final chapter of *Echoes of the Scripture in the Letters of Paul* provides a general assessment of Paul's mode of reading Scripture. Again stressing Paul's eschatological perspective, Hays observes that for Paul, "Scripture is construed metaphorically: it signifies far more than it says. Its latent sense is disclosed only to those who 'turn to the Lord.' "[28] Hays recognizes that Paul's typological exegesis "generates novel interpretations that nonetheless claim to be the true, eschatologically disclosed sense of the ancient texts."[29] Paul does not think of himself as exposing truths that should have been apparent to the original authors and agents. Paul knows that without the guidance of the Holy Spirit, he could not find these typological connections to Christ, the Church, and the sacraments in Israel's Scripture. But Paul presents his interpretation of Israel as nonetheless the true one, "the hermeneutical key that unlocks all the mysteries of God's revelation in the past."[30] By interpreting Israel's Scripture in this way, Paul taps into and imitates the intertextual allusions and echoes that characterize Israel's Scripture.[31] Paul also engages central themes in Israel's Scripture, above all the righteousness and covenant faithfulness of God.

Hays emphasizes once more that Paul does not negate or annul Israel's Scripture but instead interprets Scripture as bearing witness to the gospel. Scholars such as Adolf von Harnack and Rudolf Bultmann argue that Paul is a supersessionist both in the sense of repudiating Old Testament Israel and in the sense of caring next to nothing for the actual history of Israel. Hays points out that far from denigrating Israel's history, Paul finds a strong eschatological dynamism in the portrait of Israel's history given by Scripture. Believing that God's action in Jesus Christ and the Holy Spirit is fulfilling the eschatological dynamism of Israel's history, Paul undertakes "a dialectical struggle to maintain the integrity of his proclamation in relation to Scripture and the integrity of Scripture in relation to that proclamation, to justify his startling claims about what the God of Israel had elected to do in Jesus Christ."[32]

With the concerns of James Barr in view, Hays also observes that it might seem that Paul "offers helter-skelter intuitive readings, unpredictable, ungeneralizable."[33] Hays denies that this is the case, but he gladly affirms that Paul does not have an abstract method that he applies to all scriptural texts. Rather, Paul has a guiding principle, namely that the righteousness of God to which all Scripture attests has now been made manifest in the life, death, and resurrection of the Messiah. As Hays remarks, "Paul reads Scripture under the conviction that its story prefigures the climactic realities of his own time."[34] Paul's interpretation of Scripture is fundamentally typological.

For Hays, a proper understanding of typology gets around the question of the historical accuracy of Paul's interpretations of Israel's (or the scriptural narrative's) past. Paul has a figural chain in mind, not a causal chain. Paul's metaphors assert figural connections rather than things that happened in the past. Hays states, "Typology forges imaginative correlations of events within a narrative sequence; not all narrative sequences, however, are historical."[35] Through his "imaginative correlations," Paul aimed to show that the Church, even as communities of Gentile converts, is in continuity with Israel. His readings succeed as "historical" ones if they suggest accurately why Israel's story is the Church's story. For this reason Paul relies in particular on Deuteronomy and Isaiah, which already interpret "the history of Yahweh's dealing with Israel typologically, as a prefiguration of a larger eschatological design."[36] Since Israel's Scripture presents itself as having the power to speak anew to the present, Paul has ample grounds for his own imaginative readings of Scripture. These imaginative readings are not intended to describe what happened in the past, but instead are intended—as such readings were in Israel's Scripture itself—to form the practices of the present-day community. Given the eschatological character of the Messianic community, Paul's typological readings of Scripture are necessary so as to do justice to God's accomplishment of his plan in Christ and the Spirit. In this respect the scriptural pattern of reversal provides Paul with a way of making sense of the election of the Gentiles and the rejection of Jesus by many Jews.

Because of his eschatological perspective, Paul holds that "[a]ll that God has ever done in the past converges toward the eschatological community, and all past words of Scripture find their sense rooted in the present graced time."[37] Drawing upon the work of James Kugel, Hays suggests that this sense of time is quite different from that of Rabbinic midrash. Like the prophets, Paul believes that God is speaking through him: God has given him the mission to proclaim the gospel of Jesus Christ, and in so doing God has illumined for him the interior meaning of Israel's history, now fulfilled in Christ and the Church.

Responding to Paul's eschatological claim to be able to understand previously hidden dimensions of Israel's past, Hays affirms with Paul that the decisive eschatological event has occurred in the crucifixion and resurrection of Jesus Christ. This eschatology validates Paul's typological interpretations of Scripture, because such interpretations arise from the truth that the righteousness of God depicted in Scripture has been definitively accomplished in Jesus Christ. When Paul interprets Israel's Scripture in a manner that goes beyond what the scriptural text itself affirms, Hays rejects the historical validity of such interpretation while accepting its imaginative validity for building up the eschatological community by illuminating the "the witness of the Law and the Prophets to the gospel of God's righteousness."[38]

The final pages of Hays's book ask the question of whether Christians today are justified in reading Scripture in the way that Paul did. Richard Longenecker's negative answer to this question provides Hays with a foil. For Longenecker, Paul's typological interpretations are true both as regards Israel's past and the Church's present, but biblical scholars and pastors today do not have warrant to interpret Scripture typologically. On the one hand, Longenecker's acceptance of Paul's typological exegesis as historically accurate with respect to Israel's past seems to Hays to put "Paul on a theological pedestal," insofar as (ahistorical) theology is generally more inclined to find in Paul's "fanciful analogies" binding truth about Israel's past.[39] On the other hand, Longenecker's rejection of the use of typological exegesis today seems to Hays to cut off contemporary Christians from the very exegesis that is practiced within Scripture. He urges us to create "new figurations out of the texts that Paul read" and to weave "Paul's own writings into the intertextual web, perhaps discerning correspondences that did not occur to Paul himself."[40]

In arguing for typological exegesis today, Hays does not wish to encourage a postmodern free-for-all with regard to the meaning of Scripture. He identifies three Pauline criteria for exegetical fidelity: God's faithfulness to his covenant promises, Jesus' Pasch as the fulfillment of God's covenantal righteousness, and the power of Scripture to configure its readers "into a community that embodies the love of God as shown forth in Christ."[41] Grounded in this understanding of Scripture, good typological exegesis will "bring Scripture's witness to God's action in the past to bear as a critical principle on the present," thereby helping to form the Church in love.[42] It will enable "God's present action among us to illumine our understanding of his action in the past."[43] Hays means by this simply that we can find in Scripture, metaphorically speaking, certain "prefigurings" of God's grace, and also that we should learn to understand all of Israel's history as pointing to Christ and the Church. In this way, we can discover ourselves as living in the eschatological age or "God-dominated time," and we can learn how to be Christians not only through doctrinal logic but also with rhetorical and metaphorical imagination, granting "a broad space for the play of echo and allusion, for figurative intertextual conjunctions, and even—if our communities were sufficiently rooted in Scripture's symbolic soil—for metalepsis."[44] Along these lines, Hays argues that all truth need not be, and indeed is not, logical or doctrinal. We need more room for metaphorical truth, which (if we can avoid turning it into logical or doctrinal truth) will help us to avoid narrow literalism. He concludes that historical criticism "should not be burdened with theological responsibility for screening the uses of Scripture in Christian proclamation. If it were entrusted with such a normative task, many of Paul's readings would fail the test."[45]

As we have seen, Hays recognizes that Paul interprets Scripture as filled with types of Christ and the Church. Since Hays is committed in faith to Jesus' inauguration of the eschatological age, Hays accepts Paul's authority to interpret the whole of Scripture in light of this eschatology and under the guidance of the Holy Spirit. Hays also appreciates the rhetorical play that makes Scripture more than a wooden textbook of doctrinal propositions. But Hays conceives of typology—both Paul's and the form that would be acceptable exegetically today—fundamentally in terms of helping the present-day community of believers shape their moral practices. As a way of shaping Christian practices, typology functions to insert Christian communities within the biblical stories and to bring about a more faithful Christian witness. By contrast, Paul himself claims a good deal more than this. Paul thinks that his eschatological mandate as an apostle, filled with the Holy Spirit, enables him to interpret the events recorded in Scripture in a manner that enhances our understanding of the events. Paul's typological exegesis about the exodus—which is already typologically significant in Old Testament Scripture—has to do with Israel's past as well as with the present-day Church. When Hays limits typology in this way, he rules out Paul's own view of his eschatological mandate, and it is unclear why this limitation is not arbitrary. In this regard, despite his insistence otherwise, Hays's position is quite similar to Longenecker's, although Longenecker accepts Paul's apostolic ability to teach typologically about the past but supposes that the Holy Spirit strictly limits this ability to the apostolic age. Thus insofar as Hays's critique of Longenecker's position is persuasive, as I think it is, his critique equally applies to his own position. Given the importance that Hays has shown typology to have, is there a way to employ it without arbitrarily limiting it to moral exhortation?

## II. Peter Enns: Historical Criticism and the Meaning of the Old Testament

Before addressing the question raised by my overview of Hays's work, I wish to reflect a bit further on why typological reasoning has been eclipsed in contemporary biblical exegesis. The key problem seems again to be the nature of history and the historicity of the biblical text. This can be seen from Peter Enns's *Inspiration and Incarnation: Evangelicals and the Problem of the Old*

*Testament*, which I will survey here. The central point of Enns's book is that conservative evangelical response to historical-critical scholarship on the Old Testament shares an assumption with modern disbelievers in the Bible's authority: namely, the assumption that "the Bible, being the word of God, ought to be historically accurate in all its details (since God would not lie or make errors) and unique in its own setting (since God's word is revealed, which implies a specific type of uniqueness)."[46] Enns, however, suggests that the Incarnation of the Son of God points in the opposite direction. Just as the incarnate Word is fully human, so also the biblical word of God is fully human.[47] In revealing himself, God accommodates himself to our historical mode of existence.[48] It follows that the truth of the Old Testament, as a whole, appears not in its historical facts or its doctrines, but in the apostles' re-reading of the whole story in light of what God has done in Jesus Christ. In this regard Enns emphasizes that it is to Christ "that the Bible as a whole bears witness."[49]

Enns defends his acceptance of historical and doctrinal errors in the Old Testament partly by means of a lengthy chapter that investigates the New Testament authors' interpretation of Scripture (the Old Testament). He aims to show that with respect to the interpretation of Old Testament texts, Jesus and the apostolic authors do not display the concern for factual accuracy that modern scholars value so highly. Enns sets the stage by pointing out that many readers find the New Testament's approach to be "somewhat troubling, for it seems to run counter to the instinct that context and authorial intention are the basis for sound interpretation."[50] As a first example, he gives Jesus' debate with the Sadducees as reported in Luke 20. The Sadducees deny the resurrection of the dead, but Jesus corrects them by means of Exodus 3:6: "That the dead are raised, even Moses showed, in the passage about the bush, where he calls the Lord the God of Abraham and the God of Isaac and the God of Jacob. Now he is not God of the dead, but of the living; for all live to him" (Luke 20:37–38). In Exodus 3:6, however, God names himself "the God of Abraham, the God of Isaac, and the God of Jacob" without mentioning their resurrection, and historical-critical scholars of the Old Testament consider that the book of Exodus lacks a doctrine of the resurrection of the dead. Why then does Jesus' argument seem persuasive to his audience? To answer this question, Enns examines intra-biblical exegesis within the Old Testament as well as Second-Temple modes of interpretation.

Before doing so, he briefly reviews the positions that he is opposing. Evangelical scholars defend in three ways the New Testament's use of the Old: by arguing that the New Testament authors are responding to a contextual clue about the original author's intention; by claiming that the New Testament authors aim solely to apply, not to interpret, the scriptural text; and/or by proposing that the New Testament authors, as inspired by the Holy Spirit, can go beyond the original authorial intention and context in ways that are not in fact unfaithful to the original intention and context. These three ways, says Enns, ultimately do not work, largely because they neglect "the historical context for apostolic hermeneutics."[51] Instead, Enns hopes to show that although the New Testament authors do not care about the original authorial intention and context, they nonetheless understand themselves to be exposing what the scriptural text meant and means *in light of Christ's coming*," and their approach to the Old Testament's truth should be adopted by the Church today.[52]

Enns takes the example of Daniel's interpretation of Jeremiah's prophecy that the Babylonian captivity would last seventy years. In Daniel 9:22, the angel Gabriel comes to explain this prophecy to Daniel. Gabriel tells him, "Seventy weeks of years are decreed concerning your people and your holy city, to finish the transgression, to put an end to sin, and to atone for iniquity, to bring in everlasting righteousness, to seal both vision and prophet, and to anoint a most holy place" (Dan. 9:24). A "week" of years is seven years; thus the total is 490 years. Enns suggests that Daniel's reinterpretation of Jeremiah's prophecy parallels what we find in New Testament interpretation of Scripture. Just as Gabriel explains to Daniel the inner meaning of Jeremiah's prophecy, so also does the risen Jesus explain the inner meaning of Scripture to his two disciples on the road to Emmaus (Luke 24:25–27) and to all of his apostles in the upper room (Luke 24:44–47). To do this, Jesus "opened their minds" (Luke 24:45) so that they could perceive what would otherwise be hidden or unclear. Jesus makes clear that the (Old Testament) Scriptures have their meaning in their fulfillment in himself and in the Church that proclaims him: "Thus it is written [in the Old Testament], that the Christ should suffer and on the third day rise from the dead, and that repentance and forgiveness of sins should be preached in his name to all nations, beginning from Jerusalem" (Luke 24:46–47). As Enns points out, Jesus is not here calling upon his apostles to recognize a few proof texts (for instance, Hosea 6:2). Instead, Jesus is claiming that the whole Old Testament is about him, when read through the eyes of faith. Jesus "is saying that *all* Scriptures speak of him in the sense that he is *the climax of Israel's story*."[53]

To interpret Scripture in this way, it would seem, requires divine authority—either as one commissioned by God (such as the angel Gabriel) or as Jesus Christ, the incarnate Son. But in fact this mode of interpretation can be found in numerous Second-Temple texts. For example, in Wisdom of Solomon 10, pseudo-Solomon interprets Genesis and Exodus to show how God cares for his chosen people. Regarding Cain, pseudo-Solomon observes that "the earth was flooded because of him" (Wisdom 10:4), a causal link that Genesis itself does not explicitly state. Pseudo-Solomon also makes a connection between Abraham and Babel (Wisdom 10:5), and this connection is more explicitly made in the first-century AD *Book of Biblical Antiquities*. Again, pseudo-Solomon observes about Jacob that wisdom "kept him safe from those who lay in wait for him" (Wisdom 10:12). Genesis does not explicitly describe any of Jacob's enemies, whether Esau or Laban, as lying in wait for him. But in *Jubilees* (second century BC), we find the story of Esau preparing an ambush for Jacob. Enns gives numerous other examples from Wisdom of Solomon, and he concludes that its author drew upon interpretations that were common in the culture of his time. Enns also treats Qumran's pesher on Habakkuk 1:5, which makes the claim—somewhat similar to Jesus in Luke 24—that the true meaning of Habakkuk can only be known through the Teacher of Righteousness. The key point for Enns is that neither Wisdom of Solomon nor Qumran interprets Scripture with the purpose of discovering the original authorial intention.[54]

With this background, Enns returns to the scriptural interpretation employed by Jesus and the apostolic authors. Treating Matthew's use of Hosea 11:1, "Out of Egypt I called my son," he emphasizes that "Hosea himself is not talking about the boy Jesus, nor is he thinking of a future messiah."[55] In Hosea 11:1–4, God is bemoaning that Israel, his "son," turned away from him despite all that he did for Israel, including the exodus from Egyptian slavery. Hosea 11:1 refers to Israel's past idolatry and disobedience, not to Jesus' future coming and flight into Egypt. Admittedly, there is a possible parallel between Jesus and Hosea 11 viewed as a whole. God in Hosea 11:8 proclaims his love and compassion for Israel: "How can I give you up, O Ephraim! How can I hand you over, O Israel! . . . My heart recoils within me, my compassion grows warm and tender." As Enns says, "Israel came out of Egypt, was disobedient, deserved punishment, yet was forgiven by God (Hos. 11:8–11). Christ came out of Egypt, led a life of perfect obedience, deserved no punishment, but was crucified—the guiltless for the guilty."[56] Jesus embodies both the compassion of God for Israel, and Israel as God's "son." Enns does not deny that Matthew's use of Hosea has an internal logic that expresses Matthew's understanding of God, Jesus, and Israel. Rather, what Enns contests is that Hosea's text could be properly read in this way without faith in Christ. In its historical context, the text from Hosea means something quite different. Again, Enns's point is not that therefore we need to reject Matthew's use of Hosea. Enns aims only to show that Matthew, as a Christian interpreter of Scripture, is not worried about the authorial intention and original context of Hosea's words. The truth of Hosea's words is found not in their original context but in the light of Jesus Christ.

With similar conclusions, Enns examines Paul's use of Isaiah 49:8, "In a time of favor I have answered you, in a day of salvation I have helped you." Paul refers these words to God's grace and eschatological salvation in Jesus Christ. Enns points out, however, that Isaiah has in view the rebuilding and repopulation of Israel's war-ravaged land after the Babylonian captivity. From the same vantage point, Enns considers Paul's argument that "the promises were made to Abraham and to his offspring. It does not say, 'And to offsprings,' referring to many; but, referring to one, 'And to your offspring,' which is Christ" (Gal. 3:16).[57] Paul appears to have in mind God's promise to Abraham in Genesis 12, 13, and 24; but the Hebrew word for "offspring" is, though singular in form, plural in meaning. Furthermore, God promises Abraham land, not reconciliation. Enns affirms the point that Paul is making, namely that "Christ alone is truly Abraham's seed, the one who embodies Israel's ideal."[58] But as an interpretation of Genesis, Paul's argument cannot stand, unless we argue that the truth of Genesis is found not in its original intention and context but in its Christological fulfillment. Skipping over Enns's discussion of Isaiah 59 in Romans 11, we can mention a last example, namely the fruitful misquotation in Hebrews 3:9 of Psalm 95:10. In Hebrews 3:17, the author alludes to the correct text of Psalm 95:10, showing that the misquotation was deliberate.[59] It serves the purpose of exhibiting the relationship between Jesus, Israel, and the Church, but it is not an interpretative move that we could make today.

Enns also describes instances in which the New Testament authors adopt traditions that were current in Second Temple literature, but that had no solid basis in Scripture. For example, 2 Timothy 3:8 names the magicians of Pharaoh's court, who were unnamed in Exodus; 2 Peter 2:5 calls Noah "a preacher of righteousness" whereas Genesis does not ascribe preaching to Noah; Jude 9 mentions a dispute between the devil and the archangel Michael over Moses' body; and Jude 14–15 quotes 1 Enoch as though it conveyed the words of the scriptural figure Enoch. Among the further examples that Enns gives, 1 Corinthians 10:4 stands out for our purposes. Evidently referring to the rock that Moses struck to provide water for the Israelites on the exodus journey (Exodus 17 and Numbers 20), Paul states that "they drank from the supernatural Rock which followed them, and the Rock was Christ." Paul's argument seems to be that Christ sustained the Israelites in the wilderness, just as Christ sustains the Corinthians. Enns inquires into the source of Paul's idea that the Rock "followed" the Israelites, since Exodus and Numbers do not say that the Rock actually moved. He finds that there is widespread Second-Temple tradition about the Israelites on the exodus possessing a mobile source of water. Versions of this tradition can be found in the *Targum Onqelos* (on Numbers 20–21), in the Tosefta (*Sukkah* 3.11), and in the *Book of Biblical Antiquities*.[60] Enns once more draws the conclusion that the New Testament authors read Scripture much more loosely, as regards their attitude to the original texts, than we do today.

On the basis of faith in Jesus Christ, the New Testament authors read certain meanings into Scripture that were not the meanings that the original authors intended, and they were even willing to adjust Scripture and to read it through extra-biblical traditions. Enns explains that "the New Testament authors take the Old Testament out of *one* context, that of the original human author, and place it into *another* context, the one that represents the final goal to which Israel's story has been moving."[61] Enns thus thinks that had Hosea been in Matthew's position, Hosea would have been able to see how his words in fact speak of Jesus Christ. Nor is this merely an extrinsic connection: Enns observes that the divine author of Scripture, who is guiding the eschatological unfolding of history, can inspire words that in their own historical context mean one thing and in light of Christ mean quite another thing.

In Enns's view, it would be a mistake to find Christ in every Old Testament passage. Instead, we should recognize that the Old Testament as a whole has its fulfillment in Christ and the Church, and so we should employ a "christotelic" and "ecclesiotelic" hermeneutic. It follows that there are two acceptable ways of reading the Old Testament. First, we can read it "on its own terms," seeking the original authorial intention and context.[62] Reading in this way, we may not be able to make the connections that the New Testament authors do, but we will see that the Old Testament has a basic storyline that remains unfulfilled within the Old Testament itself. Second, we can read the Old Testament in light of its eschatological fulfillment in Christ and in the Church. This way of reading allows for interpretations that go beyond what the Old Testament says in its own contexts. These interpretations go beyond the Old Testament meaning precisely by arguing that the fulfillment has come, a fulfillment that makes present what the Old Testament authors were unconsciously pointing to. Genesis 12:7, for example, which in its own context is about descendents and land, is (as fulfilled) truly about Christ and the Church, as Paul suggests in Galatians 3.[63]

This emphasis on fulfillment gets at the core of what typological interpretation involves. Typology expresses the fulfillment in Christ and the Church of the Old Testament stories, prophecies, prayers, and wisdom. Where Enns speaks of "Christotelic" and "ecclesiotelic" hermeneutics, he might equally have spoken of typological exegesis. Thus Enns sees Romans 15:4, where Paul asserts that "whatever was written in former days was written for our instruction," as an example of reading Psalm 69:9 "in its christotelic fullness."[64] Romans 15:4 elucidates the principle behind typological exegesis. Enns recognizes that not all New Testament interpretation of Scripture is typological (or as he puts it "christotelic and ecclesiotelic").[65] His main point is that we cannot pretend that the New Testament authors shared our "grammatical-historical" approach to Scripture.

In dialogue with Richard Longenecker, Enns then takes up the issue of whether we are justified in reading Old Testament Scripture typologically today. He seeks a middle ground between simply copying the New Testament authors' exegesis, on the one hand, and rejecting it as entirely inappropriate today, on the other. His proposal is to "distinguish between *hermeneutical goal* and *exegetical method*."[66] Today we should share the New Testament authors' hermeneutical goal, namely to read the Old Testament in light of the fulfillment that Christ accomplishes. Contemporary interpreters should "bring the death and resurrection of Christ to bear on the Old Testament," by insisting that these events should inform our understanding of what the Old Testament means.[67] Moreover, we cannot suppose that our grammatical-historical exegetical method must be the universal standard for exegesis. At the same time, however, we cannot imitate the New Testament authors in changing Old Testament words or in reading Old Testament realities (such as the rock of Exodus 17:6) in a manner that goes well beyond what the Old Testament says about them.

On the basis of these reflections, he suggests that focusing on exegetical method is not the best approach. The New Testament authors did not adhere to one method or another; rather, they read Scripture through various lenses. Enns describes their scriptural interpretation as "an intuitive, Spirit-led engagement of Scripture, with the anchor being not what the Old Testament author intended but how Christ gives the Old Testament its final coherence."[68] They were excited about God's fulfillment of Israel in Christ, and they read Scripture in this new light, by which the goal of the divine author was revealed. We should do the same, rather than focusing on retrieving the Old Testament's original, historical meaning. But we do not need to follow their particular Second-Temple interpretative modes; these modes are determined by their context, as ours are by our context. God revealed himself in Christ Jesus within a particular (Second-Temple) historical context, and this context is reflected in the apostolic writings that bear witness to Christ. We have to bear witness to Christ in our own historical context, and our historical context, too, will shape our witness.

Enns also comments briefly on patristic and medieval typological exegesis, which found (for example) in Rahab's "scarlet cord" (Josh. 2:21) the blood of Christ. In Enns's view, such typological exegesis deserves the benefit of the doubt in general, even if not necessarily in specific cases, because God's word should be expected to have "multiple layers of meaning."[69] Given that the text is God's word, interpretation must go beyond analysis of the text in its ancient Near-Eastern context; interpretation must be illumined by Christ's coming. In order to be illumined in this way, interpretation must recognize its participation in an ecclesial context, "the witness of the church through time (with the hermeneutical trajectory set by the apostles as a central component), as well as the wisdom of the church in our time."[70] The goal of scriptural interpretation consists in encountering the God who reveals himself in Christ, and we encounter this God not merely individually but as a community of believers.

Enns, then, agrees with Hays that the New Testament authors often read Scripture typologically with the goal of asserting something true about the fulfillment in Christ, rather than about Israel's past. Typological exegesis belonged to the cultural context of the ancient world. It was their way of saying that "[t]he reality of the crucified and risen Christ is both the beginning and the end of Christian biblical interpretation."[71] Although we can appreciate the apostles' typological reading of Scripture, we cannot "ignore the cultural distance between us and Second Temple interpreters."[72] Despite this cultural distance, however, we must to be able to see Christ in the Old Testament. We cannot do without typology. Yet, with Longenecker, we have to admit that certain New Testament exegetical modes are no longer open to us.[75]

This approach is clearly quite similar to that of Hays, even if he lacks Hays's emphasis on mofal formation and does not exhort the Church to employ typological reasoning anew. Given his focus on distinguishing the New Testament authors' approach from that of modern historical readers, Enns demonstrates the omnipresence of typological reasoning in Scripture. As an Old Testament scholar, it matters to Enns whether Paul's (and the other New Testament authors') reading of Israel's past is accurate. He argues that we can accept Paul's reading of Scripture as true, because in God's plan Scripture (the Old Testament) does indeed point to Christ, even if the authors of the original texts were unaware of the claims that the New Testament authors make. Enns does not think that typology can inform us about Israel's past, other than in the sense that whatever happened in Israel points to Christ and the Church. Yet, I would observe that if Israel's past has really been fulfilled by Jesus Christ, then we cannot rule out that typological reasoning can speak truly about the past (as well as about the present), nor can we suppose that typology is solely a culturally conditioned exegetical mode that happened to be present around the time of Jesus. At issue is not whether typological exegesis accurately interprets the past in every instance, but rather what the Church can hope for from typological exegesis under the guidance of the Holy Spirit. Once one takes seriously the biblical-typological worldview as a truthful witness to God's work in Israel (culminating in Jesus Christ and the Church), then the truth-bearing potential of typological reasoning cannot be easily restricted.

## III.  Peter Leithart: Typology and the Fabric of History

Hays helped us to see how necessary typological exegesis is for the Church's inhabiting of Scripture; Enns showed the extent to which the New Testament authors used typological reasoning in order to understand the meaning of Scripture. I now bring these reflections to a close by briefly examining Peter Leithart's *Deep Exegesis: The Mystery of Reading Scripture*, which affirms the ability of typology to refer not only to the present but also to the past. As Leithart shows, given the nature of texts and temporality under God's providence, typological reasoning is never out of date.[76]

Leithart begins by arguing that the words of the Bible, including the particularity of the modes of biblical language, are no mere husk from which interpreters extract kernels of meaning. He reviews various Enlightenment attempts to propose that biblical texts teach spiritual truths even though the form in which they taught the truths can now be rejected as misleading. Reason sits in judgment over Scripture's husk, even while locating in the scriptural husk a kernel of enduring truth. Leithart observes that those who sought to liberate Scripture's kernel generally "shared an antipathy to priestcraft, a suspicion of the dogmas, rites, and texts of positive religion, and a conviction that the central thrust of religion is morality."[77] As a particularly clear example of this view, he examines Immanuel Kant's *Religion within the Boundaries of Mere Reason*, in which Kant identifies the husks as the Jewish elements of ecclesiastical Christianity and identifies the kernel as an ethical community rooted in universal reason.[78] Leithart comments that Kant "does not consider the possibility that the Bible is pointing us to the historicity of reason itself. He does not consider the possibility that the Bible might be indicating that we reason temporally."[79]

Leithart then turns explicitly to our topic. He quotes two lengthy passages from Richard Longenecker, in which Longenecker warns (as we have seen) against using today the modes of biblical exegesis employed by Jesus and the apostles. In Leithart's view, Longenecker is falling into the husk/kernel error. The husk here is the mode of biblical interpretation employed by Jesus and the apostles, which Longenecker links with Jewish midrash and allegory; the kernel is the doctrines that they taught. As Leithart says, for Longenecker, "We are supposed to follow Pauline doctrine, but not Pauline exegesis."[80] Leithart considers this to be a serious mistake, not least because the words of Scripture have transformative power in the particular form that God has given them. We need to study the form and to allow it to teach us how to read.

This might seem like an unpromising venture. Consider Hosea 11:1–2, "When Israel was a child, I loved him, and out of Egypt I called my son. The more I called them, the more they went from me." On what grounds, historically speaking, can one hold that the "son" in the first verse is actually Jesus (Matthew 2:15)? Likewise, although Paul claims that the Israelites "drank from the supernatural Rock which followed them, and the Rock was Christ" (1 Cor. 10:4), Exodus and Numbers do not appear to support the view that a "Rock" followed Israel. In Galatians 4, Paul allegorizes the figures of Abraham, Hagar, and Sarah; in this case Paul admits that he is allegorizing (see Galatians 4:24). But the allegory veers quite far, it appears, from the actual biblical portrait of Abraham, Hagar, and Sarah in Genesis.[81]

For Leithart, this use of typology and allegory suggests that in some way, the meaning of biblical texts (say, Exodus 12:6 or Genesis 16) can change over time. Before spelling out his solution, he first surveys the various options for handling the problem of New Testament typology. One option is to say that Paul drew on the Jewish exegesis (midrash, pesher) of his day for his understanding in 1 Corinthians 10 of the mobile Rock. Leithart grants that this is so, but notes that it merely pushes the problem one step back: on what grounds did the Jewish exegetical tradition come up with this conclusion, and why does Paul adopt their conclusion? A second option is to appeal to the fact that God and humans are equally the authors of Scripture: the divine author may intend something that the human author does not intend. Again, however, the question is why the human author—in this case Paul—felt justified in arguing in this way. Third, we can say that the apostles were inspired by the Holy Spirit and so their exegesis is accurate, even though their exegetical mode escapes us. The problem here is whether we can read Scripture adequately when deprived of the lens with which the apostles saw things in Scripture that we cannot see.

Leithart then sets forth his own solution, one that Enns considers unpersuasive: the apostles "were following hints from the Old Testament itself."[82] Regarding the Rock of 1 Corinthians 10, for example, Leithart observes that Exodus 14:19 does say that Israel was followed by a "pillar of cloud." Given that something was following Israel, how did Jewish exegetes (including Paul) conclude that this something was the "Rock"? The Song of Moses in Deuteronomy 32 repeatedly proclaims YHWH to be "the Rock." When YHWH led the Israelites out of Egypt, furthermore, Moses' Song says that YHWH made them "suck honey out of the rock, and oil out of the flinty rock" (Deut. 32:13). Furthermore, when YHWH commands Moses to strike the rock, YHWH states that he himself will stand upon the rock: "Behold, I will stand before you there on the rock at Horeb; and you shall strike the rock, and water shall come out of it, that the people may drink" (Exod. 17:6). If we recall that the Song of Moses names YHWH "the Rock," and connect this with the fact that the Israelites were being followed on the exodus and with the fact that YHWH is standing on the rock that Moses strikes, then Paul's contention (in accord with Jewish exegesis of the day) that the "Rock was Christ" seems more plausible as scriptural interpretation. What the Jewish exegetes and Paul have done is to weave together typologies and images that are present in the various scriptural texts about the exodus journey.

What about Paul's allegorical interpretation of Abraham, Sarah, and Hagar? Paul presents Sarah's son Isaac as a type of those who are "born according to the Spirit" and Hagar's son Ishmael as a type of those who are "born according to the flesh" (Gal. 4:29). Does this interpretation have a basis in Scripture? Leithart answers in the affirmative. Ishmael is born before Abraham's circumcision—which serves for Abraham as a sign of dependence on God's "everlasting covenant" (Gen. 17:13)—whereas Isaac is born after that event. Similarly, Abraham's casting out of Ishmael and Hagar into the wilderness (Genesis 21) structurally parallels Abraham's near sacrifice of Isaac (Genesis 22). Ishmael's history, too, parallels the history of Jacob/Israel; thus Ishmael also has twelve sons. As Leithart says with Paul's typology in view, "That Ishmael decreases so that Isaac might increase does not mean that Ishmael was nothing."[83] In other words, Paul's typology has a foundation in the way that Genesis relates Isaac to Ishmael.

Having defended apostolic typological reading as a legitimate weaving together of Scripture's typologies and images, Leithart then asks whether this mode of reading is legitimate only with regard to the Bible. Typological reading particularly fits the Bible due to the implications of its dual authorship, God and humans. But Leithart considers that all major texts can and should be read typologically.[84] He points out that historical events can be said to change over time, because their effects and significance change. Similarly, the same words, used in different contexts, can mean different things. Their meaning can be changed by events or by later texts. We can read the same words in different times of our lives, and gain different meanings from these words. Typology relies upon sets of relationships that develop over time, and in fact all events and texts accrue meaning over time.

After examining various historical events and literary works in this light, he returns to the biblical example of Matthew's use of Hosea 11:1. In Matthew 2, Herod, the ruler of Israel, acts like Pharaoh, and Jesus is the new Moses who redeems Israel. When Matthew says that the flight of Joseph, Mary, and their child to Egypt fulfills the prophecy that "Out of Egypt have I called my son," therefore, this means that Jesus is called out of Herod's "Egypt," and Jesus is the "son" as Israel's Redeemer. Is this a distortion of Hosea? Only if we imagine that Hosea considered himself to be speaking only for his contemporaries. In fact, however, Hosea "surely did not think that the exodus from Egypt was the final word in Yahweh's salvation. . . . Like all faithful Israelites, he hoped for a redemption far beyond what Israel had already experienced."[85] Hosea would not have been surprised by a new "exodus" in which a future "Pharaoh" would be overcome and Israel be redeemed. Thus, says Leithart, "Matthew gives new meaning to Hosea, but the meaning he gives does not violate Hosea's original meaning. The meaning changes as Hosea's prediction comes to fulfillment, but the change is consistent with the original sense."[86] Indeed, many authors anticipate being read for centuries and recognize that the passage of time will enrich the meaning of their texts in ways that they cannot now know.

With Augustine, Leithart holds that "Scripture is about Christ, but the Christ of Scripture is not only himself but also his body. The Christ who is the subject matter of Scripture is the *totus Christus*."[87] This means that the story of Cain and Abel, for example, is not only about Cain and Abel, but also about Jesus and about the persecution of the Church (both typologically figured by Abel). It means, too, that as Paul says in 1 Corinthians 10, the story of the exodus speaks of the sacraments: "The sea is baptism, and the manna and water foreshadow the Eucharist."[88] The moral application of scriptural passages to the life of Christians is justified by the fact that Scripture, in speaking of Christ, speaks also of his members. Leithart shows how this works by means of an extended analysis of John 9 in the context of the Old Testament as well as of the whole Gospel of John. Read typologically, John 9 is about the sacrament of baptism. In Leithart's view, because Jesus is the head of all things, the typological implications of John 9 can even be extended to the realm of literary interpretation, as can be seen by reading together Sophocles's *Oedipus the King* and John 9. Here the motif of blindness and sight leads onward into Nietzsche's critique of Socrates; sight is fraught with political weight. The blind man of John 9 provides typological insight into Jesus, into discipleship and power, and into the eschatological judgment and the new creation. Texts resonate with earlier texts in a manner that is inevitably and richly typological; there is no "timeless" text.

Leithart concludes that the fourfold sense of Scripture practiced by the Fathers and medievals was on the right track. He summarizes their approach: "For the medievals, the literal sense of the text opened out into a christological allegory, which, because Christ is the head of his body, opened out into tropological instruction and, because Christ is the King of a kingdom here yet also coming, into anagogical hope."[89] In defending typological exegesis, he argues not only that the biblical authors are justified in reflecting typologically upon scriptural types and images (as Paul does in 1 Corinthians 10), but also that post-biblical interpreters should learn to draw connections between the scriptural types and images. By reading typologically, post-biblical interpreters (such as the Fathers) enter into the mindset of the biblical authors themselves and see more deeply into the realities revealed in the whole Scripture. Typology, Leithart emphasizes, is not something enjoyed and practiced only by Second-Temple Jews or by other ancient cultures. Rather, it is something that is intrinsic to the temporality of texts, and to the temporality of Israel, Christ, and the Church under God's providence.

How then does Leithart think that false typological interpretations can be avoided? He emphasizes that interpreters must become attuned to Scripture's truth. We attain such attunement "[w]hen the text is seen as an event, as a joke, as music; when words are seen as players; when the letter is not seen as a husk but as a necessary and nourishing part of God's verbal bread."[90] He compares biblical interpretation to a performance, in which the performer seeks not only to get the notes right and to play them as beautifully as possible, but also awaits the judgment of the audience (the community of believers). This comparison suggests to me the function of the Church's Magisterium, properly understood as being attuned (under the Holy Spirit's guidance) to the liturgical and theological tradition of the Church rather than being merely extrinsic decision-making on the part of a pope or council.[91]

Leithart's main contributions to our study are twofold: his encouragement of typological reasoning by post-biblical interpreters without the restrictions that Hays and Enns impose; and his insistence that typological reasoning can speak truly about the past, not only about the present (even if, as I think, typology can also be "fanciful" in Hays's sense).[92] As should be apparent from my brief discussion of Leithart's book, his readings are often ingenious, and his sensitivity to biblical typology reminds us that its logic was not foreign to the biblical author even where we would not expect it. In this way, he helps us to see that typology and history are not necessarily opposed. Indeed, were we to presume such an opposition, we would rule out the historical reference of much of the New Testament. For, as Anthony Le Donne says, "one should expect among Jesus' contemporaries that the application of scriptural paradigms and typologies was an integral aspect of historical interpretation. . . . History is often seen through the lens of typology. The history of Jesus is no exception."[93]

## IV. Conclusion

In different ways, Hays, Enns, and Leithart show that contemporary Christians cannot exclude typological exegesis from the task of understanding divine revelation. Even so, Stanley Gundry warns that "whenever typology is used to show the Christocentric unity of the Bible, it is all too easy to impose an artificial unity (even assuming that there is a valid use of the basic method). Types come to be created rather than discovered, and the drift into allegorism comes all too easily."[95] It might seem that, having rejected Hays's limitation of typology to the formation of the community's practices and having argued that we cannot envision typology as merely a culturally conditioned or disposable mode of exegesis, I would lack any sympathy for these warnings against typological reasoning. On the contrary, although I value typology (and for that matter allegory as well), I think that there must be a way of measuring the truth of typological reasoning. The Church requires a way of gauging the performance of its biblical interpreters. Because of the presence of typology in the literal sense of Scripture, we should expect typological connections still to be in play among Christians in the task of understanding and proclaiming divine revelation, but such typological exegesis cannot stand on its own. It must be shown to attest to God's saving power in Jesus Christ and must have its truth confirmed liturgically and theologically by the community of believers (the Church), guided by the Holy Spirit.[96] The Church's Magisterium responds to this need.

*NOTES*

1   See John Henry Newman, *An Essay on the Development of Christian Doctrine*, sixth edition, (Notre Dame, IN: University of Notre Dame Press, 1989), p. 346. On this point see also Frances Young, "Exegetical Method and Scriptural Proof: The Bible in Doctrinal Debate," *Studia Patristica*, Vol. 29 (1989), pp. 291–304.
2   Newman, *An Essay on the Development of Christian Doctrine*, p. 343.
3   See *ibid.*, p. 339.
4   *Ibid.*, pp. 342–343. On the grounds that allegory jettisons the historical dimension, Jean Daniélou differentiated typology sharply from allegory as practiced by Philo (and by the Fathers of the Church): see Daniélou, "Symbolism and History," in Daniélou, *The Lord of History: Reflections on the Inner Meaning of History*, trans. Nigel Abercrombie, (Chicago, IL: Henry Regnery, 1958), pp. 130–146. In this vein, see Erich Auerbach, "'Figura,'" trans. Ralph Manheim, in Auerbach, *Scenes from the Drama of European Literature: Six Essays* (Gloucester, MA: Peter Smith, 1973), pp. 11–76, especially pp. 49–60; K. J. Woollcombe, "The Biblical Origins and Patristic Development of Typology," in G. W. H. Lampe and K. J. Woollcombe, *Essays on Typology* (Naperville, IL: Alec R. Allenson, 1957), pp. 39–75. Henri de Lubac, S.J. challenged Daniélou's sharp distinction: see de Lubac, "'Typologie' et 'allégorisme',"  *Recherches de science religieuse*, Volo. 34 (1947), pp. 180–226. See also Hans Boersma, *Nouvelle théologie and Sacramental Ontology: A Return to Mystery* (Oxford: Oxford University Press,

2009), ch. 5. Although a clear division between allegory and typology is not always possible or necessary, I think that some such distinction is helpful.

5   For an introduction to "typology" in Scripture and the Fathers, see, e.g., Anthony Le Donne, *The Historiographical Jesus: Memory, Typology, and the Son of David* (Waco, TX: Baylor University Press, 2009); Benjamin J. Ribbens, "Typology of Types: Typology in Dialogue," *Journal of Theological Interpretation*, Vol. 5 (2011), pp. 81–96; Jean Daniélou, S.J., *From Shadows to Reality: Studies in the Biblical Typology of the Fathers*, trans. Dom Wulstan Hibberd, O.S.B., (London: Burns & Oates, 1960); E. Earle Ellis, *Paul's Use of the Old Testament* (Edinburgh: Oliver and Boyd, 1957), pp. 126–35. Richard B. Hays argues that neither typology, nor other categories such as midrash or allegory, do justice to the scope of Paul's exegesis, which generally relies on dialectical intertextuality: Hays, *Echoes of the Scripture in the Letters of Paul* (New Haven, CT: Yale University Press, 1989), pp. 173–178.

6   Richard B. Hays, *First Corinthians* (Louisville, KY: John Knox Press, 1997), p. 173; cf. Hays's "The Conversion of the Imagination: Scripture and Eschatology in 1 Corinthians," in Hays, *The Conversion of the Imagination: Paul as Interpreter of Israel's Scripture* (Grand Rapids, MI: Wm. B. Eerdmans Publishing Company, 2005), pp. 1–24. See also the moving evocation of the power of typological reading to draw readers into the biblical story, in G. W. H. Lampe, "The Reasonableness of Typology," in Lampe and Woollcombe, *Essays on Typology*, pp. 9–38, at pp. 9–14.

7   Hays, *First Corinthians*, p. 160.

8   *Ibid.*

9   *Ibid.*, p. 161. Frances Young similarly dissociates typological reasoning from historical claims: see Young, "Typology," in *Crossing the Boundaries: Essays in Biblical Interpretation in Honour of Michael D. Goulder*, ed. Stanley E. Porter, Paul Joyce, and David E. Orton, (New York, NY: E. J. Brill, 1994), pp. 29–48, at p. 48.

10  Hays, *First Corinthians*, p. 173. See also James W. Aageson's *Written Also for Our Sake: Paul and the Art of Biblical Interpretation* (Louisville, KY: Westminster/John Knox Press, 1993).

11  Hays, *First Corinthians*, p. 173.

12  *Ibid.*, p. 162.

13  *Ibid.*, p. 151.

14  *Ibid.*, p. 160.

15  *Ibid.*, p. 167.

16  *Ibid.*

17  *Ibid.*, p. 168.

18  Hays, *Echoes of the Scripture in the Letters of Paul*, p. 91.

19  *Ibid.*

20  *Ibid.*

21  *Ibid.*

22  *Ibid.*

23  *Ibid.*

24  *Ibid.*, p. 95.

25  *Ibid.*, p. 96.

26  *Ibid.*, p. 97.

27  *Ibid.*, p. 100–101.

28  *Ibid.*, p. 154.

29  *Ibid.*, p. 155.

30  *Ibid.*

31  Hays draws on the work of Michael Fishbane: see especially Fishbane, *Biblical Interpretation in Ancient Israel* (Oxford: Oxford University Press, 1985). For intertextual (and typological) connections in the New Testament, see, e.g., Rikk E. Watts, *Isaiah's New Exodus in Mark* (Grand Rapids, MI: Baker Academic, 1997); Joel Marcus, *The Way of the Lord: Christological Exegesis of the Old Testament in the Gospel of Mark* (Louisville, KY: Westminster John Knox, 1992).

32  Hays, *Echoes of the Scripture in the Letters of Paul*, p. 159.

33  *Ibid.*, p. 160.

34  *Ibid.*, p. 161.

35  *Ibid.*

36  *Ibid.*, p. 164.

37  *Ibid.*, p. 170.

38  *Ibid.*, p. 178.
39  Ibid., p. 181.
40  *Ibid.*, p. 187. As an example, he reads Romans 9:6–9 in the context of the allegory in Galatians 4:21–31. This reading is not exactly typological, but it does extend Paul's mode of thought through intertextual echoes.
41  *Ibid.*, p. 191.
42  *Ibid.*, p. 183; cf. pp. 191–192.
43  *Ibid.*, p. 183.
44  *Ibid.*, p. 186.
45  *Ibid.*, p. 190. In a response to Hays's criticism of his position, Longenecker argues that Hays mistakenly downplays Paul's use of midrash, pesher, and allegory, none of which would today be suitable for understanding the apostolic witness to Jesus Christ. For Longenecker, Hays's encouragement of imaginative and ecclesial readings of Scripture would lead us back into the "disastrous results" that Christians have obtained when they have "claimed to be inspired by Christ living within me, by the Spirit illumining me, or by the Church conditioning me." See Richard N. Longenecker, "Preface to the Second Edition, in his *Biblical Exegesis in the Apostolic Period*, second edition, (Grand Rapids, MI: Wm. B. Eerdmans Publishing Company, 1999), pp. xiii–xli, at p. xxxiv. From a different perspective, but with a similar result, see Friedrich Baumgärtel, "The Hermeneutical Problem of the Old Testament," trans. Murray Newman, in *Essays on Old Testament Hermeneutics*, ed. Claus Westermann, (Richmond, VA: John Knox Press, 1964), pp. 134–159, at pp. 143–144.
46  Peter Enns, *Inspiration and Incarnation: Evangelicals and the Problem of the Old Testament* (Grand Rapids, MI: Baker Academic, 2005), p. 47; cf. pp. 17, 21.
47  For concerns about this analogy, see Lewis Ayres and Stephen E. Fowl, "(Mis)reading the Face of God: The Interpretation of the Bible in the Church," *Theological Studies*, Vol. 60 (1999), pp. 513–528.
48  For related discussion of "accommodation," including its role in the Fathers, see Kenton L. Sparks, *God's Word in Human Words: An Evangelical Appropriation of Critical Biblical Scholarship* (Grand Rapids, MI: Baker Academic, 2008), pp. 229–259. See also Nicholas Wolterstorff, *Divine Discourse: Philosophical Reflections on the Claim That God Speaks* (Cambridge: Cambridge University Press, 1995), pp. 206–212. G. K. Beale offers an extended critique of Enns's position in Beale, *The Erosion of Inerrancy in Evangelicalism* (Wheaton, IL: Crossway Books, 2008), especially pp. 25–122. For further criticism see D. A. Carson's review essay on John Webster's *Holy Scripture*, N. T. Wright's *The Last Word*, and Peter Enns's *Inspiration and Incarnation*: Carson, "Three More Books on the Bible: A Critical Review," *Trinity Journal*, Vol. 27 (2006), pp. 1–62.
49  Enns, *Inspiration and Incarnation*, p. 110.
50  *Ibid.*, p. 114.
51  *Ibid.*, p. 116.
52  *Ibid.* (emphasis his).
53  *Ibid.*, p. 120.
54  James L. Kugel gives numerous examples of this mode of interpretation: see James L. Kugel, *The Bible as It Was* (Cambridge, MA: Harvard University Press, 1997), pp. 123–127, 363. By contrast, indebted to Harold Bloom's theory of the "anxiety of influence," Herbert Marks claims that "Paul's subordination of the Jewish scriptures to their 'spiritual' understanding is a paradigmatic instance of revisionary power realized in the process of overcoming a tyranny of predecession. In historical terms, this approach leads to conclusions that might be characterized vaguely as Marcionite" (Marks, "Pauline Typology and Revisionary Criticism," *Journal of the American Academy of Religion*, Vol. 52 [1984], pp. 71–92, at p. 72). Hays responds to Marks in *Echoes of the Scripture in the Letters of Paul*, pp. 95–102, 156–160.
55  Enns, *Inspiration and Incarnation*, p. 133.
56  *Ibid.*, p. 134.
57  *Ibid.*, p. 136.
58  *Ibid.*, p. 138.
59  For a careful survey of this "interpretive rendering" of original texts in Paul and his Greco-Roman contemporaries, see Christopher D. Stanley, *Paul and the Language of Scripture: Citation Technique in the Pauline Epistles and Contemporary Literature* (Cambridge: Cambridge University Press, 1992).

60    See also the reflections of Aageson, *Written Also for Our Sake*, pp. 121–125; Ellis, *Paul's Use of the Old Testament*, pp. 66–70.
61    Enns, *Inspiration and Incarnation*, p. 153.
62    *Ibid.*, p. 154.
63    For a similar approach to the Old Testament see Walther Eichrodt, "Is Typological Exegesis an Appropriate Method?," trans. James Barr, in *Essays on Old Testament Hermeneutics*, ed. Claus Westermann, (Richmond, VA: John Knox Press, 1964), pp. 224–245.
64    Enns, *Inspiration and Incarnation*, p. 155.
65    *Ibid.*
66    *Ibid.*, p. 158.
67    *Ibid.*, p. 159.
68    *Ibid.*, p. 160.
69    *Ibid.*, p. 161.
70    *Ibid.*, p. 162.
71    *Ibid.*, p. 163.
72    *Ibid.*, p. 157.
73    *Ibid.*, p. 159.
74    *Ibid.*, p. 160.
75    *Ibid.*, p. 161. James Barr is equally concerned not to focus on particular methods, but he underscores the integrity of the Old Testament in itself: see Barr, *Old and New in Interpretation: A Study of the Two Testaments* (New York, NY: Harper & Row, 1966), pp. 139–140. More recently, see Christopher Seitz's remark in his *The Character of Christian Scripture: The Significance of a Two-Testament Bible* (Grand Rapids, MI: Baker Academic, 2011), pp. 23–24: "The witness of the OT is far more manifold, far more theologically ambitious, far more temporally challenging than can be comprehended by recourse to *Vetus Testamentum in Novo receptum*." Attention to this insight would enhance what Enns is trying to do.
76    See Peter J. Leithart, *Deep Exegesis: The Mystery of Reading Scripture* (Waco, TX: Baylor University Press, 2009).
77    *Ibid.*, p. 22.
78    See Immanuel Kant, *Religion within the Limits of Reason Alone*, trans. Theodore M. Greene and Hoyt H. Hudson, (New York, NY: Harper & Row, 1960).
79    Leithart, *Deep Exegesis*, p. 29.
80    *Ibid.*, p. 34.
81    For further discussion see Ben Witherington III, *Grace in Galatia: A Commentary on St Paul's Letter to the Galatians* (Grand Rapids, MI: Wm. B. Eerdmans Publishing Company, 1998), pp. 321–340; Hays, *Echoes of the Scripture in the Letters of Paul*, pp. 111–121.
82    Leithart, *Deep Exegesis*, p. 37; see Enns, *Inspiration and Incarnation*, p. 115.
83    Leithart, *Deep Exegesis*, p. 38.
84    Although Leithart's perspective differs from Gerhard von Rad's, one might compare Leithart's view at this juncture with von Rad's remark in his "Typological Interpretation of the Old Testament," trans. John Bright, in *Essays on Old Testament Hermeneutics*, ed. Claus Westermann, pp. 17–39, at p. 17: "typological thinking is an elementary function of all human thought and interpretation." For von Rad, Old Testament typology has to do with "the eschatological correspondence between beginning and end" (*ibid.*, p. 19), without undermining the linear (rather than cyclic) progression of history. The New Testament continues this typological reasoning, which von Rad distances from allegory. Von Rad adds a plea for the return of typology, which he considers to have been wrongly marginalized by Michaelis's *Entwurf der typischen Gottesgelahrtheit* (1755), which concerned itself not with events but "with 'the religious truths' symbolically enshrined in the Old Testament" (*ibid.*, p. 22). On von Rad's view of typology see Barr, *Old and New in Interpretation*, pp. 111–112, 137.
85    Leithart, *Deep Exegesis*, p. 65.
86    *Ibid.* See also John Sailhamer, "Hosea 11:1 and Matthew 2:15," *Westminster Theological Journal*, Vol. 63 (2001), pp. 87–96. Dan G. McCartney and Peter Enns respond in the same issue of *Westminster Theological Journal*: "Matthew and Hosea: A Response to John Sailhamer," pp. 97–105.
87    Leithart, *Deep Exegesis*, p. 173.
88    *Ibid.*, p. 174.

89   *Ibid.*, p. 207. For discussion see especially Henri de Lubac, S.J., *Exégèse médiévale. Les quatre sens de l'écriture*, three volumes of which have appeared in English translation as *Medieval Exegesis: The Four Senses of Scripture* (the first volume translated by Mark Sebanc, and the second two volumes by E. M. Macierowski) (Grand Rapids, MI: Wm. B. Eerdmans Publishing Company, 1998–2009).

90   Leithart, *Deep Exegesis*, p. 207.

91   For Leithart's ecclesiology, see especially his *The Priesthood of the Plebs: A Theology of Baptism* (Eugene, OR: Wipf and Stock, 2003) and his *Defending Constantine: The Twilight of an Empire and the Dawn of Christendom* (Downers Grove, IL: IVP Academic, 2010).

92   Michael D. Goulder argues that the biblical authors' typological reasoning necessarily mired them in myth-making: see Goulder, *Type and History in Acts* (London: SPCK, 1964), pp. 181, 205.

93   Le Donne, *The Historiographical Jesus*, p. 136.

94   Everett Ferguson, "The Typology of Baptism in the Early Church," *Restoration Quarterly*, Vol. 8 (1965), pp. 41–52, at p. 52.

95   Stanley Gundry, "Typology as a Means of Interpretation: Past and Present," *Journal of the Evangelical Theological Society*, Vol. 12 (1969), pp. 233–240, at p. 235. For further cautions, see Ellis, *Paul's Use of the Old Testament*, p. 134; W. Edward Glenny, "Typology: A Summary of the Present Evangelical Discussion," *Journal of the Evangelical Theological Society*, Vol. 40 (1997), pp. 627–638.

96   Thus Enns argues that we share in the apostles' encounter with the risen Christ within "the witness of the church through time"—where the "church" means both "congregation, denomination, or larger tradition" and more broadly "a global reality," dependent in all cases on "the direct involvement of the Spirit of God" (Enns, *Inspiration and Incarnation*, p. 162).

# Part III

# Reading in Contemporary Context

# 8

# THE SELF-CRITIQUE OF THE HISTORICAL-CRITICAL METHOD: CARDINAL RATZINGER'S ERASMUS LECTURE

MICHAEL MARIA WALDSTEIN

## 1. What is Dearest to Us?

The beginning of Cardinal Ratzinger's 1988 Erasmus Lecture takes the bull by the horns with dramatic intensity, but also with the distance of ironic wit:

> In Vladimir Solovyov's Tale of the Antichrist, one of the chief strategies by which the Redeemer's definitive Adversary seeks to ingratiate himself with the faithful is to point out that he has been awarded an [honorary] doctorate in theology by Tübingen and that he has written what the experts acknowledge as a pioneering exegetical work. The Anti-Christ as a famous exegete—with this paradox Solovyov has thrown light almost a hundred years ago on the double-edged [sword] of modern methods of interpreting Scripture.[1]

The Anti-Christ makes this announcement during the great ecumenical council convened by him to gain the support of Christians. To each divided confession of Christians he offers what is dearest to them. To Catholics he offers world-wide moral authority for the common good of peace and justice, making his offer in virtue of his autocratic authority as the successor of Constantine the Great. To Protestants he offers a richly endowed university for free research into Scripture, and it is to them directly that he breaks the news of a recent letter from the University of Tübingen, the greatest of all

*Heaven on Earth?: Theological Interpretation in Ecumenical Dialogue*, First Edition.
Edited by Hans Boersma and Matthew Levering.
© 2013 Blackwell Publishing Ltd. Book compilation © 2013 Blackwell Publishing Ltd.

centers of theological learning in Germany, that proposes awarding him an honorary doctorate in theology, in recognition of a work of Scripture scholarship he completed as a young man. To the Orthodox, finally, he offers a museum of Christian archeology and the reinstitution of sacred customs.

Many accept his offer, but Pope Peter II, Professor Pauli from Germany and the Elder John from Russia, each with a small group around them, drawing ever closer to each other, refuse. The climax of the scene follows immediately after their refusal:

> In a grieved voice the Emperor addressed them: "What else can I do for you, you strange men? What do you want from me? I cannot understand. Tell me yourselves, you Christians, deserted by the majority of your brothers and leaders, condemned by popular sentiment: What is it that is dearest to you in Christianity?"
>
> At this the Elder John rose up like a white candle, and said in a quiet voice: "Great Emperor! Dearest to us in Christianity is Christ Himself—He in His person. Everything else comes from Him, for we know that in Him dwells the fullness of the Godhead bodily. But we are ready, Great Emperor, to accept any gift from you as well, if only we recognize the holy hand of Christ in your generosity."[2]

With great precision, Solovyov places the main question at the center. What is it that is dearest to us in Christianity? Everything in biblical studies, as everywhere else, depends on the answer to this question. "That for the sake of which is the best and tends to be the end."[3] "The end is most powerful in everything."[4] "This kind of cause is chief among the other causes: for the final cause is the cause of the other causes,"[5] also in biblical scholarship.

At this point, I wish to recall a vivid memory of Fr. Francis Martin.[6] We were both in the audience at a conference of the Catholic Biblical Association. The speaker was Norman Gottwald, author of a famous book about the early tribal history of Israel.[7] He interpreted Scripture as encoding an oppressed people's practical impetus of emancipation and liberation. The word "God" seemed to be for him much like the word "please," a performative utterance. God talk only *does* something; the term does not *refer* to anything. It cannot be true or false.

The lecture's argument did not seem liberating to me at all. I experienced it as an attempt to squeeze my mind into the most oppressive form of reductionism. God, the origin and end of all things, Gottwald was asking me to embrace as a mere social push and pull, grander than the word "please" perhaps, but just as vacuous. It was as if someone had said to me, "Your wife doesn't really exist. Forget about her. Use her name to do things, to accomplish certain social goals." The most appropriate response to this proposal are the words of the Elder John. "Dearest to me in my marriage is my wife, she herself in person."

At the end of the lecture I sat there rather depressed, especially since Gottwald's lecture seemed to have met with general approval. Then something wonderfully liberating happened. Fr. Francis rose up like a white candle, and in a quiet voice raised the question of the transcendent goodness of God. Gottwald answered, "I recognize no form of transcendence except that of human action."

His answer was perfectly in line with Karl Marx. "*Die Philosophen haben die Welt nur verschieden interpretiert, es kömmt drauf an, sie zu verändern.* Philosophers have only interpreted the world in different ways: the point is to change it."[8] "All social life is essentially practical. All mysteries that mislead theory into mysticism find their rational solution in human action and in the understanding of that action."[9] Aristotle refutes this view with a brilliantly simple argument. "It is absurd (ἄτοπον) to think that politics or practical knowledge is the most excellent, unless man is the best of all that exists."[10]

## 2. Clarifying the Geography of the Conflict

The hard-hitting opening paragraph about the Antichrist as exegete reflects a judgment Cardinal Ratzinger has expressed publicly for many years. Raymond Brown, the most prominent Catholic Scripture scholar in the US at the time of the Erasmus Lecture, had been invited to the lecture and the seminar that followed it. A number of faithful Catholics had publicly petitioned the Vatican to condemn Brown for arguing, for example, that the infancy narratives in Matthew and Luke had little to do with history and that the New Testament contained no conclusive evidence that Mary was a Virgin when she gave birth to Jesus, affirming at the same time the Catholic dogma of the Virgin birth. At a press conference, crowded with journalists from major news outlets, the Cardinal appeared together with Brown. He took the embattled exegete under his wing and praised him as a scholar for whom the Church's faith was still normative.

In January of 1988, when the conference and seminar took place, I was still a student in the New Testament Department at Harvard Divinity School, though I had accepted a position to teach at the University of Notre Dame. From the perspective of my Harvard experience, the Cardinal's defense of Brown seemed just. Brown is indeed an island of sanity and integrity in the faith compared with much else that goes on in biblical studies. Most important, what is dearest to Brown is the infinite goodness of God poured out in Christ, particularly in the Eucharist.

Nevertheless, there are two Raymond Browns, not just one, and they stand in profound tension with each other. It seemed evident to me that one of the purposes of the Erasmus Lecture was to address the second Brown, the Brown who had angered many faithful Catholics. The lecture argues that biblical exegesis needs to pass through a "self-criticism of historical reason."

This self-criticism needs to reflect on "the attempt to apply methods and models of natural science also in the area of history."[11] It is here, in this attempt, the Cardinal argued, that the key philosophical premises of the historical-critical method lie hidden. They needed to be brought out into the open and addressed thematically:

> At its core, the debate about modern exegesis is not a dispute among historians: it is rather a philosophical debate. Only in this way can it be carried on correctly; otherwise we continue with a battle in the mist. In this respect, the exegetical problem is identical with our time's struggle about the foundations as such. . . .
>
> The exegete should approach the exegesis of the text not with a ready-made philosophy, not with the dictate of a so-called modern or scientific worldview, which determines in advance what is permitted to be and what is not permitted to be.[12]

Raymond Brown's response to this invitation was disappointing, both in the Seminar and in his written "Addenda" submitted after the debate to the Seminar volume. He shrugged off the Cardinal's invitation and asserted that these philosophical issues were irrelevant in his case, because his practice of historical criticism did not derive from any philosophical theory. It never became fully clear to me whether this response was simply an attempt to avoid an issue he did not feel prepared to think through or whether it was the genuine naïveté of a "scientist" who is truly unaware of his presuppositions, because he considers them so self-evident that he does not need to trouble himself about them. The second possibility seems more likely, judging from Brown's response:

> Much of Cardinal Ratzinger's paper is directed against the philosophy that he detects in historical-critical exegesis. . . . The Cardinal argues, "The debate about modern exegesis is not a dispute among historians; it is rather a philosophical debate.". . . .
>
> To explain my divergence here I must speak of my training. *I obtained a master's degree in philosophy, writing on the philosophical background of Einstein,* before I did any graduate biblical studies. . . . Yet, like many Americans and Anglo-Saxons who did not do their graduate biblical studies in Germany, *I never had laid out for me a master philosophy* according to which should practice exegesis. My biblical training was highly historical critical. . . .
>
> I recognize that what the Cardinal has described has been the philosophy of many practitioners of the method, but *the fact that I could learn the method entirely differently calls into question whether the flaws are in the method itself.* I do recognize philosophical questions about the historical critical method, but in my judgment *they are not questions about the possibility of the supernatural.* . . .

I hope that such a practical rather than a philosophical approach is not simply an American versus a German way of thinking.[13]

What is it that Brown is saying here? Let me draw a caricature. Caricatures are always too simple and therefore unjust, but they can be useful for bringing out a point. "The invitation to a self-criticism of historical reason, which you are extending to me, Your Eminence, is inappropriate in my case. I have an immaculate perception as a scientist. I am simply in touch with facts. I am not a historian burdened with some theory from the German clouds. Germans may revel in philosophy, particularly in Kant. We Americans are more practical. In our interpretation of Scripture, we are simply interested in facts. Like Einstein, we only do philosophy as far as we need it for science. This necessary minimum of philosophy does no harm to our interpretation of Scripture."

Einstein, however, was deeply imbued with Neo-Kantian ideas that follow out the impetus of Bacon and Descartes. These thinkers did indeed supply him with the master philosophy. America, de Tocqueville observes in his chapter on "Philosophical Method of the Americans," is the country "where the precepts of Descartes are least studied and are best applied. . . . The Americans do not read the works of Descartes . . . but they follow his maxims."[14] Brown's attempt to shrug off Cardinal Ratzinger's invitation to a critique of historical-critical reason was thus an eloquent testimony to the need for that invitation.

One generation later, the author of the Erasmus Lecture is still with us. In his 2006 Regensburg Lecture he unfolds the most comprehensive perspective that is needed to understand the invitation extended to Raymond Brown. It clarifies the true geography of the conflict far beyond the Erasmus Lecture. It brings to light the true source of the inner division in Brown's work.

The conventional map of the debate in present-day culture is to distinguish two countries at war with each other:

- One of them is the country of religious faith, allied with conservative, repressive politics. The Catholic Church, traditional forms of Protestantism and Islam inhabit that country.
- The other is the country of science, of rationality, and of liberal politics. The dominant culture of the West, shaped by the school system, the universities, and the mass media, inhabits that country.

The Regensburg Lecture radically reconfigures this map:

- One of the countries is the country of authentic reason and of Christian faith. Greek philosophy, especially Socrates, Plato, Aristotle, Plotinus, etc. inhabit that country, as does the Catholic Church.
- The other is the country of voluntarism, that is, of the primacy of will and power over reason. Islam, medieval nominalism, the Reformation, modern natural science, and liberal politics inhabit that country.

*3. Three Aspects of Greek* Logos

Let us turn first to Pope Benedict's point about Greek philosophy:

> Is the conviction that acting unreasonably contradicts God's nature merely a Greek idea, or is it always and intrinsically true? I believe that here we can see the profound harmony between what is Greek in the best sense of the word and the Biblical understanding of faith in God.
>
> Modifying the first verse of the Book of Genesis, the first verse of the whole Bible, John began the prologue of his Gospel with the words: "In the beginning was the *Logos*." This is the very word used by the emperor: God acts with *Logos*. *Logos* means both reason and word—a reason which is creative and capable of self-communication, precisely as reason. John thus spoke the final word on the Biblical concept of God, and in this word all the often toilsome and tortuous threads of Biblical faith find their culmination and synthesis. In the beginning was the *Logos*, and the *Logos* is God, says the Evangelist.
>
> The encounter between the Biblical message and Greek thought did not happen by chance. The vision of Saint Paul, who saw the roads to Asia barred and in a dream saw a Macedonian man plead with him: "Come over to Macedonia and help us!" (cf. *Acts* 16:6–10)—this vision can be interpreted as a "distillation" of the intrinsic necessity of a rapprochement between Biblical faith and Greek inquiry. . . .
>
> The New Testament was written in Greek and bears the imprint of the Greek spirit. . . . The fundamental decisions made about the relationship between faith and the use of human reason [in the New Testament and the early Church] are part of the faith itself; they are developments consonant with the nature of faith itself.[15]

What does this mean? What, specifically, are the main marks of Greek *Logos*?

**The Openness of Human Logos to All of Being**

According to Socrates, "[t]hose who welcome each being (ἕκαστον τὸ ὂν) should be called lovers of wisdom (philosophers) rather than lovers of opinion."[16] Aristotle has a similar understanding of the universality of human *logos*. "The soul is in a certain way all beings," namely, in the sense of being open to knowing all that exists.[17] To be rational (to have *logos*) means to face all being; it means to ask questions about the meaning, good and source of each being and of being as a whole; it means, therefore, to place no limits, to be open to infinite being; it means, above all, to welcome in a receptive and contemplative gaze (*theoria*), whatever being makes known of itself.

**The Absolute Primacy of Theoria Over Praxis**

In the *Apology*, Socrates expresses the principle of his activity in the city: "The unexamined life is not livable for man."[18] Human life is in movement, propelled by the desire for a life about which one can say, "That life is good." What needs to be applied to human life in the examination proposed by Socrates is above all the truth about the good.

In the examination of life, there is a radical and absolute primacy of the theoretical or contemplative order (*theoria*) over the practical order (*praxis*). It is never right to go against one's conscience and to submit to power, to mere imposition of will, not even one's own will. Once *theoria* has grasped something of the truth about the good, it binds *praxis* to that truth.

In Plato's *Gorgias* the Sophists hold up the ideal of the manly man who has big appetites and the power to satisfy them. Since he has such power, he is free, because he can do whatever he wants, particularly if he has become tyrant over the city.[19] In the tyrant's life, *praxis* has primacy over *theoria*.

Socrates argues in response that human freedom depends entirely on the primacy of *theoria*. The tyrant can do what he wants only if he knows the truth about the good. If he is deceived about the good, he might by mistake do what he would not really want to do. The Sophists grant the argument step by step, but when the conclusion is reached they find it absurd. It is utterly opposed to their naked will to power.

One of them asks Socrates in astonishment, "So you would want to suffer what is unjust rather than do it?" Socrates answers, "I certainly would not want either, but if it had to be one or the other, I would choose suffering over doing what is unjust."[20] The radical commitment to *logos* as the rule of life, the primacy of *theoria* over *praxis*, could not be expressed more forcefully and dramatically than in this testimony. Socrates *did* suffer when Athens executed him for denying the gods of the city and corrupting the young.

### The Infinite Longing of Human Logos

The openness of *logos* to being as a whole and its application to human acts implies an open longing that cannot be satisfied by any finite being, not even by moral virtue, by justice. *Logos* reaches out with desire toward the infinite, toward the divine origin of all beings. The building of a truly human city must take into account, above all, the common good that is the object of this longing. This common good, the divine source of all being, is what is dearest to us.

### 4. *The Denial of Greek* Logos: *Islam, Scotus, Ockham, Bacon, and Descartes*

Let us now turn to Pope Benedict's account of the country at war with Greek *logos*. Many in the Islamic world reacted with passionate anger against the Regensburg Lecture, because it quotes the Byzantine emperor as criticizing Mohammed's practice of conversion by fire and sword. This practice, the lecture argues, implied a priority of will and power over reason. It is surprising that the Western liberal audience of the Regensburg Lecture, which was pleased with Pope Benedict's critique of power in Mohammed, overlooked that the same criticism appears only a few paragraphs later on a much deeper level, directed precisely against the form of rationality embraced by the West:

> In all honesty, one must observe that in the late Middle Ages we find trends in theology which would sunder this synthesis between the Greek spirit and the Christian spirit. In contrast with the so-called intellectualism of Augustine and Thomas, there arose with Duns Scotus a voluntarism which, in its later developments, led to the claim that we can only know God's *voluntas ordinata*. Beyond this is the realm of God's freedom, in virtue of which he could have done the opposite of everything he has actually done. . . .[21]

The voluntarism identified by Pope Benedict reached its most radical form in Scotus' student William of Ockham. Ockham sees the order of created beings as an order God happens to have imposed on them from the outside, one among many orders he could have imposed. He regards natural beings as artifacts, not as natural beings, not as having an interior principle of order toward the good.

Charles Taylor points out, "This line of thought even contributed in the end to the rise of mechanism: the ideal universe from this point of view is a mechanical one."[22] Similarly, he comments:

> The super-agent who is God relates to things as freely to be disposed of according to his autonomous purposes. . . . The purposes of things are extrinsic to them. The stance is fundamentally one of instrumental reason. . . . The shift will not be long in coming to a new understanding of being, according to which, all intrinsic purpose having been expelled, final causation drops out, and efficient causation alone remains. There comes about what had been called "the mechanization of the world picture." And this in turn opens the way for a view of science in which a good test of the truth of a hypothesis is what it enables you to effect. This is the Baconian view.[23]

Ockham's voluntarist philosophy passed through the Ockhamist Gabriel Biel to Luther. This approach also impacted Calvin, and from Calvin it moved to Francis Bacon, who himself was raised as a strict Calvinist.

Bacon took the logical step of transferring the logic of power from divine to human knowledge. It was a decisively new step, a step not taken before by any philosopher. The only legitimate purpose of knowledge, he argues, is to gain power over nature and improve the human condition by technological progress: "Human knowledge and power coincide in the same. . . . Nature is conquered by obeying."[24] "And so these twin intentions, namely, those of human *knowledge and power*, truly coincide in the same."[25] On this point, Bacon's secretary Thomas Hobbes agrees with his employer and friend: "Knowledge is for the sake of power."[26]

Bacon considers seeking knowledge for its own sake immoral. It is the equivalent of enjoying the beauty of a prostitute for pleasure instead of honorably using one's wife to beget children and secure the comforts of life: "Knowledge should not be as a prostitute for pleasure . . . but as a wife for honorable generation, fruit and comfort."[27] In this respect, Marx is a faithful follower of Bacon: "Philosophers have only interpreted the world in different ways: the point is to change it."[28]

## 5. *The Choice of Mechanics*

If the goal of knowing is power over nature, the choice of a particular discipline as the master-discipline follows almost automatically. "The end is most powerful in everything."[29] The Science of power *par excellence* is mechanics. This science was known already to the Ancients, as demonstrated by the *Questions of Mechanics*, a text written probably by one of Aristotle's students.[30] The prologue to the *Mechanics* says,

> When we have to do something contrary to nature, the difficulty of it causes us perplexity and we need technology (*technē*). The technology which helps us in such perplexities we call Mechanics. The words of the poet Antiphon are quite true: "By technology we are powerful even where nature would defeat us." . . . Mechanical problems . . . have something in common both with mathematical and with physical theorems; for while Mathematics shows "the how," Physics shows "the concerning what."[31]

Bacon himself testifies that he adopted his mechanist proposals for science directly from the Aristotelian Mechanics, which he attributes to Aristotle himself: "Aristotle [said it] best. Physics and Mathematics give rise to Practical Science and Mechanics."[32] Whenever possible, Bacon argues accordingly, the laws of nature should be expressed mathematically in accord with precise measurements made in experiments: "Everything in nature relating both to bodies and powers must be set forth (as far as may be) numbered, weighed, measured, determined. For it is works we are in pursuit of, not speculations. Physics and Mathematics, in due combination, give rise to practical science."[33]

It is important to notice that this instruction is not a theoretical judgment based on evidence, but a choice that acts as a non-cognitive selective principle to exclude many modes of being grasped in ordinary experience. Bacon does not draw attention to the moral character of this first and most fundamental choice. It is this self-concealment that gave and still gives to the "objective" mathematical view of nature its strength as a quasi self-evident theoretical starting-point.

It is even more important, however, to insist that the science of physical mechanics is a legitimate science with its own inner coherence. Its success has been stupendous, like a great avalanche that begins with a small movement in the snow near the top of a mountain and in short time manages to gather fullness and speed until it has become a thundering giant of overwhelming energy. One need only think of the Large Hadron Collider built near Geneva, or the research on the human genome, in which innumerable laboratories have become involved. These achievements must not be denied. A true discovery is and remains a true discovery.

The problem with the proposal of mechanics as the master-science is that it was intended to marginalize or eliminate other ways of knowing—and succeeded. In his recent book, *The Grand Design*, Stephen Hawking, who had the Lucasian Chair of Mathematics at the University of Cambridge from 1997 to 2009, occupied from 1669–1702 by Sir Isaac Newton, offers a striking example of this cognitive imperialism:

> How can we understand the world in which we find ourselves? How does the universe behave? What is the nature of reality? Where did all this come from? Did the universe need a creator? Most of us do not spend most of our time worrying about these questions, but almost all of us worry about them some of the time. Traditionally these are questions for philosophy, but philosophy is dead. Philosophy has not kept up with modern developments in science, particularly physics. Scientists have become the bearers of the torch of discovery in our quest for knowledge.[34]

The statement, "Philosophy is dead," is not an observation in the field of quantum mechanics, but a philosophical statement. It therefore proves its exact opposite. "The report of my death," philosophy herself says in Hawking's words, "was an exaggeration."[35]

The conventional narrative of the scientific revolution portrays it as the sudden awakening of human minds to the observation of the facts of nature, leaving behind the overpowering influence of Aristotle's writings, which had been imposed by the Church to buttress its own power. The actual origin of the new science is almost the exact opposite. The will to power over nature led Bacon to choose one particular tractate in the *Corpus Aristotelicum* as relevant to that will, the Mechanics, and to brush aside the rest of the *Corpus* as irrelevant:

> Seek knowledge, and knowledge will give you power. But . . . it would be more accurate to say that the new science sought *first* power over nature, and *derivatively*, found a way to reconceive nature that yielded the empowering kind of knowledge: Seek power, and you will devise a way of knowing that gives it to you. The result can be simply put: knowledge permitting prediction and (some) control over biological *events* has been purchased at the cost of deep ignorance, not to say misunderstanding, of *living beings*, ourselves included.[36]

In *Spe salvi*, Benedict XVI offers a similar account of the scientific revolution.

We must take a look at the foundations of the modern age. These appear with particular clarity in the thought of Francis Bacon. . . . What is the basis of this new era? It is the new correlation of experiment and method that enables man to arrive at an interpretation of nature in conformity with its laws and thus finally to achieve "the triumph of art over nature" (*victoria cursus artis super naturam*). . . .[37]

Anyone who reads and reflects on these statements attentively will recognize that a disturbing step has been taken: up to that time, the recovery of what man had lost through the expulsion from Paradise was expected from faith in Jesus Christ: herein lay "redemption." Now, this "redemption," the restoration of the lost "Paradise," is no longer expected from faith, but from the newly discovered link between science and praxis. . . .

This programmatic vision has determined the trajectory of modern times and it also shapes the present-day crisis of faith which is essentially a crisis of Christian hope. Thus hope too, in Bacon, acquires a new form. Now it is called: *faith in progress*.[38]

## 6. Three Consequences

### The Split Between Fact and Value

One of the most important consequences of the adoption of mechanics as the master-science, as Charles Taylor points out in the passages quoted above, is the elimination of the good and of final causality from the objectively real world. This elimination is inescapable, because the good does not and cannot play any role in a science that works on a mathematical basis. On this point, Aristotle once again supplies the key point: "The mathematical sciences make no arguments about goods and evils."[39] A science of nature that is primarily or exclusively mathematical in method necessarily loses sight of what the divine vision at the beginning saw with full clarity. "God saw everything . . . and indeed, it was very good" (Gen. 1:31).

If mechanics is the master-science, then science must be value-free. And if science is value free, then the truly real world, the world of matter, motion and force, must be value-free as well. The consequence is a profound split between facts and values. The human body for example, is simply a bio-chemical machine that happens to have come to be by chance. In itself, it has no meaning and no goodness. Various sorts of values can be imposed on it, but these are a matter of choice or social construction, not of truth.

### The Primacy of Choice

Descartes studied Bacon early in his career, as documented in several letters, the first one dating from 1630,[40] before he began his first major work in natural philosophy, *Le Monde* (written 1630–1633) almost a decade before his *Meditations on First Philosophy* (1641). He became a particularly effective proponent of Bacon's proposal.

Descartes is fully aware that in following Bacon he makes a fundamental choice at the very roots of philosophy. His difficulty with Aristotelian philosophy is not that it is false, but that it is not useful as an instrument of power:

It is possible to reach knowledge that will be very useful to life and instead of the speculative philosophy which is now taught in the schools [that is, Aristotelian philosophy] we can find a practical one, by which, knowing the force and the actions of fire, water, air, stars, the heavens, and all the other bodies that surround us as distinctly as we know the various skills of our artisans we can employ them in the same way for all the uses for which they are fit, and so *make ourselves masters and possessors of nature.*[41]

Ockham's voluntarist philosophy already gives primacy to choice as the highest kind of freedom. This primacy of choice is intensified if the end of knowledge is power. Accordingly Descartes writes:

Now freewill is in itself the noblest thing we can have because it makes us in a certain manner equal to God and exempts us from being his subjects; and so its good use is the greatest of all the goods we possess, and further there is nothing that is more our own or that matters more to us. From all this it follows that nothing but freewill can produce our greatest contentments.[42]

What Descartes proposes in this text is the hard core of a technological liberalism, technological long before it is metaphysical, political and moral. There seems to be a mutual harmonic reinforcement between the exaltation of free choice and the Baconian-Cartesian program. What distinguishes the master and possessor of nature above all is that he can decide freely what to do with nature. He is not bound by any pre-existing purposes in nature, but sets his own purposes. Compare, by contrast, what Wojtyła says about the freedom of choice and the fuller freedom gained by love:

Love consists of a commitment which limits one's freedom—it is a giving of the self, and to give oneself means just that: to limit one's freedom on behalf of another. Limitation of one's freedom might seem to be something negative . . . but love makes it a positive, joyful and creative thing. *Freedom exists for the sake of love. . . .* Man longs for love more than for freedom—freedom is the means and love the end.[43]

**Total Emancipation**
The emancipation of the person from all that is simply received and not produced as a direct result of personal choice is a necessary implication of Descartes' technological liberalism. Already in 1963, in his inaugural lecture at the University of Münster, Prof. Ratzinger pointed to this implication with astonishing clarity and prescience:

We must see right through traditional value systems and expose them.

In technical rationality we become our own creators and the creators of a world built on the basis of our own inventions. We construct ourselves and reality anew in the unconditional transparence of our rationality. This commitment finds philosophical expression in the idea that there is no pre-given human nature, so that we are free and in fact compelled by our freedom to invent ourselves, to determine what a human being will be in the future.

The strongest form of this detachment from the earth, from the given that carries us, is the complete power over life and death and the abolition of the difference between man and woman.[44]

## 7. *The Challenge of the Regensburg Lecture*

Pope Benedict's analysis is helpful for understanding the tension in Raymond Brown's work. It is a work that attempts to be loyal to both countries at war with each other, to the Catholic Church and the voluntarist movement of the late Middle Ages, which shaped the scientific revolution. When one examines Brown's work in light of the Regensburg Lecture, it becomes clear that it does not sufficiently appreciate the importance of Greek philosophy and the need to resist the voluntarist and nominalist undercurrent of the scientific establishment. The battle line between the two countries, the country of the primacy of truth and the country of the primacy of the will to power, runs through his work itself.[45]

Let us return to the point of departure, to the question, "What is dearest to us?" Dearest to us is Christ, because in him dwells the fullness of the Godhead bodily. He himself, he in person, inseparable from the Father and the Spirit, is our ultimate common good and end. He is the Logos, the divine wisdom, made flesh. This is the discernment that most deeply defines Catholic intellectual life.

If one seriously loves this common good as the end that most deeply forms the pursuit of knowledge, what is required is a radical rethinking of all academic disciplines. It is only in this context that one can hope for a renewal of biblical scholarship. We exegetes depend very much on what happens in the physics department, as Raymond Brown shows in his naïve adherence to Einstein.

Pope Benedict XVI concludes his Regensburg Lecture with a challenge:

The courage to engage the whole breadth of reason, and not the denial of its grandeur—this is the program with which a theology grounded in Biblical faith enters into the debates of our time. "Not to act reasonably, not to act with *logos*, is contrary to the nature of God," said Manuel II, according to his Christian understanding of God, in response to his Persian interlocutor. It is to this great *logos*, to this breadth of reason, that we invite our partners in the dialogue of cultures.[46]

What is needed is a systematic attempt across all university disciplines to work toward the unity of knowledge and to integrate the mechanistic aspects of nature into a fuller understanding. The intellectual problem does not lie in defects of the mathematical natural sciences themselves. Discoveries are and remain discoveries. The problem lies in the tendency of many practitioners of these sciences to marginalize or eliminate every other mode of knowing. The difficulties on this path are enormous, yet the common good of Christ himself, the good that consists of Himself in person, the greatest and most noble common good, makes it worth facing all difficulties.

The difficulties are not only intellectual, but moral and political as well: "The contemporary debates within modern political systems are almost exclusively between conservative liberals, liberal liberals and radical liberals."[47] Liberal suspicion is particularly acute in the case of "the common good." Our culture invests its energies mainly in private goods: money, consumer articles, power, pleasure, etc. Particularly in its conservative version, liberalism tends to react with visceral aversion against the very idea of "common good," because it suspects that "common good" really comes down to depriving individuals of their private goods. "Common good," this is the suspicion, is a rhetorically sophisticated way of persuading those who have the only real goods there are, namely private goods, to give them up so that some bureaucrat can distribute them to others.

The effects of the fact-value dichotomy are also devastating in any proposal of a common good. The ultimate reason for visceral aversion and suspicion toward "common good" in our culture is that we cannot conceive "good" in objective terms, as truly residing in things, but only as an imposition of "value" by individuals or communities. Assertion of a common good will therefore be answered by the counter-pressure, "Who are you to impose your values on me?"

St. Augustine's critique of Rome, "the lust for domination dominates (*dominandi libido dominatur*) that city,"[48] has an object that is easily recognizable as an instrument of power, namely, the military and political apparatus of the Roman Empire. The critique of the origins of natural science in the *libido* for domination is much more difficult to propose, because this *libido* hides itself behind the screen of scientific objectivity. It is unaware of itself as *libido*, unaware of its roots in a highly problematic moral choice that has only very partial cognitive legitimacy.

Scientists work on the cutting edge of their disciplines. They look toward the future. It is difficult to ask them to look back into the past of their disciplines in order to examine the fundamental choices that shaped their very nature as disciplines and marginalized other disciplines with which they should stand in close relation. This point applies not only to physics, chemistry and biology, but also to biblical studies, inasmuch as they attempt to throw the mantle of scientific objectivity over their own shoulders, as Brown does.

Toward the end of the Regensburg Lecture Pope Benedict leaves his audience with a positive note of hope:

The scientific ethos, as you yourself mentioned [addressing the University's Rector], is the will to be obedient to the truth, and, as such, it embodies a fundamental attitude which belongs to the essential decisions of the Christian spirit. The intention here is not one of retrenchment or negative criticism, but of broadening our concept of reason and its application.[49]

Pope Benedict's challenge may be difficult, but it must be taken up. The challenge goes to the most essential point as we search for the right way of reading Scripture.

## NOTES

1 Joseph Ratzinger, "Schriftauslegung im Widerstreit: Zur Frage nach Grundlagen und Weg der Exegese heute," in *Wort Gottes: Schrift—Tradition—Amt*, ed. Peter Hünermann and Thomas Söding (Freiburg: Herder, 2005), pp. 83–116, at p. 83.
There are three independent English translations of the Erasmus Lecture, of which Adrian Walker's is the best.
(1) The lecture as delivered in 1988 in New York City, which is shorter than the published German version: "Biblical Interpretation in Crisis: On the Question of the Foundations and Approaches of Exegesis Today," in Richard J. Neuhaus, ed., *Biblical Interpretation in Crisis: The Ratzinger Conference on Bible and Church* (Grand Rapids MI: Wm. B. Eerdmans Publishing Company, 1989), pp. 1–23.
(2) Adrian Walker's translation of the longer German text: "Biblical Interpretation in Conflict: On the Foundations and the Itinerary of Exegesis Today," in José Granados, Carlos Granados, and Luis Sánchez-Navarro, eds., *Opening up the Scriptures: Joseph Ratzinger and the Foundations of Biblical Interpretation* (Grand Rapids MI: Wm. B. Eerdmans Publishing Company, 2008), pp. 1–29.
(3) Henry Taylor's translation of the same longer German text: "Biblical Interpretation in Conflict: The Question of the Basic Principles and Path of Exegesis Today," in Joseph Ratzinger, *God's Word: Scripture—Tradition—Office* (San Francisco, CA: Ignatius Press, 2008), pp. 91–126.
2 Vladimir Solovyov, *War, Progress and the End of History, Including a Short Story of the Anti-Christ: Three Discussions* (London: London University Press, 1915), pp. 213–214.
3 Aristotle, *Physics*, 2. 3, 195a.24–25.
4 St. Thomas Aquinas, III *Sent.* d. 33, q. 2, a. 1A, c.
5 St. Thomas Aquinas, *Commentary on Aristotle's Physics*, 2. 5, Marietti #186.
6 This article was first presented as a paper at a conference held in honor of Fr. Francis Martin on the theme of "Reading God's Word: Ratzinger's Erasmus Lecture a Generation Later," sponsored by Ave Maria University, Ave Maria, Florida, February 11, 2012. Fr. Francis Martin's testimony at the Catholic Biblical Association is for me a shining beacon in the search for a right reading of Scripture. It pervades all of his rich legacy as a scholar. I thank him with all my heart for this testimony.
7 Norman K. Gottwald, *Tribes of Yahweh: A Sociology of the Religion of Liberated Israel, 1250–1050 BCE* (Sheffield: Sheffield Academic Press, 1999).
8 Karl Marx, *Theses on Feuerbach*, original version (1845), Thesis 11.
9 Marx, *Theses on Feuerbach*, Thesis 8.
10 Aristotle, *Nicomachean Ethics*, 1141a20–22.
11 Erasmus Lecture, in Ratzinger, "Schriftauslegung im Widerstreit," p. 102; Neuhaus, *Biblical Interpretation in Crisis*, p. 14; Walker, trans., "Biblical Interpretation in Conflict," pp. 17–18.
12 Erasmus Lecture, in Walker, trans., "Biblical Interpretation in Conflict," pp. 16 and 19.

13   Raymond E. Brown, "Addenda," in Richard J. Neuhaus, ed., *Biblical Interpretation in Crisis: The Ratzinger Conference on Bible and Church*, pp. 37–49, at pp. 44–47; emphasis added.

14   Alexis de Tocqueville, *Democracy in America*, 2 vols., ed. Phillips Bradley (New York, NY: Vintage, 1945), 2.4.

15   Benedict XVI, *Regensburg Lecture*, December 12, 2006.

16   Plato, *Republic*, translated by Allan Bloom, second edition, (New York, NY: Basic Books, 1991), 480a.

17   "ἡ ψυχὴ τὰ ὄντα πώς ἐστι πάντα." Aristotle, *De Anima*, 431b.21. See Josef Pieper, *Leisure, the Basis of Culture* (South Bend IN: St. Augustine's Press, 1998), p. 86.

18   Plato, *Apology*, 38a.

19   See Plato, *Gorgias*, 492c.

20   Plato, *Gorgias*, 469b–c.

21   Benedict XVI, Regensburg Lecture, December 12, 2006.

22   Charles Taylor, *Sources of the Self: The Making of the Modern Identity* (Cambridge, MA: Harvard University Press, 1989), p. 82.

23   Charles Taylor, *A Secular Age* (Cambridge, MA: Harvard University Press, 2007), pp. 97–98.

24   Francis Bacon, *The New Organon*, Aphorism 1.3.

25   Francis Bacon, *The Great Instauration*, Plan of the Work.

26   Thomas Hobbes, *Elementa Philosophiae*, 1.1, *De Philosophia*, par. 6.

27   Francis Bacon, *The Advancement of Knowledge*, 1.

28   Karl Marx, *Theses on Feuerbach*, Thesis 11.

29   St. Thomas Aquinas, III *Sent.* d. 33, q. 2, a. 1A, c.

30   Lawrence Rose and Stillman Drake, "The Pseudo-Aristotelian Questions of Mechanics in Renaissance Culture," *Studies in the Renaissance*, Vol. 18 (1971), pp. 65–104.

31   Aristotle, *Mechanics*, prologue, 847a10–28.

32   Bacon, *Advancement of Knowledge*, 3.6.

33   Francis Bacon, *Preparation for Natural and Experimental History*, Aphorism 7.

34   Stephen Hawking and Leonard Mlodinow, *The Grand Design* (New York: Bantam Books, 2010), p. 5.

35   Mark Twain, *New York Journal*, June 2, 1897.

36   Leon Kass, "The Permanent Limitations of Biology," in *The Ambiguous Legacy of the Enlightenment*, ed. William A. Rusher, (Lanham, MD: University Press of America: 1995), p. 125.

37   Bacon, *New Organon*, Aphorism 1.117.

38   Benedict XVI, *Spe salvi*, 16–17.

39   Aristotle, *Metaphysics*, 996a35–996b1.

40   The documentary evidence for Descartes' relation to Bacon is gathered in the final volume of Adam and Tannery, *Oeuvres de Descartes*, 12.479, footnote a.

41   René Descartes, *Discourse on Method*, 6; Adam and Tannery, 6.61–62, emphasis added.

42   René Descartes, *Letter to Christina of Sweden*, Adam and Tannery, 5.85; cf. *Meditations*, IV.8. Translation following Taylor, *Sources of the Self*, p. 147. Taylor's translation affirms that freedom "exempts us from being his [that is, God's] subjects." Descartes writes, in fact, a little more cautiously, "*semble* nous exempter de luy estre suiets . . . *seems* to exempt us from being his subjects." Emphasis added.

43   Karol Józef Wojtyła, *Love and Responsibility* (San Francisco, CA: Ignatius Press, 1993), pp. 135–136.

44   Joseph Ratzinger, *Theologische Prinzipienlehre: Bausteine zur Fundamentaltheologie* (München: Erich Wewel Verlag, 1982), pp. 96–97. English: *Principles of Catholic Theology: Building Stones for a Fundamental Theology* (San Francisco, CA: Ignatius Press, 1987), p. 93.

45   See Michael Maria Waldstein, "*Analogia Verbi*: The Truth of Scripture in Rudolph Bultmann and Raymond Brown," *Letter & Spirit*, Vol. 6 (2010), pp. 93–140, at pp. 108–126.

46   Benedict XVI, Regensburg Lecture, December 12, 2006.

47   Alasdair MacIntyre, *Whose Justice? Which Rationality?* (Notre Dame, IN: University of Notre Dame Press, 1988), p. 392.

48   Augustine, *De Civitate Dei*, 14.28.

49   Benedict XVI, Regensburg Lecture, December 12, 2006.

# 9

# PROFILING CHRIST: THE PSALMS OF ABANDONMENT

## FRANCESCA A. MURPHY

### 1. Introductory: Profiling

Thomas Merton said that because the "psalms are theology . . . they place us in direct contact with God, through the assent of faith to his revelation. . . . [B]ecause of this theological and dynamic effect . . . the psalms are steps to contemplation. . . . If we chant the psalms with faith, God will manifest Himself to us; and that is contemplation."[1] The psalms are composed of little scenes or images. These images can be perceived from many angles. A theological interpretation of the psalms is one that contemplates the scene from the angle provided by God. The whole image is taken from the angle that profiles Christ.

The term "profile" is familiar to us from Sokolowski's use of it in his interpretation of the Eucharist. In his terms, a profile is a "view" which is not simply chosen by the viewer, but also given by the object. An object's key profile is that angle *through* which it best shows itself. Sokolowski states that "In the Eucharist we look back at the death of Jesus . . . as profiled through the Passover anticipation by Christ."[2] We read or "see" the death of Jesus in the light of the Last Supper. Likewise, we see and hear the images and scenes in the psalms in the light of Christ's prayer. In this way, the psalms are mediated to us through his profile.

We can use some elementary examples from the cinema to elucidate this theological interpretation of the psalms. In cinema, diverse camera angles produce a scene with a different meaning: a high angled shot symbolizes something different from a close up. For instance, a famous shot from the film "High Noon," zooming in from the back on one of the protagonists who goes out to meet his opponents single-handed, is high-angled, and

*Heaven on Earth?: Theological Interpretation in Ecumenical Dialogue*, First Edition.
Edited by Hans Boersma and Matthew Levering.

thereby draws out the absolute nature of the conflict portrayed in the movie.

Any cinematic image profiles its objects in a way which supplies its meaning or tells us what to attend to. This cinematic way of approaching the subject is both connatural to most of us, and it is not arbitrarily imposed on the biblical text. When Robert Alter wanted to explain biblical plot conventions in *The Art of Biblical Narrative*, he instinctively reached for the gunslinger in the classical Western, whose moves an audience knows how to anticipate.[3] The directors of those early Westerns knew their Bibles. There was a biblical inflection in the clear and graphic way they assembled their scenic images. The use of light and dark as symbolic colors is natural in the photographically based medium of cinema, and likewise the basic biblical use of color symbolism is light and dark. The aesthetics of cinema could make a reasonable fit with traditional theological reading of Scripture. In the ancient Church, Icons, with their foregroundings and enlargements, captured the primitive, illustrative style of Scripture. For us, cinema can make "natural" that same style, with its artistically ranged and focused shots.

The traditional theology of the psalms imagines them as spoken in Christ by his members. This is the *totus Christus* interpretation of the psalms, for which the psalms are "the language spoken to the Father by the humanity redeemed in Christ."[4] Let's consider Psalm 26, as an example, using the Book of Common Prayer version:

Psalm 26   *Judica me, Domine*
Be thou my judge, O Lord, for I have walked innocently.
My trust hath been also in the Lord; therefore shall I not fall.
Examine me, O Lord, and prove me; try out my reins and my
heart. For thy loving-kindness is ever before mine eyes; and
I will walk in thy truth.
I have not dwelt with vain persons; neither will I have fellowship
with the deceitful. I have hated the congregation of
the wicked, and will not sit among the ungodly. I will wash
my hands in innocency, O Lord; and so will I go to thine altar,
that I may show the voice of thanksgiving, and tell of all
thy wondrous works. Lord, I have loved the habitation of thy
house, and the place where thine honour dwelleth. O shut
not up my soul with the sinners, nor my life with the bloodthirsty,
in whose hands is wickedness, and their right hand is
full of gifts.
But as for me, I will walk innocently; O deliver me, and be
merciful unto me. My foot standeth right; I will praise the
Lord in the congregations.

This psalm is a *profession* of innocence.[5] If you want to read or say that psalm as "me speaking to God" you run into immediate problems. As C.S. Lewis notes, it seems utterly Pharasaical, as spoken to God by "me."[6] This is where profiling the psalms through Christ helps us out: only under the cover of Christ's sinless humanity, we can speak these words to God the Father.

Another example of the *totus Christus* reading can be shown from Psalm 32, given here in the New King James version:

**A *Psalm* of David. A Contemplation.**
[1] Blessed *is he whose* transgression *is* forgiven,
   *Whose* sin *is* covered. . . .
[5] I acknowledged my sin to You,
   And my iniquity I have not hidden.
   I said, "I will confess my transgressions to the LORD,"
   And You forgave the iniquity of my sin. Selah

Robert Alter defines this psalm as a confession in the "perfect tense": the speaker acknowledges his fault, and states that God has forgiven him. In this example, the *totus Christus* is not about our covering ourselves in Christ's innocence as we speak the psalm, but about Christ taking up our sin. Dietrich Bonhoeffer says this about such psalms of repentance: "Not for the sake of his sins, but for the sake of our sins . . . does Jesus pray for the forgiveness of sins. He positions himself . . . for us. He wants to be a man before God as we are.

So he prays also the most human of all prayers with us and thereby demonstrates . . . that he is the true Son of God."[7]

## 2. Realism vs. Symbolism in Biblical Exegesis

But do we not want to say that this scene in Psalm 32 refers to the repentance of the very real humanity of David? In the King James Bible the psalm is attributed to him, and we know that David had much of which to repent. The realistic or literally minded scholar wants to read the psalms "historically," although, as we know, this may ultimately entail eschewing reference to David. For several centuries, the historically minded critics seized the land, expelling the original inhabitants into foxholes, like Merton's Trappist monastery and Bonhoeffer's prison cell. Today, symbolist exegesis has begun to recapture the territory. Battle for the land has recommenced. To many of us it is obvious which of the pair is Israel and which the Philistines, which is David and which is Goliath.

The term "Philistines" is useful, because it is in part an imaginative struggle, a contest over whether it is best to imagine the Scriptures literally or symbolically. Such a disagreement was apparent within the first decade of movie making, in the 1890s, with the Lumière brothers realizing the potential of cinema for recording movement, and delighting cinema audiences by capturing the arrival of trains into stations, but on the other hand, with Georges Méliès recognizing the power of cinema for production of illusion, and making a movie about a trip to the moon.[8]

Realist cinema found its champion in Siegried Kracauer, a refugee from Nazi Germany who was convinced that symbolic use of the cinema reached its apogee in *The Triumph of the Will*, a documentary about the Nuremberg rally. Kracauer argued that cinema is based on photography and is therefore connaturally a realistic art form. He claimed that cinema could redeem modern people from sliding into abstraction and ideology by reminding us of the physical world about us. The "large waves roused in the soul" by this

cinematic vision of reality "bring ashore propositions regarding the significance of the things we fully experience. Films which satisfy our desire for
such propositions", may, Kracauer thought, "reach into the dimension of
ideology. But if they are true to the medium, they will . . . not move from a
preconceived idea down to the material world in order to implement that
idea" but rather "set out to explore physical data and, taking their cue from
them, work their way up to some problem or belief." "The cinema", he
affirmed "is materialistically minded; it proceeds from 'below' to 'above.' "[9]
There he speaks, analogously, for those who delight in the Bible's documentary realism, of its historical or history-like character. Realist directors prefer
the long shot, and likewise the historical biblical critic wants to include in the
frame the intra- and extra- biblical evidence, treating the biblical angle as one
amongst others on the Ancient Near Eastern world.

On the other hand, the expressionistic or symbolic character of cinema was
most ably defended by Rudolf Arnheim. Arnheim's best piece of armoury
was the *edited* quality of cinema, the fact that what the camera shows us
differs from anything an unediting human eye can perceive. The professional
camera is deliberately selective, or symbolizing. Expressionist cinema
favours the close-up, and camera angles which turn objects into symbols. The
director becomes the *auteur* of an alternate reality which he controls. The
theological reader of Scripture is not perhaps very interested in a chain of
hypothetical editors, but he is concerned about the fact that the Bible as
revelation is the product of an *auteur*, a demanding Director, and is skillfully
edited for that reason.

My native sympathies are with Kracauer. I took my first steps in theological
exegesis by writing about I Samuel. When I began work on the psalms, I
assumed that David would continue to be the star of the show. The interpretation of the character of David in I and II Samuel has become narrowly
focused on his political exploits and misadventures. This is partly because
historical critics no longer imagine David as a psalmist as well as a king, a
poet as much as a giant slayer. So in taking up the exegesis of the psalms, I
gravitated to the question of whether David wrote the psalms ascribed to him
in Scripture.

In our Bibles, Psalms 3–41, 51–66, 68–70, 86, 101 and 103, and 108–110,
122, 124, 131 and 138 to 145 are attributed to David. Some psalms also
contain in their "headers" little pointers to which episodes in David's life
the psalm depicts. This picture of David as psalmist is backed up by
Chronicles, which describes David as a maker of musical instruments and as
instituting a choir in the temple. But the key to it is the "superscriptions,"
the little headers containing the phrase *ledawid*. David ceased to be perceived as a psalmist when modern scholars began to discount the superscriptions as late additions. Conversely, today's conservative historical
Biblical scholars regard it as theologically indispensable to demonstrate that
*ledawid* means "of David"—that is, written by David, the shepherd and chap

we meet in 1 and 2 Samuel. Without Davidic authorship, they contend, the Christological exegesis of the psalms is not anchored in the historical experience of a specific individual.

### 3.  *Liturgy: Why the Psalms are a Specific Case*

Is David and his authorship really so central to the contemplative reading of the psalms which Merton and countless monks and friars before him espoused? One reason why one may seriously doubt it is that if one is reading the psalms as an Anglican, from the Prayer Book, or as a Catholic, from the Breviary, one encounters a text which has no superscriptions.

Even before they were incorporated into the Hebrew Scripture, the psalms belonged to the worship of the Second Temple. Psalms were fitted into use in Jewish festivals: Psalms 113–118, the Hallel psalms, were sung at Passover, and the "Psalms of Ascent" were used for the pilgrimage festivals. Some scholars claim that, just as the Pentateuch was read in the Temple in a three-year cycle, so, too, the "five books of Psalms" were put through a triennial cycle. Upon achieving a placement in the liturgy, each psalm was thereby somewhat displaced from its historical context. Early Christian usage follows the same trajectory. Psalm 32, about repentance and forgiveness, was, according to Cyril of Jerusalem, sung after Baptisms. Cyril of Alexandria says that the line in Psalm 26 about cleaning one's hands and going to the altar was spoken by the celebrant at Mass at the "lavabo", where the celebrant dips his fingers in water.[10] He is speaking in Christ, or quoting him. David is rinsed out of it. By Augustine's time, specific psalms were attached to the ordinary and special days of the Christian liturgical calendar.[11] By the sixth century, with the Bendictines of Monte Cassino, we have the beginning of the "Office of Readings", with specific psalms prescribed for each hour of the monk's liturgical day. This practice is not broken at the English Reformation: the prayer book assigns psalms for morning and evening prayer, the glory of Anglican spirituality, and covers the Psalter in a monthly liturgical "cycle". From earliest times, in both Jewish and Christian liturgical spirituality, the psalms have been displaced from any original historical context and recontextualised in relation to the liturgical calendar. This happens both in the breviary and in the Missal.

The Missal takes single lines from the psalms, and makes them the antiphons to specific Masses. An antiphon is like an extreme close up: "The Lord hath said unto me, Thou art my son; this day have I begotten thee" condenses Psalm 2 into its seventh verse. Psalm 2:7 was from early times the antiphon for Christmas day. Often the title of the Mass is taken from the first line of the psalm prescribed for that day.

The entire thrust of the liturgical usage of the psalms is thus toward symbolic rather than literal or historical interpretation. You could say the same is true of any part of Scripture: Christians experience it first and fore-

most in the liturgy, displaced from its original historical context. The Lectionary as a whole is "cyclical", and also displaces events and stories from their
context within their given Biblical books. But, when you hear a prose portion
of the Scripture read in Church, you may reasonably connect that Scripture
with an actual event in the life of Christ, or wonder how or whether such
things actually happened. It seems much less natural to make that mental
move of linking the psalms, in their liturgical experience, with the life of
David. It is more obvious to read poetry symbolically than prose. We easily
think of the simplest songs as bearing allegorical meanings. The psalms are a
special case, if not the archetypal case. Perhaps, with the Fathers, the Psalms
were too much of an archetypal case, symbolic reading of the historical prose
of Scripture following on too smoothly from allegorical reading of the
psalms. Thomas Merton puts the difference quite strongly: "the psalms have
an accidental advantage over the New Testament. We *pray* them. We chant
them together. They form part of an action into which the whole Church
enters, and in ... that prayer, the Spirit of Love who wrote the Psalms
... raises us up to God."[12] That is, with some historical portions of Scripture,
a "top down", allegorical reading may in fact impose an ideological abstraction on the text, whereas with the psalms symbolic reading *is* the concrete,
bottom up reading.

## 4. Symbolic Reading as Montage

In cinema, montage can be literally overlaying one image on another, where
both remain visible: directors from Eisenstein to Woody Allen have used it
to great effect. Montage can also mean assembling a series of images in
such a way that viewers automatically do the "superimposing" for themselves, grasping the series as a single image: "To be able to find the requi-
site order of shots or pieces, and the rhythm necessary for their
combination—that is the ... director's art. This art we call *montage*—or
constructive editing."[13]

The New Testament writers apply these lines from Psalm 2 to Jesus:

Yet
have I set my King upon my holy hill of Sion.
I will preach the law, whereof the Lord hath said unto me,
Thou art my Son, this day have I begotten thee.

This biblical usage can be considered as theological montage.

The Psalter is the Old Testament book which the authors of the New
Testament quote most often. By the first century, messianic meanings or a
"future orientation" had gravitated to the Davidic psalms.

The original meaning of royal psalms, such as Psalm 2, had become a locus
of messianic hope. The book of Acts depicts Paul as citing Psalm 2:7 in his

sermon at Pisidia. Already in the mouth of Jesus, the royal psalms acquire a meaning directed away from David and towards himself. In Matthew 22, Jesus refers to the first line of Psalm 110: "What do you think about the Christ? Whose son is he?" "The son of David," they replied. He said to them, "How is it then that David, speaking by the Spirit, calls him, 'Lord'? For he says,

> 'The Lord said to my Lord:
> "Sit at my right hand
> until I put your enemies under your feet." '

If then David calls him 'Lord', how can he be his son?" (Matthew 22:42–45; Mark. 12:35–37; Luke 20:42–44).[14] The point of this elliptical saying is that the Lord God would not refer to David as "my Lord." He must be speaking not to a human king but to a heavenly Lord. But David doesn't disappear completely: David's inspiration, as author of the psalm, is assumed, and messianic hope presupposes his siring a line of kings, who left the throne vacant after the Babylonian conquest, for one who was to come. Although we think of promise and fulfillment, which are historical, linear things, linear or temporal arrows do not make cogent a transition from an earthly king to a divine monarch, or an adopted human "son of God" to a divine Son of God.

Here it is better to conceive of what is being done to the image as "montage" rather than as linear imagery: in montage one picture is superimposed on another without obliterating it. The way Mel Gibson uses montage in the *Passion of the Christ*, where he superimposes the last Supper on the image of the Crucifixion is a good way to imagine what happens with the "Davidic" and Christological images in the psalms. Some may say the movie combines the worst of graphic literalism with the worst of expressionist symbolism, but I think the various "montages" in the film capture something of the way Christians pray the passion in the psalms.

### 5. Symbolic Reading of the Psalms: Merton on the Totus Christus

Psalm 34 takes us deeper into a "montage" conception of Scripture. This is Robert Alter's translation:

> 1  For David, when he altered his good sense before
>    Abimelech
>       who banished him, and he went away.
> 2  Let me bless the LORD at all times,
>       always His praise in my mouth.
> 3  In the LORD do I glory.
>       Let the lowly hear and rejoice.

4   Extol the LORD with me,
        Let us exalt His name one and all.
5   I sought the LORD and he answered me,
        and from all that I dreaded He saved me.
6   They looked to Him and they beamed,
        and their faces were no longer dark.
7   When the lowly calls, God listens
        and from all his straits rescues him.
8   The LORD's messenger encamps
        round those who fear Him and sets them free.
9   Taste and see that the LORD is good,
        happy the man who shelters in Him.
10  Fear the LORD, O His holy ones,
        for those who fear Him know no want.
11  Lions are wretched, and hunger,
        but the LORD's seekers lack no good.
12  Come, sons, listen to me,
        the LORD's fear will I teach you.
13  Whoever the man desiring life,
        who loves long days to see good,
14  keep your tongue from evil
        and your lips from speaking deceit.
15  Swerve from evil and do good,
        seek peace and pursue it.
16  The LORD's eyes are on the righteous
        and His ears to their outcry.
17  The LORD's face is against evildoers,
        to cut off from the earth their name.
18  Cry out and the LORD hears,
        and from all their straits He saves them.
19  Near is the LORD to the broken-hearted,
        and the crushed in spirit He rescues.
20  Many the evils of the righteous man,
        yet from all of them the LORD will save him.
21  He guards all his bones,
        not a single one is broken.
22  Evil will kill the wicked,
        and the righteous man's foes will bear guilt.
23  The LORD ransoms His servant's lives,
        they will bear no guilt, all who shelter in Him.

The superscription to Psalm 34 relates it to the episode in 1 Sam. 21, where David had fled from the frying pan to the fire, from murderously jealous Saul to Philistine Gath, where he has to pretend to be crazy to prevent King Achish from killing him. It is the only psalm with a Davidic superscription to be categorized as a "thanksgiving": the rest are "laments". Psalm 34 is a psalm of terror and desolation, and simultaneously a psalm of joy. David, the original singer, praises God whilst still panting from his narrow escape. The personal quality which makes David so empathetically appealing is his cheerfulness in a crisis. He is and knows he is closest to God in a disaster: the worse things are the more God shelters him. It is this theological quality which makes David prefigure Christ, who in his human soul is capable of enduring the greatest distance from God *because* of his unique filial intimacy with the Father. As von Balthasar puts it, "[T]he Church's understanding of the relationship between Cross and joy is to be found in the realm of the mystery of Jesus' Cross: only in virtue of his filial intimacy with the divine Father can he suffer total abandonment by the Father and taste that suffering to the last drop."[15] If it is the "glorified humanity" of Jesus which is "chanting" such a psalm "in heaven"[16] this Jesus still bears the marks of the wounds of the passion. Merton speaks of faith in Christ's presence in the psalms as "transform[ing] the Office from a routine into a constant joy."[17]

The Gospel passion narratives draw on Psalm 34, and by Chrysostom's time it was detailed for Holy Week.[18] This theological montage educates the believer to discover Christ in the Psalm by "recognizing both Him and ourselves in the sufferings of David, of Israel."[19] It directs us imaginatively to identify the desolation and joy of Jesus in the Passion, and our own desolations and joys, with that of David. So the *totus Christus* reading is not about finding a verbal typological equivalence between parts of Scripture, but about enacting or living the Body of Christ in historical reality. It means Christ's actions are profiled through the lives of the people who belong to his "mystical body", as his life reflects and assimilates that of David. As Merton puts it, the "spiritual understanding of the Psalter . . . will tell us . . . that we are Christ in this world, and that He lives in us, and that what was said of Him . . . is fulfilled in us. . . ."[20] The community between Christ and David as sharers in one single act of desolation and joy extends into a coinherence between Christ's desolation and joy and our own.

### 6. The Dynamism of the Psalms

Dietrich Bonhoeffer said of Psalm 22, "We pray this Psalm, not on the basis of our fortuitous personal suffering, but on the basis of the suffering of Christ which has also come upon us."[21] In the *Nova Vulgata*, Psalm 22 begins:

1 *Magistro chori. Ad modum cantici "Cerva diluculo." PSALMUS. David.*
2 Deus, Deus meus, quare me dereliquisti?
  Longe a salute mea verba rugitus mei.

Augustine remarks that Psalm 22 was used in the liturgy on Passion Friday "even amongst the Donatists".[22] It fits perfectly into the format biblical scholars have devised for the lament, perhaps because that category was modeled upon it! First the speaker complains against God:

> ¹ My God, My God, why have You forsaken Me?
>      *Why are You so* far from helping Me,
>      *And from* the words of My groaning?
> ² O My God, I cry in the daytime, but You do not hear;
>      And in the night season, and am not silent.

Second, the speaker complains against his foes and opponents:

> ⁷ All those who see Me ridicule Me;
>      They shoot out the lip, they shake the head, *saying*,
> ⁸ "He trusted in the LORD, let Him rescue Him;
>      Let Him deliver Him, since He delights in Him!"
> ¹² Many bulls have surrounded Me;
>      Strong *bulls* of Bashan have encircled Me.
> ¹³ They gape at Me *with* their mouths,
>      *Like* a raging and roaring lion.

And third, the speaker complains against himself[23]:

> ⁶ But I *am* a worm, and no man;
>      A reproach of men, and despised by the people.
> ⁷ All those who see Me ridicule Me
> ¹⁴ I am poured out like water,
>      And all My bones are out of joint;
>      My heart is like wax;
>      It has melted within Me.
> ¹⁵ My strength is dried up like a potsherd,
>      And My tongue clings to My jaws;
>      You have brought Me to the dust of death.
>
> [New King James Version]

Most of us know this psalm in the "capsule" version given in Mark's depiction of the crucifixion, but there is more to it than Mark cites, and what he cites implies what is uncited:

Psalm 22 *Deus, Deus meus*
My God, my God, look upon me; why hast thou forsaken me, and art so far from my health, and from the words of my complaint? O my God, I cry in the daytime, but thou hearest not; and in the night-season also I take no rest. And thou continuest holy, O thou worship of Israel. Our fathers hoped in thee; they trusted in thee, and thou didst deliver them. They called upon thee, and were holpen; they put their trust

in thee, and were not confounded.

But as for me, I am a worm, and no man; a very scorn of
men, and the outcast of the people. All they that see me laugh
me to scorn; they shoot out their lips, and shake their heads,
saying, He trusted in the Lord, that he would deliver him; let
him deliver him, if he will have him.

But thou art he that took me out of my mother's womb;
thou wast my hope, when I hanged yet upon my mother's
breasts. I have been left unto thee ever since I was born; thou
art my God even from my mother's womb. O go not from
me, for trouble is hard at hand, and there is none to help me.
Many oxen are come about me; fat bulls of Bashan close me
in on every side. They gape upon me with their mouths, as it
were a ramping and a roaring lion.

I am poured out like water, and all my bones are out of
joint; my heart also in the midst of my body is even like melting
wax. My strength is dried up like a potsherd, and my
tongue cleaveth to my gums, and thou shalt bring me into the
dust of death. For many dogs are come about me, and the
council of the wicked layeth siege against me. They pierced
my hands and my feet; I may tell all my bones. They stand
staring and looking upon me. They part my garments among
them, and cast lots upon my vesture.

But be not thou far from me, O Lord; thou art my succour.
Haste thee to help me. Deliver my soul from the sword, my
darling from the power of the dog. Save me from the lion's
mouth; thou hast heard me also from among the horns of the
unicorns.

I will declare thy Name unto my brethren; in the midst of
the congregation will I praise thee. O praise the Lord, ye that
fear him; magnify him, all ye of the seed of Jacob, and fear
him, all ye seed of Israel. For he hath not despised nor abhorred
the low estate of the poor; he hath not hid his face
from him, but when he called unto him, he heard him.

My praise is of thee in the great congregation; my vows
will I perform in the sight of them that fear him. The poor
shall eat, and be satisfied; they that seek after the Lord shall
praise him. Your heart shall live for ever.

All the ends of the world shall remember themselves, and
be turned unto the Lord; and all the kindreds of the people
shall worship before him. For the kingdom is the Lord's, and
he is the Governor among the people. All such as be fat upon
earth have eaten and worshipped. All they that go down into
the dust shall kneel before him; and no man hath quickened

his own soul. My seed shall serve him; they shall be counted
unto the Lord for a generation. They shall come, and shall
declare his righteousness unto a people that shall be born,
whom the Lord hath made.

In Mark's Gospel, Jesus prays this psalm as he dies on the Cross. Mark gives
a "close up" of the psalm, citing just a couple of verses. A close up is not just
the same as a freeze frame. For "the cinematic close-up," such as in Dreyer's
*Passion of Joan of Arc*, can convey just as much or more movement as the most
sweeping vistas in long shot. "[T]here is . . . more movement in a close up
showing tears running down a person's face than there is in an extreme long
shot of a man running thirty feet."[24] By citing just the one verse, Mark does
not abrogate the tendency to rapid movement present from the beginning of
his Gospel. Movement, or *kinesis*, the word from which we get cinema, is
typical of Mark and of the Psalms, and not only in analogous ways. As Robert
Alter says, "The fluidity of genres of many of the psalms is an expression of
their psychological dynamism—they express not one static attitude but an
inner evolution or oscillation of attitudes. Perhaps the prayer itself served as
a vehicle of transformation from acute distress to trust."[25] This Psalm has an
epic sweep, from scenes of the singer's demonic humiliation on earth to the
startling praise of God by "those who go down into the dust" or as Alter
translates, "the netherworld's sleepers". Startling because the Psalter is insis-
tent that the dead cannot praise God: "the poet, having imagined God's
dominion extending to the far ends of the earth, also wants to extend it
downward . . . into the very underworld."[26] Hence, even Mark's crucifixion
scene is not simply a scene of desolation: given Mark's use of several psalms
which "testify to Yahweh's vindication of his messianic king"[27] it is most
likely that Resurrection from the dead is built into his "capsule" version: joy
is implicitly present in this abandonment.

Merton interprets the Psalm in the same way, with his *totus Christus* exegesis: "[I]n such a Psalm, the soul, . . . comprehending in its own black mirror
the fearful darkness of revelation, is confronted in its own depths with the
face of the murdered Christ. This is . . . an identification. We have entered into
a Baptism of darkness. . . . We now know that this darkness, which seems
to annihilate us, is not the darkness of death but . . . the darkness of
life. . . . [T]his frightful death is our first taste of glory."[28]

Flannery O'Connor's story, "Revelation", is an exegesis of Psalm 22 which
seems to draw on Merton's exegesis of the psalm. As with Mrs. Turpin, "[i]t
can sometimes happen that we too are brought down by Christ's love, into
the dust of death. Then we know, somewhat as He knew, what it is to be
'poured out like water'. . . . It is the frightful taste of a humility that is not
merely a virtue but the very agony of truth. This ghastly emptying" and
"gutting of our own appalling nonentity, takes place under the piercing light
of the revealed word, the light of infinite Truth."[29] It is strange to think that

O'Connor took Merton's words about the "dark night of the soul" and turned them into a blackly comic story about the overly complacent wife of a farmer of cows and pigs. But it is vastly stranger that the misdeeds and merriments of Israel's first king should form the template for the temporal abandonment of the son of God. This is where David has his unalterable place in the Psalter. We cannot imagine the abandonment of Christ, the son of God. David's psalms of lament and abandonment give us a human mirror and human words with which to imagine, picture and verbalise the unimaginable. Bonhoeffer says truly that "even David did not pray out of the personal exuberance of his heart, but out of the Christ who dwelled in him."[30] But it is equally true that we can best conceive that exuberant abandonment as profiled through David. In other words, both the literal, historical "original" of the psalms of abandonment, that is, David in his plight, and his symbolic double, Christ, are necessary to the appreciation of these psalms.

*NOTES*

1   Thomas Merton, *Bread in the Wilderness* (New York, NY: New Directions, 1953), pp. 14–15.
2   Robert Sokolowski, *Eucharistic Presence: A Study in the Theology of Disclosure* (Washington, DC: Catholic University of America, 1993), p. 26.
3   Robert Alter, *The Art of Biblical Narrative* (New York, NY: Basic Books, 1983), pp. 48–49.
4   Laurence Kriegshauser O.S.B., *Praying The Psalms in Christ* (Notre Dame, IN: University of Notre Dame Press, 2009), p. 12.
5   Robert Alter, *The Book of Psalms: A Translation and Commentary* (New York / London: W.W. Norton, 2007), p. 88.
6   C.S. Lewis, *Reflections on the Psalms* (San Diego/New York/London: Harcourt, 1958, 1986), pp. 66–67.
7   Dietrich Bonhoeffer, *Psalms: The Prayer Book of the Bible*, translated by Daniel W. Bloesch and James H. Burtness, (Minneapolis, MN: Augsburg Press, 1970), pp. 51–52.
8   Louis D. Giannetti, *Understanding Movies* (Englewood Cliffs, NJ: Prentice-Hall, 1972), p. 185.
9   Siegfried Kracauer, *Theory of Film: The Redemption of Physical Reality* (Oxford: Oxford University Press, 1960), pp. 308–309.
10  John Alexander Lamb, *The Psalms in Christian Worship* (London: Faith Press, 1962), p. 33.
11  C. Hasell Bullock, *Encountering the Book of Psalms: A Literary and Theological Introduction* (Grand Rapids, MI: Baker Academic, 2001), p. 94.
12  Merton, *Bread in the Wilderness*, p. 107.
13  V. I. Pudovkin, *Film Technique and Film Acting*, translated by Ivor Montagu (London: Vision Press, 1929, revised edition 1958), p. 169.
14  Bullock, *Encountering the Book of Psalms*, p. 183.
15  Hans Urs von Balthasar, *Truth Is Symphonic: Aspects of Christian Pluralism*, translated by Graham Harrison, (San Francisco, CA: Ignatius Press, 1987), p. 169.
16  Merton, *Bread in the Wilderness*, p. 92.
17  *Ibid.*, p. 118.
18  Lamb, *The Psalms in Christian Worship*, p. 35.
19  Merton, *Bread in the Wilderness*, p. 91.
20  *Ibid.*, p. 38.
21  Bonhoeffer, *Psalms*, p. 37.
22  Lamb, *The Psalms in Christian Worship*, p. 35.
23  Bullock, *Encountering the Book of Psalms*, p. 122.
24  Giannetti, *Understanding Movies*, p. 51.
25  Alter, *The Book of Psalms*, p. 38.
26  *Ibid.*, p. 76.

27   George J. Brooke, "The Psalms in Early Jewish Literature in the Light of the Dead Sea Scrolls," in Steve Moyise and Maarten J. J. Menken (eds), *The Psalms in the New Testament* (Edinburgh: T & T Clark, 2004), p. 44.
28   Merton, *Bread in the Wilderness*, p. 122.
29   *Ibid.*, p. 120.
30   Bonhoeffer, *Psalms*, p. 19.

# 10

# READING THE BOOK OF THE CHURCH: BONHOEFFER'S CHRISTOLOGICAL HERMENEUTICS

## JENS ZIMMERMANN

*1. Introduction: The Legitimacy of Theological Interpretation*

Theological interpretation is becoming a common practice among Catholic and evangelical theologians, but one occasionally criticized for neglecting the historical and social setting of the text in order to pursue a spiritualizing reading that is arbitrary, prejudiced and unscientific.[1] Not infrequently, this criticism is combined with the conviction that especially patristic theological exegesis departs from the historical, inner-biblical context because world denying influences of Greek philosophy have crept into Christian theology and its interpretive practices. According to this view, Greek metaphysical longings and concepts have eclipsed the more earthbound Hebraic imagination and distorted actual meanings of New Testament texts. This argument implies that an objective, truly text-oriented, philological approach to the biblical texts would not commit such subjective flights of fancy and bind itself more faithfully to a historical framework and Christianity's Judaic roots. As the following example from the history of biblical exegesis illustrates, however, there is no such guarantee.

We are turning to the early twentieth century, when theological interpretation made a comeback in Germany after the long reign of the historical-critical school.[2] Dietrich Bonhoeffer deliberately participated in this recovery of theological exegesis. The following paragraphs are meant to contextualize his approach to the Bible and to affirm it by establishing the continuing legitimacy of theological interpretation. We will then turn to his actual interpretive practice in the remaining sections of this article.

*Heaven on Earth?: Theological Interpretation in Ecumenical Dialogue*, First Edition.
Edited by Hans Boersma and Matthew Levering.
© 2013 Blackwell Publishing Ltd. Book compilation © 2013 Blackwell Publishing Ltd.

The return of theological interpretation in Germany was spearheaded by Karl Barth's Commentary on Romans. His criticism of the historical-critical school, and his openly theological interpretation of the text triggered a passionate, critical response from those who had devoted their lives to objective, historical scholarship of the Biblo and the Christen tradition. The classic debate between theological hermeneutics and supposedly factual exegesis took place between Barth and the church historian Adolf von Harnack.

Not unlike some critics of theological interpretation today, von Harnack rejected Karl Barth's theological exegesis as Romanticism and dangerous theologizing unmoored from scientific textual exegesis. Yet, it was the supposedly objective historian, Adolf von Harnack, who sought to appropriate Marcion's rejection of the bloodthirsty Old Testament God for modern Protestantism.[3] It was Harnack's alleged "scientific" exegesis that unhinged the New Testament from the Old, a move that aided theological anti-Semitism later on during the church struggle in Germany. This brief example shows that the question of what makes something "biblical" interpretation cannot be decided by any kind of positivism, by retreating behind the empirically verifiable, obvious, or objective meaning of the text. In fact, the delusion of achieving neutral, unbiased exegesis has been generally recognized by biblical scholars in the latter half of the twentieth century. And biblical critics have recognized this not because they no longer value objective truth, but because they have realized that objectivity is not obtained by presuming an uninvolved stance toward our object of investigation. The question is no longer whether we approach the texts with presuppositions, but rather what kind of presuppositions are adequate for the sort of text and the subject matter we want to examine. In the words of Martin Heidegger, "it is never a question of avoiding the hermeneutical circle, but to enter it in the right way."[4] In other words, any discussion concerning the legitimacy of theological reading, and of the Bible as the book of the church, has to begin with examining our presuppositions about epistemology and cosmology, or, to put it more simply, by interrogating our views on how we know and how we construe the reality within which God makes himself known to us. Thus, the reason that theological and spiritual readings of the scriptures were commonplace among the church fathers but later were derided has much less to do with the supposed superiority of modern exegetical tools (even though such superiority exists), than with the shift from participatory metaphysics in the ancient world to the separation of nature and supernature in our times.

Frances Young, who studied the development of patristic exegesis, confirms that the differences between pre-modern and modern exegesis depend on different conceptions of reality:

> An authoritative text is understood to refer to the world in which people live, and so its meaning is bound to be received or contested in the light of the plausibility structures of the culture which receives the text. A culture

which can conceive of the material universe as interpenetrated by another reality, which is transcendent and spiritual, will read the reference of scripture in those terms. That is far more significant for the differences between ancient and modern exegesis than any supposed 'method.' Methodologically, exegesis involves many of the same procedures.[5]

Exegesis in the ancient world among pagans and Christians was based on a view of reality in which textual meaning participated in spiritual realties beyond the text. On the basis of this worldview, the church fathers could develop a sacramental view of language, according to which, following the pattern of the incarnation, the self-communication of a transcendent God was mediated through finite human language.[6] Thus patristic exegetes could speak about a unifying reality behind the text, about the "the mind of the text" that allowed for coherent overall meaning.[7]

The assumption of a meaningful transcendent reality to which the text referred permitted, in turn, mimetic interpretations of the text. Mimetic interpretation was common in the ancient educated world, and entailed the reading of texts in a typological fashion as teaching moral and doctrinal precepts. As Young explains, "in the ancient Church *mimesis* or 'representation' was important. It underlay the enactment of the saving events of the sacraments, as well as the 'exemplary' use of scripture."[8] Mimesis also helps us understand ancient use of typology as a form of allegory. So Job, for example, was a "type" prefiguring Christ. His life pre-enacted, as it were, an experience that Christ then filled with meaning. Both are models of patience to be followed. As Young points out, because the ancient world embraced a sacramental view of reality—that is, a participatory metaphysics—it is misleading to oppose allegory and typology by identifying the latter with historical occurrences and the former with fanciful spiritualizing of history.[9] Such distinctions rest on modern notions of history and nature as divorced from spiritual realities that were unthinkable to the ancient world. The real question is, of course, whether we, today, are still bound by this separation.

The answer is, "it depends." For even while we no longer inhabit an ancient cosmology in which the natural and supernatural easily interpenetrate, there is nothing that absolutely compels us to bracket spiritual realities from our reading of texts. At the very least, something approaching a sacramental view of language has been reintroduced through hermeneutic theory as developed by Martin Heidegger, Hans-Georg Gadamer, and Paul Ricoeur, all of whom rejected an instrumental view of language and positivistic conceptions of truth. Perhaps Gadamer most clearly expresses this change when he argues that while the link between the human and the divine mind may have become untenable to modern consciousness, language still ties our minds to the universal rationality of the human spirit as it is mediated through human traditions. In fact, Gadamer thinks that Christianity's belief in the incarnation makes possible a truly hermeneutical conception of human knowledge by establishing the linguisticality of human understanding. In Greek thought, true correspondence between thought and word was impossible since every concept was merely a copy of its perfect form. Yet Christianity's claim that the eternal Word was incarnated in human form without any loss to His integrity laid the foundation for the notion that particular languages could truly reflect universal human insights.[10] Contrary to Greek philosophy, for which the move from intellectual idea to external word entails a sense of loss and disunity, the Christian incarnation allows for the unity between thought and speech, between universal concepts and their particular expressions.[11] Such correspondence in no way implies full comprehension of universals on our part, but it does mean that the uttered word truly participates in and reliably reflects the concept. It is true that "no human word can express the mind completely," because our intellect is finite. Nonetheless, the multiplicity of words and interpretations always remain truly connected to, or in union with, the thing we are trying to express.[12] In this way, Gadamer concludes, "Christology prepares the way for a philosophy of man, which mediates in a new way between the mind of man in its finitude and the divine infinity. Here what we have called the hermeneutical experience finds its own special ground."[13] Hermeneutic theory thus opens once again the way to a sacramental view of language and to the legitimacy of theological interpretation. This is not to say that biblical scholars as a whole are happily returning to theological readings of the scriptures. Yet even those committed to reading the Bible purely as a literary artifact are reflecting more deeply on the interpretive presuppositions of their craft.

The well-known biblical scholar John Barton, for example, seeks to defend biblical criticism as a strictly literary discipline that is neither hermeneutically naïve by supposing neutral objectivity, nor theologically committed to reading the Bible as a sacred text. Instead, Barton champions biblical criticism as the preparatory philological foundation that establishes the meaning of the text on which subsequent confessional readings can build. Against caricatures of biblical critics as dissecting the text with a positivist scalpel in order to reconstruct history 'as it really happened,' Barton argues that "biblical criticism is not a matter of *processing* the text, but of *understanding* it."[14] His emphasis on understanding renders questionable, however, Barton's affirmation of biblical criticism as a preparatory discipline for establishing the plain sense of the text prior to ecclesial or other readings.[15] As Gadamer made clear in *Truth and Method*, our understanding is inseparable from the applicatory expectations and questions we bring to the text.[16] Even in the case of the Bible, these questions need not, it is true, necessarily concern Christian belief. Moreover, Barton is certainly correct to claim that the biblical critic is not a mere clinician but motivated by love for truthful meaning.[17] Yet surely, while recognition of the reader's shared humanity with the author is important,[18] the specific understanding required by the biblical text involves more than a general passion for meaning, especially if, as Barton insists, we aim at a kind of interpersonal understanding, of "human heart speaking to human heart."[19] After all, the Christian Bible as sacred text is a record and reflection of human experience and self-understanding as shaped by an actual encounter with God in real time and history, and by the ultimate revelation of this God in Jesus the Christ. If the biblical authors are inspired by the Spirit of God, and as those who, in the New Testament, are reshaped as God's people, moving from communion with God through the observance of Temple worship into communion with God through Jesus the Christ, then is not the church the proper framework for reading these scriptures?

Gadamer insists that understanding a text requires that the questions we put to the text are guided primarily by the subject-matter of the text.[20] More precisely, the hermeneutic task is to reconstruct the question to which the text offers an answer, for each text is really an answer to a question.[21] And while purely literary critics surely can be very successful in allowing themselves to be shaped by the biblical text, there is a difference between the Bible and a literary text. The difference is that the Bible is especially (though not exclusively for them) a literary text inspired by a people's experience with God, and this God still actively shapes the present community of his people by the power of his Spirit. To use Gadamer's vocabulary, the fusion of horizons between the past horizon and the present application of the biblical text is enabled and directed by more than a common humanity, because God's own personal presence within tradition shapes the process of reception and understanding. Another way of expressing the unique character of the scriptures is to describe them as the book of the church, and to acknowledge Christ as the key to their interpretation.

Christians have argued since the beginning of Christian hermeneutics that the fulfillment of Old Testament prophecies through the incarnation of God in Christ is the hermeneutical focus of the Christian Bible.[22] In Origen's words, a new light shines forth on the scriptures with the advent of Christ,[23] the same Christ whose Spirit moulds a new humanity, the people of God represented by the church. While it is entirely plausible to read the Bible like any other text and to "bracket out questions of truth" in a sort of "procedural neutrality,"[24] it is hard to see how bracketing out the christological focus assumed by early Christians does not distort the questions we put to the text and thus skew our understanding. In other words, the kind of "procedural distinction between discovering what texts mean and evaluating or using them"[25] suggested by Barton is questionable, since our use co-determines what we consider permissible readings. For the same reason, it also seems odd to advance a purely literary reading of the Bible as preparatory reading for a more confessional approach on the assumption that theological interpretations are gnostic, accessible only to insiders. With these claims, Barton lapses into exactly the kind of modernist assumptions he wants to repudiate.

Barton rightly points to the fact that biblical criticism as such has philological roots in antiquity, making it implausible to equate biblical criticism with Enlightenment rationalism.[26] Yet this very fact of co-existing spiritual interpretation and historical-critical tools in pre-modern exegesis indicates that biblical criticism, along with its critical tools, requires a hermeneutic framework that views the Bible as the book of the church. Like many other biblical scholars, Barton remains too much wedded to the German cultural movement that expatriated the Bible from the church, making it the posses-sion of the academy, a purely cultural and literary artifact. Michael Legaspi has succinctly summarized this development and shown that establishing the Bible as a cornerstone of Western culture and its universal values required the "death of scripture." By becoming the domain of academic philologists and literary critics, the Bible was divested of its scriptural character and domesticated into a cultural treasure.[27]

These historical and hermeneutical reflections on the biblical text show us that attempts to sever biblical criticism from the text's native environment in the believing and practicing church community stem from the false opposi-tion of tradition and objective knowledge, which hermeneutic theory has rightly criticized. As Yves Congar has argued, in the Christian life, the scrip-tures are an intricate part of a living stream of tradition within which the Christian faith is communicated and the Christian is shaped into god-likeness.[28] And this tradition is alive in the people of God as community, in the church. In short, the Bible can and ought to be read as the book of the church, and this is how Bonhoeffer insists on reading it.

Given the hermeneutical dynamic of human understanding we have just described, for the Christian to profess Christ as the center of scriptural exegesis is not a cowardly sheltering from radically open inquiry, but rather constitutes a stance of intellectual integrity in conformity with the workings of textual interpretation. Because all questions emerge from our human exist-ence as an interpretation of the world, and are therefore never neutral or disengaged, the question concerning the center of biblical exegesis is already theological[29] and emerges from a Christian experience of the world, which, as a human experience of the world governed by a certain interpretive frame-work, is as valid and open to rational discussion as any other worldview. Ingolf Dalferth has made this hermeneutical point clearly: "Jesus Christ," he writes, "constitutes the compass and destination of evangelical interpretation of the scriptures because he is also the compass and destination for the Christian interpretation of the self, of the world, and of God."[30] Christian biblical interpretation is Christological and inherently seeks to transcend the historical letter toward the presence of God as mediated by the letter: "Faith is not directed to the scriptures but to Jesus Christ, and by attuning itself to this center of the scriptures, [the reader] doesn't focus on a handed down 'once upon a time' or 'back then' but on the effective now and today of God's presence."[31] The biblical text is not itself an object of devotion but a means of meeting and speaking with God as he reveals himself in Christ. Conse-quently, Christian biblical exegesis has to take place within a consciously

Christological hermeneutic. Dietrich Bonhoeffer offers such a hermeneutic, and he does this as one seeking to overcome the limitations of historical-criticism with its implicit dualistic view of reality and its consequent separation of reason from faith. Bonhoeffer sees with total clarity that biblical exegesis depends on how we understand the relation of "history, and spirit."[32] He recognizes that historical criticism rests on the philosophical foundations of a "natural-scientific-mechanical worldview" and its scientific epistemology that excludes dogmatic considerations from reading the text.[33] Such historical criticism fragments the biblical documents until it destroys any unified reading of the text.[34] Bonhoeffer seeks to move beyond this failure of historical-critical exegesis to a theological, edifying reading, based on a Christological hermeneutic. Therefore, his work provides an important contribution to the retrieval of theological exegesis in our day.

## 2. *Dietrich Bonhoeffer's Christological Hermeneutic*

Dietrich Bonhoeffer's own defense of spiritual (he called it "pneumatic")[35] interpretation owes much to Karl Barth's view of the Bible. In his *Church Dogmatics*, Barth stressed the importance of the incarnation for biblical interpretation. Just as in the incarnation real divinity dwells in real humanity, so God mediates himself through the human words of the Bible. Truly human words in all their fallibility and historical context[36] are used by God to make himself present to the reader. Yet, according to Barth, this self-presencing of God does not reside in the text as if by magic,[37] is never automatic, and never at the command of the reader. For these reasons, the reader should not attempt to differentiate between the divine and the human word. To do so would be to rebel against the miracle, against "the hard thought" of the incarnation.[38] The sovereign grace of God, by which He took up humanity in complete freedom, is equally at work when the Bible becomes a vehicle for His presence. Bonhoeffer shares Barth's incarnational view of the scriptures. The written words of revelation are a true image (*Abbild*) of the Person of Jesus Christ himself, of the eternal word become flesh. Every word of scriptures, says Bonhoeffer, is "a true image of the person of Jesus Christ," presenting the reader with a historical reality and its divine inner reality that transcends this historical element.[39] For this reason Bonhoeffer, like Barth, rejects as presumptuous any distinction between human and divine words in the scriptures. Such distinctions inevitably destroy the unity of God's word along lines drawn by our own ideologies, separating, for example, Jesus' miracles (now deemed credible only to a pre-modern, unscientific imagination and hence no longer believable) from His ethics (timeless universal truths).[40] Bonhoeffer concludes that, indeed, "the divine and the human word are commingled in the scriptures, but in such a way that God himself says where his word is, and he does so *within the human word.*"[41] Otherwise, warns Bonhoeffer in a letter to his skeptical brother-in-law, Rüdiger Schleicher, we will merely meet our own thoughts in the Bible instead of being transformed by it.[42] This incarnational approach to the scriptures allows Barth and Bonhoeffer to avoid the pitfalls of verbal inspiration theories on the one hand, and of the Bible's reduction to a mere historical document on the other.

Yet while Bonhoeffer inherited from Barth a high view of scripture and a conviction that it requires theological exposition, he more clearly and succinctly integrates the theological interpretation of the scriptures into a general sacramental framework, in which the Christian life revolves around God's becoming present within church and world. To be sure, *both* theologians understood faith to be an encounter with a personal, Trinitarian God. *Both* reject the liberal Protestant view of the Christian faith as cognitive assent to propositions or universal moral values. Yet Bonhoeffer, more than Barth, offers an understanding of faith as genuine participation in Christ. To be sure, Barth's emphasis on God's revelation of Himself in Christ as "God for us" and even as "one of us" also seeks to establish faith as a real communion with God. Yet Barth's stress on God's freedom and sovereignty still suggests a gap between our identity as Christians in God and our historical being. We have to "believe in our faith,"[43] says Barth, whereas Bonhoeffer proclaims our "being in Christ." He criticizes the early Barth for implying that "God is always the 'arriving' but never the 'present' (*daseiende*) God."[44] But God, says Bonhoeffer, has promised to be "with us," to be "haveable" (*habbar*) or present in his church.[45] For this reason, Bonhoeffer defines faith as participation in Christ, a "being-in-Christ" that is equally a being-in the church as a member of Christ's body, so that the transcendent and ontological realities of Christian existence are held together.[46]

This understanding of faith as a mode of being that defines our human identity holistically as new creation constitutes the heart of Bonhoeffer's Christological hermeneutic. God nourishes this new identity by presencing himself in the church through baptism, Eucharist and preaching, and the goal of this communion with God is the formation of Christ in each believer and the church as a whole through the power of the Spirit. The Bible as God's word is central to the Christian's education into true humanity. The church, as Bonhoeffer phrases it, is "Christ existing as community," and biblical exegesis is one way by which the community understands its identity as formation into the new humanity for whose creation God became human and whose prototype is Jesus the Christ, the perfect image of God. For Bonhoeffer, salvation is the attainment of our true humanity in Christ.[47] True humanity, however, does not exist in isolation, but is marked by the kind of unity and solidarity the church ought to represent. The new human being is not a single individual but "the church community, the body of Christ."[48] These sentiments align Bonhoeffer with the Christian humanism that determined the theology of the church fathers, and that underlies a number of Roman Catholic documents, such as the Second Vatican Council's *Dogmatic Constitution on Divine Revelation* (or Pope Benedict's Apostolic Exhortation,

*Verbum Domini*),[49] linking the interpretation of scripture to the vocation of the church as the new humanity in Christ. We can summarize the ethos of this Christian humanism with the motto that "God became human so that human beings could attain their true and full humanity, their god-likeness."[50]

Bonhoeffer's Christological hermeneutic follows the church fathers in placing God's written word and its interpreter within a genuinely logos-centric, a Word-centered reality. The Bible is not merely an old book of great cultural relevance but a primary witness to the living, eternal *Logos* that sustains creation and became human in Christ. Incarnational Christology is the centre not only of scriptural interpretation but of understanding reality in general. Bonhoeffer's concept of "one Christ-reality" places the Christian interpreter within a unified world determined through its creation in the eternal logos and its reconciliation to God in Christ. Faith and reason are unified by Christ, who is "the center and the power of the Bible, of the church, of theology, but also of humanity, reason, justice, and culture."[51] Christology, ecclesiology and general epistemology are in this sense all sustained by the same Word of God, and our response to this word constitutes "action in accordance with reality."[52] Reality in the highest sense as ultimate purpose and meaning is not some abstract, neutral thing but "the *real one*, the God having become human. In the incarnate, crucified, and resurrected Christ, everything factual obtains its ultimate foundation (*Begründung*) and its ultimate relativization (*Aufhebung*), its ultimate contradiction and its ultimate yes and its ultimate no."[53] The Christian is the quintessential realist because he lives out of his participation in Christ, in whom God reconciled the world to Himself. Thus "Christ-centered action is realistic action," because Christ summed up in himself all of reality.[54] Bonhoeffer thus anticipated Pope Benedict's recent affirmation of a Christological realism. In his apostolic exhortation *Verbum Dei*, Benedict writes, "The Word of God makes us change our concept of realism: the realist is the one who recognizes in the Word of God the foundation of all things."[55] With Bonhoeffer, Benedict holds that "the Christ event is at the heart of divine revelation,"[56] wherefore the Bible itself is the word of God only in a derivative sense[57] as witness to divine realities.[58] Bonhoeffer's linking of Christology, ecclesiology and biblical interpretation also finds echoes in Benedict's affirmation that the church is "built upon the word of God" that "she is born from and lives by that word."[59] At the very least, then, Catholics and Protestants share the conviction that the Bible, as Bonhoeffer put it, is "the book of the church" and has to be interpreted as such.[60]

## 3. Reading the Bible as the Book of the Church

Without question, Bonhoeffer is heir to the *sola scriptura* tradition of Protestantism. Yet his reason for this position differs from traditional Protestant affirmations of the internal coherence of the Bible, its verbal inspiration, or its supposed perfection in the original documents. Instead, Bonhoeffer argues from an incarnational model of the scriptures as both spirit and flesh, as historical document whose proper meaning is revealed only through the Spirit's power, who creates spiritual understanding in the reader, a gift that is received every time anew.[61] Reading the Bible as the book of the church means first of all that exegesis follows a circular movement, whereby interpretation of biblical texts requires prior familiarity with the spirit in which they are written. The paradox of the Bible is that only through God can God be known.[62] This paradox, claims Bonhoeffer, is described by Luther's famous dictum "scriptura sacra est sui ipsius interpres." The maxim that scripture interprets itself was not intended as a grammatical principle but as a description of the need for spiritual illumination, and an assertion of spiritual interpretation.[63] Being drawn into communion with God through Christ by an act of grace, the theological exegetes are taken into a reality that is independent of the Bible, into a living relation with God, and yet they only learn the nature of this relation through reading the biblical text. Bonhoeffer is not saying, of course, that one cannot read the Bible unless one is a Christian. Such a claim would contradict his conviction that the Bible is written in truly human words arising within their socio-historical fields of reference.[64] He is saying, however, that the biblical authors employ the cultural language of their day to express a particular experience of God,[65] wherefore their meaning cannot be grasped fully nor become contemporaneous with us without participation in the same divine reality. Just as faith does not oppose but goes beyond reason, so spiritual exegesis does not negate but goes beyond mere historical-critical reading in seeking the spiritual referent of the human words.[66]

In advocating theological interpretation, Bonhoeffer seeks to strike a balance between a historical-critical approach[67] to the Bible in which he was schooled and a pneumatical (spiritual) approach to scripture as a vehicle for God's transformative grace: "Theological interpretation," as he once put it, "regards the Bible as the book of the church and interprets it as such. Its method is this assumption and entails a continual referring back of the text (which has to be ascertained with all the methods of philological and histori-cal research) to this presupposition."[68] Historical criticism is justified because the Word became flesh, and so the spiritual exegete has to wrestle with the historical dimension of the text, because the Bible is at one level a human word about God. Yet historical criticism is limited by the very fact that God entered history and that his Spirit is needed to reveal his divine Word in the human word.[69] For this reason, problems concerning the redaction and genesis of texts are ultimately less important than the actual subject-matter of the scriptures as God's word to his people.

Based on this conviction, Bonhoeffer even suggests that belief in the histori-cal veracity of the virgin birth is less important than grasping its theological import, namely that in Jesus God has become human.[70] Bonhoeffer is here rigorously true to his incarnational principle: in entering humanity, God has also entered the ambiguity of language and history. His divine reality shines forth through the unstable medium of human communication. Textual ambiguities and even conflicting views of Jesus's actions are part of the scandal constituted by the incarnation and *kenosis* of God. For this reason, textual clarity itself cannot be the final criterion for belief. If Christians insist that an unbeliever's doubt of the virgin birth constitutes an obstinate refusal to accept clear textual evidence, they confuse dogmatic theology with textual criticism. Equally bad, they are blind to the incarnational nature of the biblical text.[71]

Together with the New Testament writers and the greater Christian tradition, Bonhoeffer assumes that reading the Bible as the book of the church is to read it Christologically. His conviction that Christ is the inner logic of the scriptures that unifies the Old and New Testaments[72] prompts Bonhoeffer to adopt Luther's hermeneutical key of "whatever promotes Christ," and he even argues for an open canon based on this principle.[73] For Bonhoeffer, Christological reading, however, is also an eschatological reading, a reading in light of the end: "The church of the holy scripture—and there is no other church—lives in light of the end. For this reason, she reads the entire holy scripture as the book about the end, about the new, about Christ."[74] The Bible as the book of the church has to be read from the point of view of the fulfillment of all things in Christ. The incarnation, death and resurrection of God in Christ is the hermeneutical center from which anything preceding or following this event gains its meaning.[75] For example, from a historical-critical perspective, one can speculate about what the concept of God meant in the Genesis account for pagan or pre-Christian hearers. These anofair, historical questions that move within the legitimate penultimate realm of religious history. Yet pneumatic exegesis read these penultimate considerations in light of God's ultimate self-revelation in Christ. Theologically, neither who God is, nor the purpose of the Genesis account within scripture as a whole, can be understood apart from Christ.[76] And the full meaning of God's self-interpretation in Christ has itself to be worked out by the church with the help of theological exegesis. Such theological exegesis in turn is always oriented toward the question "who is Jesus Christ for us today?" Within the penultimate fallen world and all its ambiguities, the church lives out its vocation as the new humanity in response to this question, always in light of God's ultimate reconciliation of the world to Himself. The relation of historical-critical and theological interpretation is thus governed by the same ultimate-penultimate relation that shapes Bonhoeffer's entire theology as an eschatological understanding of reality.[77]

This ultimate-penultimate tension also ties together Old and New Testament. In no way has the Old Testament become superfluous, nor is it to be read as an important but merely secondary source. Rather, the Old Testament has its' own relative autonomy and validity as the penultimate reality precisely because it is now carried and fulfilled by the ultimate word of God in Christ. To combat the theological anti-Semitism of his day, Bonhoeffer argues that the historical reality of the incarnate God in the Jewish Messiah Jesus ties Christianity and the occident indissolubly to the Old Testament and Judaism.

Reading the Old Testament with the Jews keeps open the question of who Christ is.[78] At the same time, the Christian reader, if Christ is truly God's incarnate Word, will have to read the Old Testament story and its sources in light of this revelation.[79]

Bonhoeffer has left us two published examples of theological exegesis, both of the Old Testament: his theological interpretation of Genesis chapters 1–3,[80] and his short treatise on the Psalms as the prayer book of the Bible. We will briefly examine the latter. Without once mentioning his name, Bonhoeffer follows in Augustine's footsteps by reading the Psalms ecclesiologically as the prayers of Christ and the church. Bonhoeffer justifies this approach by citing Christ's own claim that the Psalms predict his ministry and Christ's deliberate use on the cross of phrases from the Psalms, as well as the claim by the writer of Hebrews that Christ himself speaks in the Psalms of David.[81] The Psalms are, as it were, the voice of Christ already pregnant with the church.[82] By working through the Psalms christologically, the church learns to pray with the voice of Christ. All Psalms are to be read from the point of view that in Christ all things have been fulfilled.[83] Yet, how is the Christian to pray through the imprecatory Psalms? Bonhoeffer thinks that we can still pray that the wrath of God may be poured out over all of His enemies, but with the Psalmist, we should turn the judgment of others over to God. God himself, however, has focused all the wrath of sin and evil on Christ at the cross, who defeated them through his death and resurrection. Hence through a Christological lens, the message of wrath becomes one of grace: "Jesus Christ himself asked for the execution of God's punishment on his own body, and thus he leads me daily back to the somberness and grace of his cross for myself and for all the enemies of God."[84] Bonhoeffer argues that the Psalms should guide our individual prayers, but as the prayer book of the new humanity in Christ, they should really be part of the liturgy and shape communally our understanding of who God is and who we are to become.

## 4. Conclusion: The Sacrament of the Word

This liturgical aspect of spiritual exegesis takes us to our final point, namely the subservience of biblical exegesis to preaching and the Eucharist. This sacramental aspect of Bonhoeffer's theology should once and for all obviate any criticism of his exegetical approach as following a dualistic epistemology by removing God's presence from the real realm of history.[85] The opposite is the case, but Bonhoeffer insists that history and temporality have to be understood from God's rather than our perspective.[86] For Bonhoeffer, preaching of the Word and the Eucharist are two different modes of God's becoming present among his people. Preaching, in fact, is for him a third sacrament, the sacrament of the word (*sacramentum verbi*).[87] Theology is merely the church's guarding, ordering memory of the Word,[88] a necessary but merely descriptive discipline. Preaching, on the other hand, is a sacrament that makes possible the direct encounter with God and his address to us: "the scriptures belong essentially (*wesentlich*) to the preaching office; the congregation, however, to the sermon. Scripture wants to be interpreted and preached. It is not, in the first instance, an edifying book for the community."[89] Instead, exegesis is subservient to preaching Christ and preaching legitimates itself as the incarnation of Christ: "The sermon derives from the incarnation of Jesus Christ and is determined through the incarnation of Jesus Christ. It does not originate in any general truth or experiences. The word of the sermon is the incarnate Christ himself. The incarnate Christ is God. Hence the sermon is Christ himself. God *as* human being, Christ *as* word. As word he walks among his community."[90] In preaching, the congregation encounters the cosmic *Logos* in whom all things co-inhere and in whom the church subsists. Just as the Eucharist unifies the body of believers and impresses on them the cruciform being of Jesus, the sacrament of the Word draws the listener toward Christ-likeness. Both sacraments belong inseparably together.

Since the same Christ is present in both sacraments through the power of the Holy Spirit, preaching and the Eucharist are related means of conforming the believer to Christ-likeness. In other words, the ancient theme of deification resurfaces also in preaching: God became man so that man could become like God. Luther puts it this way: "You see that God pours himself and Christ, his beloved son, into us and, conversely, draws ourselves into him, so that he becomes completely human and we completely divinized."[91] The sacraments of the Word and of the Eucharist are thus both means for the believers' divinization and thus for their becoming most fully human in the image of the God-man. The church, to put it in Bonhoeffer's terms, "is the place where the taking shape of Jesus Christ is proclaimed and where it happens. Christian ethics stand in service to this proclamation and event."[92]

Because God makes *Himself* present through preaching, the theological exegesis underlying the sermon should not be motivated by the attempt to make the scriptures relevant. The claim that the Bible has to be made relevant for the present already fails to understand that the Christ who is present in the Scriptures determines what reality actually is.[93] It is wrong to read the scriptures, including the New Testament, as templates for current actions or as manuals of wisdom. For the scriptures proclaim the incarnation, death, and resurrection of Christ,[94] and the concrete issues besetting a congregation have to be transposed into the universal situation of humanity before God. For example, when in the exegesis of the Word, Christ himself becomes present, "the one who formerly considered himself important as a man, national socialist, or Jew, becomes someone who considers himself now only sinner, called one, or forgiven one."[95] In this way, the door is opened for the authentic situation of a human being before God, and room is made for the Holy Spirit to speak into our concrete situation. Because of this Christ-reality, the texts, when followed carefully, will become relevant all by themselves because they will speak out against abuses of humanity. Relying on this living presence and power of Christ in the reading of his word will save us from trying to establish eternal norms on the basis of our own cultural situation that may become unworkable for posterity.[96] In drawing attention to this intrinsically applicatory dimension of reading, Bonhoeffer reminds us that biblical exegesis is essentially "translation," that is, the making present to *our* particular circumstances the one Christ-reality. In this sense, the interpretation of scripture indeed does link heaven and earth by supporting the church in fulfilling its vocation as a place of God's presence and thus as the only true source for the renewal of our humanity.

## NOTES

1  It may be useful to distinguish between theological and spiritual exegesis, insofar as some biblical critics may agree that even philological work for establishing the meaning of the text requires sensibility to theological conceptions and yet they remain indifferent to the spiritual realities expressed by these theological concepts.

2  For the purposes of this article, I distinguish between the "school of historical criticism" with its modernist and Enlightenment presuppositions cloaked in the guise of objectivity on the one hand, and historical-critical tools of exegesis which are, of course indispensible, on the other hand. In Germany, the historical-critical school or method came under serious attack in Barth's day and was declared officially as untenable by Gerhard Maier in the seventies. Maier argued that "the historical critical method, in its actual application, has become an impenetrable screen which simply does not allow certain statements any more, even though they may be proved a thousand times in the experience of the believers. This is not evil intent but the helplessness into which a falsely selected method blunders." The historical-critical method is finished because its supposed objectivity has revealed itself as biased ideology. See Gerhard Maier, *The End of the Historical-Critical Method*, trans. Edwin W. Leverenz, (St. Louis, MO: Concordia Publishing House, 1977), pp. 11–12.

3  Martin Rumscheidt, *Adolf von Harnack: Liberal Theology at Its Height* (Philadelphia, PA: Fortress Press, 1991), p. 27.

4  Martin Heidegger, *Ontology: The Hermeneutics of Facticity*, trans. John Van Buren (Bloomington, IN: Indiana University Press, 1999), p. xx.

5  Frances M. Young, *Biblical Exegesis and the Formation of Christian Culture* (Cambridge: Cambridge University Press, 2007), p. 139.

6  *Ibid.*, p. 160.

7  *Ibid.*, p. 129.

8  *Ibid.*, p. 209.

9  The difference was rather greater attention to narrative context in Antiochene typological exegesis, and to the spiritual content beyond narrative in Alexandrian allegorical exegesis. In the ancient world, "language was symbolic, and its meaning lay in that to which it referred ... [t]he difference between 'literal' and 'allegorical' references was not absolute, but lay on a spectrum" (*ibid.*, p. 120). Therefore neither literalism nor greater historicity distinguished ancient typology from allegory. Rather, the Antiochene school objected to the neglect of narrative coherence by Alexandrine allegory. Both schools, however, used similar tools and engaged in spiritual interpretation (*ibid.*, p. 176).

10  Hans-Georg Gadamer, *Truth and Method*, trans. Joel Weinsheimer and Donald G. Marshall, (New York, NY: Continuum, 1994), pp. 418–428.

11  *Ibid.*, p. 421.

12  *Ibid.*, pp. 426–427.

13  *Ibid.*, p. 428.

14  John Barton, *The Nature of Biblical Criticism* (Louisville, KY: Westminster John Knox Press, 2007), p. 57.

15  *Ibid.*, p. 6.

16  Gadamer, *Truth and Method*, pp. 306 ff.

17  Barton, *The Nature of Biblical Criticism*, p. 59.

18  *Ibid.*

19  *Ibid.*, p. 59.

20  Gadamer, *Truth and Method*, pp. 362 ff.

21  *Ibid.*, p. 374.

22  See Karlfried Froehlich, "Introduction" to *Biblical Interpretation in the Early Church* (Phila-delphia, PA: Fortress Press, 1984), pp. 1–39, 9. As Froelich points out, the apostle Paul establishes the precedent for Christian interpreters of scriptures by claiming that "the fulfillment of messianic prophecy in the coming, death, and resurrection of Jesus made the Jewish Scriptures the book of the Christians, the essential key to their understanding of the events which had taken place among the disciplines of the first generation." Jesus as the center of God's history with humanity meant "[a] new reading of God's history with his people . . . which contrasted with the old reading like Spirit and Letter, even life and death (2 Cor. 3:6 ff)." See also F. G. W. H. Lampe's assertion: "[l]ike the New Testament writers, the Fathers approach the Old Testament in the conviction that the divine purposes in history are revealed in a pattern of promise and fulfillment, and that this means that the Old Testament can in principle be applied at every point to Christ and the Church." F. G. W. H. Lampe, "The Exposition and Exegesis of Scripture to Gregory the Great," in *The Cambridge History of the Bible: The West From the Fathers to the Reformation* Vol. 2, (Cambridge: Cambridge University Press, 1975), pp. 155–183; at p. 163.

23  Origen, "On First Principles: Book Four," cited in Froehlich, *Biblical Interpretation in the Early Church*, p. 53.

24  Barton, *The Nature of Biblical Criticism*, pp. 178–179.

25  *Ibid.*, p. 188.

26  *Ibid.*, p. 189.

27  Michael Legaspi, *The Death of Scripture and the Rise of Biblical Studies* (Oxford: Oxford University Press, 2010), p. 9. For Legaspi's comments on Barton's position in this context see pp. 167 ff.

28  Yves Congar, *The Meaning of Tradition*, translated by A. N. Woodrow with a foreword by Avery Cardinal Dulles, (San Francisco, CA: Ignatius Press, 2004), p. 41–43. Congar argues that the living presence of God within tradition does not obviate its historical and interpre-tive character: "it is not enough to say that there is a living subject. It must be added that this subject lives *in history* and that historicity is one of its inherent features without, however, implying that its truth is relative or that it is nothing more than the changing thought of men" (*ibid.*, p. 114).

29  Heidegger, *Ontology: The Hermeneutics of Facticity*, p. 181.

30  Ingolf Dalferth, "Die Mitte ist außen " in Christof Landmesser, Hans-Joachim Eckstein, and Hermann Lichtenberger, eds., *Jesus Christus als die Mitte der Schrift. Studien zur Hermeneutik des Evangeliums* (Berlin: Walter de Gruyter, 1997), pp. 173–198; at p. 181.

31  *Ibid.*, p. 193–194.

32  "Referat über historische und pneumatische Schriftauslegung" in *Dietrich Bonhoeffer: Jugend und Studium 1918–1927* Dietrich Bonhoeffer Werke, edited by Eberhard Bethge, Ernst Feil, Christian Gremmesl, Wolfgang Huber, Hans Pfeifer, Albrecht Schönherr, and Heinz Eduard Tödt. Volume 9 (Gütersloh: Christian Kaiser Verlag, 1986), pp. 305–325; at p. 304. Further volumes are henceforth abbreviated as DBW, followed by volume and page numbers.

33  *Ibid.*, p. 306–307.

34  *Ibid.*, p. 307.

35  The German is "pneumatische Auslegung" in DBW 9, p. 312.

36  Barth rejects verbal inspiration on this incarnational basis. Neither prophets nor apostles have channeled God's word but rather conveyed it through their fallible human words truthfully: "In accordance with the Scriptures' testimony about human beings, which also pertains to them [the prophets and apostles], they *could* err with every word and *did* err with every word, and according to the same scriptural testimony, they did nevertheless speak God's word, justified and sanctified by grace alone, based on this very fallible and erring human word." See Karl Barth, *Die Kirchliche Dogmatik. Drittes Kapitel: Die Heilige Schrift* (Zürich: Theologis-cher Verlag Zürich, 1986), p. 588. This and following passages are my translations of Barth.

37  *Ibid.*, p. 589: "The presence of God's Word itself, however, that is, his actual, present being-said and being-heard, is not identical with the existence of this book as such." The Bible is rather an "instrument" used by God.

38  *Ibid.*, p. 588.

39  "Refereat über historische und pneumatische Schriftauslegung" in DBW 9, p. 316.

40   DBW 14, p. 407.
41   *Ibid.*, p. 408 (italics Bonhoeffer's).
42   *Illegale Theologenausbildung in Finkenwalde*, DBW 14, p. 145.
43   See for instance Karl Barth, *Kirchliche Dogmatik* I, 1 §5, "Das Wesen des Wortes Gottes," p. 190: "[W]e have to believe in our faith no less than in the believed Word." Barth laudably intends to ensure that faith depends completely on grace. Even when we confess our faith, this is solely the work of God. Faith certainly is also a human (i.e. ontological) experience but this experience is decided not on the basis of our faith but comes from the Word of God. Barth's concern is to avoid any method that could secure the presence of God. Human experience can never secure (*sicher stellen*) the presence of the Word of God, at least not in a way "that they [human experiences] can be unambiguously signs of his reality" (*ibid.*, p. 191).
44   Dietrich Bonhoeffer, *Act and Being*, DBW 2, p. 85.
45   Bonhoeffer, *Act and Being*, p. 90. See here the related criticism by Alan Torrance that Barth's desire to guard God's otherness leads him to adopt a revelational model that prevents him from adopting categories of personhood for the Trinity. Consequently, Barth cannot properly integrate the immanent and economic Trinity and thus ends up with impersonal Trinitarian "relations" (*Beziehungen*) rather than with more dynamic, personal intercommunion that allows for real human-divine participation. See Alan Torrance, *Persons in Communion: Trinitarian Description and Human Participation* (Edinburgh: T&T Clark, 1996), pp. 260–261.
46   Dietrich Bonhoeffer, "Sein in Christus ist Gerichtetsein auf Christus, das nur möglich ist als 'Schon-Sein' in der Gemeinde Christi " DBW 2, p. 154. By defining faith as "being-in-Christ" Bonhoeffer seeks to unite transcendental and ontological approaches to revelation (*ibid.*). In *Ethics* Bonhoeffer increasingly employs participatory language with words such as "Teilhabe" and "Teilnahme" to express this mode of being (DBW 6, pp. 151, 173, 436).
47   "Christian life means being human in the power of Christ's becoming human, [it means] being judged and pardoned in the power of the cross, living a new life in the power of the resurrection." "Ultimate and Penultimate Things" in *Ethics*, Dietrich Bonhoeffer Works, edited by Clifford Green. Vol. 6. translated by Reinhard Krauss, Charles West, and Douglas W. Stott, (Minneapolis, MN: Fortress Press, 1996), pp. 146–171; at p. 159. Henceforth abbreviated as DBWE (Dietrich Bonhoeffer Works English) and volume number. See also *Letters and Papers from Prison*, DBWE 8, p. 480.
48   Dietrich Bonhoeffer, *Nachfolge*. DBW 4, p. 219. See also *ibid.*, p. 233: "not the justified and sanctified individual is the new human being but the community of faith (*Gemeinde*), the body of Christ, Christ."
49   *Gaudium et Spes*, ch. 4, "Role of the Church in the Modern World", p. 185 ("Christ the New man" restoring our God-likeness") and p. 207 (the church's common journey with humanity). The document also refers to "Christ as the goal of human history" and "center of humanity" (*ibid.*, p. 216).
50   For a fuller description of the connection between Christian Humanism and deification, see Jens Zimmermann. *Humanism and Religion: A Call for the Renewal of Western Culture* (Oxford, UK: Oxford University Press, 2012), pp. 66–68.
51   DBWE 6, p. 341.
52   DBWE 6, p. 263.
53   DBW 6, p. 261.
54   *Ibid.*, p. 262.
55   Post-Synodal Apostolic Exhortation *Verbum Domini* of the Holy Father Benedict XVI (Vatican City: Liberia Editrice Vaticana, 2010), p. 22.
56   *Ibid.*, p. 17. See also Vatican II on Revelation in *Dei Verbum* which refers to Christ "who is himself both the mediator and the sum total of revelation." *Dei Verbum*, in Austin P. Flannery, ed., *Vatican Council II: The Basic Sixteen Documents: Constitutions, Decrees, Declarations* (Northport, NY: Costello Publishing Company, 1996), pp. 97–117, at p. 98. Benedict also sees, like Bonhoeffer, the direct import of the relation between reason and faith for the interpretation of scripture. The division between theological and historical-critical exegesis stems from too narrow a view of reason that rules out "in advance the self-disclosure of God in history" (*Verbum Domini*, p. 65).
57   *Ibid.*, p. 18.
58   The view expressed by Bonhoeffer and Benedict represents the official position of the Roman Catholic Church on revelation: "The writings of the New Testament stand as a

perpetual and divine witness to these [divine] realities." See, *Dei Verbum*, p. 110. Again, like Bonhoeffer, the authors of *Dei Verbum* assert the sacramental qualities of the scriptures, so that, their human qualities notwithstanding, "in the sacred books the Father who is in heaven comes lovingly to meet his children, and talks with them" (*ibid.*, p. 112).

59  *Verbum Domini*, p. 6.

60  Dietrich Bonhoeffer, *Creation and Fall: A Theological Interpretation of Genesis 1–3*. DBWE 3 (Minneapolis, MN: Fortress Press, 1997), p. 22.

61  Dietrich Bonhoeffer, "Referat über historische und pneumatische Schriftauslegung," in DBW 9, pp. 305–323, 314. Bonhoeffer's position here is close to Barth's notion of the text as becoming God's word through an act of divine grace we cannot control or predict. See Karl Barth, "Die Lehre vom Worte Gottes" in *Kirchliche Dogmatik* 5. 1,2, §19–21 (Zürich: Theologischer Verlag, 1986), pp. 586–587.

62  Bonhoeffer, "Schriftauslegung," p. 313.

63  *Ibid.*, p. 312. More recently, Oswald Bayer has confirmed this possible interpretation of Luther's axiom. Rather than an "argument for internal interpretation in the sense of a concordance-method," the statement means that "the scripture is not interpreted by me. Rather it is capable of interpreting itself, in that it interprets me, inscribes and judges my life history, so that the God who is identical with the author of the Holy Scriptures is the author of my life history." Oswald Bayer, "Hermeneutical Theology" in Petr Pokorný and Jan Roskovec, *Philosophical Hermeneutics and Biblical Exegesis* Wissenschaftliche Untersuchungen zum Neuen Testament (Tübingen: Mohr Siebeck, 2002), pp. 103–120, 118.

64  As Bonhoeffer puts it, "Of course one can *also* read the Bible like any other book, and thus from the viewpoint of textual criticism etc. One cannot object to that. Only, one cannot access the true nature of the Bible that way, but merely its surface. . . . Only if we dare to engage the Bible as if here the God who loves us really speaks to us, and does not leave us alone with our questions, only then will be derive joy from the Bible" ("Letter to Rüdiger Schleicher" in DBW 14, p. 145).

65  Bonhoeffer, "Schriftauslegung," DBW 9, p. 316.

66  Bonhoeffer's distinction is between *Sachbeziehung* (reference to the subject matter) and *Geistesbeziehung* (reference to spirit). Only the former is necessary and built into human language. The latter is the work of the divine Spirit (Bonhoeffer, "Schriftauslegung," DBW 9, p. 315).

67  It is necessary to distinguish between the historical-critical school of interpretation as an ideological approach to the Bible, and the historical grammatical tools of exegesis that may be employed within different hermeneutical frameworks. In German terminology, one distinguishes between *historisch-kritischer exegese* (the school) and *historisch grammatischem Ansatz* (historical grammatical "tools" of exegesis).

68  Bonhoeffer, *Creation and Fall*, DBWE 3, p. 22.

69  Bonhoeffer, "Schriftauslegung," DWB 9, p. 319. Hence Bonhoeffer's Barthian statement that the Bible is merely a literary-historical source for the historical critic but *witness* for spiritual exegesis (*ibid.*, p. 320). See also DBW 14, p. 404: "The most concrete element of the Christian message and textual interpretation is not a human act of presencing (*Vergegenwärtigung*) but always God Himself, the holy Spirit."

70  Bonhoeffer, "Vorlesung: Christologie" in *Berlin 1932–33*, DBW 12, pp. 279–348, 341.

71  In Bonhoeffer's words it is not the "how" question but the "what" (does it mean) question that is more important. It is helpful to read his statement on the virgin birth in light of similar remarks made by Bonhoeffer with regard to the Eucharist. Not how God is present, but that he is present is of greater importance. In other words, one cannot doubt Bonhoeffer's insistence on God's real presence at the Eucharistic table, nor his belief in the divinity of Christ. In the last phase of his thinking, Bonhoeffer reiterates his view on miraculous doctrines. Revelation occurred in this world and for this world, and thus warrants a theocentrically grounded anthropocentrism "not in the sense of liberal, mystical, pietistic, ethical theology, but in the biblical sense of creation, and the incarnation, crucifixion and resurrection of Jesus Christ." To make the virgin birth and the Trinity equally important pieces of a theological system that one has to accept in order to be able to call oneself a Christian ("Friss Vogel oder stirb") is the kind of Barthian revelational positivism that Bonhoeffer criticizes as unbiblical, because it does not do justice to levels or stages of knowledge. See Bonhoeffer, "Stufen der Erkenntnis," *Widerstand und Ergebung*, DBW 8,

p. 415. Clearly, at this point, Bonhoeffer's approach is open to the role of tradition and doctrinal development as guarded by the church in determining biblical meaning.

72   As Martin Kuske has shown, "Bonhoeffer perceives in the Old *and* the New Testament the Word of God, because it is the *one* God, who speaks in both Testaments." Thus the whole Bible is the Word of God when read with reference to Christ, and therefore, "for Bonhoeffer, the problem of having to legitimate the Old Testament in contrast to a predetermined and unproblematic authority of the New Testament does not exist." This unified view of the Bible distances Bonhoeffer from his teachers Harnack and Seeberg, and puts him closer to Karl Barth, and, indeed, Martin Luther. See Martin Kuske, *Das Alte Testament als Buch von Christus: Dietrich Bonhoeffers Wertung und Auslegung des Alten Testaments* (Göttingen: Vandenhoeck & Ruprecht, 1971), p. 26.

73   Dietrich Bonhoeffer, "Biblical Interpretation" in *The Young Bonhoeffer 1918–1927*, DBWE 9 (Minneapolis, MN: Fortress Press, 1986), p. 297.

74   DBWE 3, p. 22.

75   "The name Jesus Christ, in which God reveals himself, interprets itself in the life and death of Jesus Christ. After all, the New Testament does not consist in an endless repetition of the name Jesus Christ, but that which this name encompasses is interpreted (*ausgelegt*) in events, concepts and sentences that are understandable for us." *DBW* 6, p. 338.

76   *Ibid.*, pp. 22–23.

77   See Bonhoeffer, "Ultimate and Penultimate Things," *Ethics*, DBWE 6, pp. 146–171.

78   I take this to mean that Old and New Testament are to be read in a penultimate-ultimate tension that takes seriously the possibility of not believing that Jesus is the Jewish Messiah, while at the same time reading the Old Testament as fulfilled in the New Testament (see DBW 6, pp. 94–95).

79   Bonhoeffer thus avoids any simple successionism in his approach to the Old Testament. For a similar Catholic attempt, see Benedict's *Verbum Domini*, p. xx.

80   Bonhoeffer, *Creation and Fall: A Theological Exposition of Genesis 1–3*. DBWE 3 (Minneapolis, MN: Fortress Press, 1997).

81   Heb. 2:12; 10:5. DBW 5, p. 111.

82   For parallels with Bonhoeffer's Christological reading, see Michael Fiedrowicz' general introduction to Augustine's *Exposition on the Psalms*. Augustine, *Exposition of the Psalms*, Vol. 1, *Psalms 1–32*. In *The Works of Saint Augustine: A translation for the 21st century*, ed. John E. Rotelle, (Brooklyn, NY: New City Press, 1990), pp. 13–66, especially p. 55.

83   Dietrich Bonhoeffer, *Prayerbook of the Bible*, DBWE 5 (Minneapolis, MN: Fortress Press, 1996), pp. 158–159, 175.

84   Bonhoeffer, DBWE 5, p. 175.

85   Richard Weikart arrives at this conclusion in "Scripture and Myth in Dietrich Bonhoeffer," *Fides et Historia*, Vol. 25 (1993), pp. 12–25, at p. 13. Weikart does not grasp the hermeneutical concerns of Bonhoeffer's refusal to go beyond the word of scripture to the real events (p. 19). Bonhoeffer realizes the interpretive quality of knowledge and rightly rejects the historical-critical separation between facts and interpretation by insisting that the gospel accounts are theological interpretations of events. Thus Bonhoeffer's approach is not "irrationalist" (p. 16) but rather "anti-rationalist."

86   See his Christology lectures on this topic in DBW 12, pp. 294–295.

87   Bonhoeffer, DBW 14, p. 507.

88   Bonhoeffer, DBW 2, p. 130: "Theology is a function of the church; for church is not without preaching, preaching not without memory; theology, however, is the memory of the church."

89   Bonhoeffer, DBW 6, p. 397.

90   Bonhoeffer, "Schreitet durch seine Gemeinde" (DBW 14, pp. 502–503).

91   The German terms are *vermenschet* and *vergottet* respectively. Martin Luther, *D. Martin Luthers Werke. Kritische Gesamtausgabe* (Weimar, 1883–), Vol. 20, pp. 229–230. Cited as a 1526 sermon in Kurt E. Marquart, "Luther and Theosis," in *Concordia Theological Quarterly*, Vol. 64 (2000), pp. 182–206, at p. 185.

92   Bonhoeffer, DBWE 6, p. 102.

93   Bonhoeffer, DBW 14, p. 405.

94   Bonhoeffer, DBW 14, pp. 411–412.

95   Bonhoeffer, DBW 14, p. 410.

96   Bonhoeffer, DBW 14, p. 415.

# 11

# "ASCENDING THE MOUNTAIN, SINGING THE ROCK: BIBLICAL INTERPRETATION EARTHED, TYPED, AND TRANSFIGURED"

## KEVIN J. VANHOOZER

*I. Introduction: Does Evangelical Protestantism Rest Upon a Mistake?*

Evangelicals and Catholics together affirm divine authorship, yet they differ in how they understand its implications for biblical interpretation, with Catholics typically claiming that it entails spiritual or allegorical interpretation and Evangelicals typically denying it. Evangelicals are wary of implying that what God says in Scripture today differs from what God spoke through the prophets in the past, or of following Thomas Aquinas in attributing multiple senses to Scripture: "One way according as to how things are signified through words; and in this consists the literal sense. The other way according to which things are figures of other things, and in this consists the spiritual sense."[1] It is through allegory that earthly things—rocks and mountains, for example—take on heavenly meanings.

"The world is charged with the grandeur of God"—so Gerard Manley Hopkins in 1877. A century later, another poet, Annie Dillard, has to ask: *Do the things of this world have meaning?* Her answer is sobering, to poets and believers alike: "Everywhere Christianity and science hushed the bushes and gagged the rocks . . . drain[ing] the flow of meaning right off the planet. . . . The direction of recent history is toward desacralization, the unhinging of materials from meaning."[2]

"The letter kills, but the Spirit gives life" (2 Cor. 3:6). Is this an indictment of the literal sense, and hence literal interpretation, or is it perhaps an indication of the impotence of a certain stage of redemptive history? Conversely,

*Heaven on Earth?: Theological Interpretation in Ecumenical Dialogue*, First Edition.
Edited by Hans Boersma and Matthew Levering.
© 2013 Blackwell Publishing Ltd. Book compilation © 2013 Blackwell Publishing Ltd.

is the Spirit's life-giving to be associated with the spiritual sense, practices of spiritual interpretation, or the new covenant? This article explores the third option, suggesting that the "mystery" of salvation attested by Scripture— arguably the goal of spiritual interpretation—is not a secret for which one needs some kind of Greek allegorical decoding key, but rather the book of Hebrews and its construal of redemptive history as God's publicly making good on his covenant promise in the history of Jesus Christ, a history that includes Pentecost—which is to say, the church.

### Protestantism and the Desacralization Thesis

There are several versions of what we may call the "desacralization thesis." One popular account locates the fountainhead in fourteenth-century nominalism, whence it received further boosts from the Neo-Thomist Scholastic idea of "pure nature" separate from the order of grace and the Reformation notion of a right to private judgment separate from authoritative church tradition. On this telling, the Reformation was the gateway for the ascendancy of both the Book of Nature and the "natural" sense of Scripture, thus making possible not only modern science but also modern biblical criticism.

Stories are powerful, especially when they are identity narratives. Hans Boersma's redaction of the story of modern theology raises searching questions about the extent to which evangelicals are implicated in the Protestant rejection of allegorizing, and with it, the vision of creaturely participation in heavenly realities. Though Boersma does not assign sole responsibility to the Reformers for modern secularism, capitalism, and individualism, he nevertheless views the Reformation as a tragedy because "it split the unity of the church while it failed to address the problematic decline of the Platonist-Christian synthesis."[3]

That was then. What of the future, and in particular the newfound enthusiasm in some Protestant quarters for "theological interpretation of Scripture"? Evangelicalism is best viewed as a renewal movement within confessional Protestantism, just as Protestantism is best viewed as a renewal movement within Catholicism. Evangelicals today find themselves at a three-pronged fork in the hermeneutical road: they can maintain the grammatical-historical methods of old (i.e., "early modern") Protestants, go "po-mo" (always conversing/emerging but never coming to a statement of the truth), or follow the Roman brick road of ancient-*nouvelle* Catholic sacramentalism.

### An Ontological Deficit

Boersma rightly identifies one of the crucial deficits in contemporary Evangelicalism: an anemic ontology. Langdon Gilkey had identified a similar problem a few decades earlier in connection with the Biblical Theology Movement.[4] What Boersma laments about the Reformation is its failure to recover the premodern mindset "in which the realities of this-worldly existence pointed to greater, eternal realities in which they sacramentally shared."[5] The real problem with Protestant theology is its underlying non-participatory ontology in which things are just things. This "Dragnet" ("Just the facts, ma'am") mentality misses the underlying mystery, sequestering Nature (created reality) from grace (the eternal mystery of the uncreated self-giving love of God). All Hallows Eve shrivels into Halloween and, like Charlie Brown, Protestants find themselves holding their trick-or-treat bag, complaining: "I got a *rock*—a plain, de-grandeured igneous rock." Protestants may not be flat-earthers, but they look to Boersma like earth-*flatteners*, which is equally dangerous.

## II. Sexting the Song: "Earthing" Biblical Interpretation

Have modern exegetes indeed absorbed the modern tendency to "flatten" things out, viewing history as a purely immanent, this-worldly sequence of atomistic events, rather than as a field of divine action in which creatures participate? It is not enough for exegetes to attend to the *length* of history only; they must also attend to its mystery, its *height, breadth*, and *depth*: "the historical includes a participation in the realities known by faith."[6]

### The Prime Hermeneutical Imperative

Evangelical exegetes have by and large tended to focus less on the theological realities about which the text speaks than on determining the meaning of the Bible's human authors with grammatical-historical interpretation. Their prime hermeneutical imperative: to "earth" biblical interpretation, grounding exegesis in an authorial intention discerned by examining the grammar and the immediate historical context (i.e., the world-behind-the-text), usually in its horizontal (i.e., linear, this-worldly) dimension only.

It is not a mistake to "earth" biblical interpretation. The gospel is an eminently *historical* (and hence contextual) affair: "He is risen." Nor were the Reformers wrong in wanting to do justice to what the human authors were saying/doing with their words (i.e., the literal sense) by ascertaining the historical context. If hermeneutics is "the art of discerning the discourse in the work,"[7] then the Evangelical Protestant instinct to earth the divine discourse in human discourse is essentially sound. The question, however, is whether divine authorship is simply human discourse writ holy.

### Whose Discourse? Which Context?

Protestant biblical interpretation displays the influence of Renaissance philology in its passionate commitment to studying how authors use words in their particular contexts.[8] Luther and Calvin are representatives of what Nicholas Wolterstorff terms "authorial discourse" interpretation, where meaning is a function of what authors are saying, and doing, with their words.[9] If the author is speaking metaphorically, then the literal sense—"the way the words run"—is metaphorical. Of course, to recognize whether a stretch of words is meant metaphorically, one has to know what the speaker is talking about—and who the speaker is. The future of spiritual interpretation is inextricably tied up with this latter question: does the divine address coincide with that of the human author without remainder or is there a surplus of meaning?[10]

When Christians confess Scripture to be "the word of the Lord," they acknowledge a mystery and imply that Scripture is more than merely human discourse. "Discourse" is the operative ontological term. As discourse, Scripture is language *in use*—"something someone says (at some time and in some way) to someone about something for some purpose"—and involves many aspects, including verbal "sense" (semantic content; the "what" of meaning) and "reference" (the "about what" of meaning).[11] A sentence's semantic content will always underdetermine reference to the extent that we are unsure *whose discourse* it is.[12] Hence the real point at issue in spiritual interpretation—the mystery of Jesus Christ—involves not only the verbal *sense* of the text but also some indication of *who* is speaking, *about what* (i.e., the referent), and to *whom* (i.e., the intended audience).

### The "Swinburne Test"

The Song of Songs represents the acid test for deciding whether it is reasonable for Christians to read the Bible in terms of the original meaning (i.e., human authorial discourse) only. Swinburne thinks it ludicrous to suppose that even the most literal-minded church father would have read the Song as having "its meaning as a book on its own."[13] It is worth parsing what he means by "on its own."

Swinburne thinks that we should take the biblical text in its literal sense unless "it would be obviously false or inappropriate in the context."[14] Everything thus depends on what we take as the context: "If God is the ultimate author of the Bible and the Church of many centuries its intended audience, then that context will include central Christian doctrines, including those developed in the New Testament."[15] This seems counter-intuitive to evangelical biblical scholars more inclined to say that, while the Bible was written *for* us, it is not written *to* us, which is precisely why we have to muck about in ancient Near Eastern history—so that we can hear the text the way the first audience heard it. By contrast, Swinburne thinks that Christian readers would do better to attend to later, creedal contexts, especially if one views tradition as the Spirit-enabled, "ever-deepening onward flow of the sense of Scripture itself."[16] For Swinburne, then, the meaning of the Song of Songs is "determined by future context" (to use one of his section headings).[17] Divine authorship here implies that Scripture's intended audience is the church of future centuries, an audience that knows better than to take the Song of Songs literalistically.

Origen and Gregory of Nyssa construed the meaning of the Song in terms of God's love for the church. Indeed, for some nineteen centuries the dominant approach to the Song was the allegorical, where interpreters read the Song as meaning something other than what modern readers think it obviously seems to say.[18] Only in the nineteenth century do we see the waning of the allegorical approach and what we might call the "sexting" of the Song (i.e., reading it as an ode to erotic love). Note that the controversy is not over what the Song says (i.e., its semantic content) but what it is *about* (i.e., its reference). Hence the key question: *Who* is the communicative agent directing the words to run this way rather than that?[19]

Tremper Longman, a leading evangelical Old Testament scholar, maintains that there is nothing in the Song itself "that hints of a meaning different from the sexual meaning."[20] He is unimpressed with Hippolytus's suggestion that "Your two breasts are like two fawns" (4:5) is a reference to the Old and New Testaments.[21] To ascribe a spiritual meaning to the bride's two breasts cannot but appear arbitrary, not least because other possible referents—the twin precepts of love of God and neighbor; the sacramental Blood and Water—are all within the bounds of Nicaea and the Rule of Faith.[22] Longman himself, noting parallels with Egyptian and Mesopotamian texts, takes the Song as an anthology of love poems affirming intimacy, sensuality, and sexuality: "the Enlightenment, often rightly vilified by evangelical Christians as robbing us of a sense of the supernatural, may have been a help to *proper* interpretation of the Song of Songs."[23] It would appear that "sexting" has won the exegetical day: "Overwhelmingly, modern interpreters read the book as purely secular love poetry, even soft pornography."[24]

We seem to be at an impasse. Swinburne thinks it obvious that the Song in its creedal context cannot really be about human sexuality; Longman finds it just as obvious that the Song in its original historical context cannot really have been about anything else. Ironically, the divorce between heaven and earth is best illustrated in the divergent ways that various Christians interpret this song celebrating union. The way forward, I submit, is to realize that what the Song is finally *about* depends on *whose discourse* it finally is. The other two aspects—the "about what" and "to whom"—follow from this.

While the Song makes for an excellent litmus test, my primary case study lies elsewhere, in Paul's claim that the rock in the wilderness from which water flowed to quench Israel's thirst "was Christ" (1 Cor. 10:4). There are properly Protestant resources by which to affirm the spiritual sense of Scripture, without having to say that the meaning "changes," resources with which to keep the text earthed even as we discern its heavenly mystery. We shall see that spiritual interpretation is a three-dimensional affair, involving (1) divine discourse, (2) the "what" and the "about what" of meaning, and (3) the church's reading Scripture to gain Christ-mindedness ("to whom" and "for what purpose"). My claim will be that Protestants helped develop an approach for interpreting Scripture theologically—what I shall call "transfigural" interpretation—which Evangelicals, and Catholics, need to recover in order for the Spirit to effect union and communion in Christ. There is a properly Protestant moment to *ressourcement*.

## III.  *Singing the Rock: "Typing" Biblical Interpretation*

### The Spiritual Rock: 1 Cor. 10:1–4

1 Corinthians 10:1–4 is Paul's gloss on Israel's wilderness wanderings, and in particular the peculiar incident of water from the rock mentioned in both Exodus 17:1–7 and Numbers 20:2–13: "For I want you to know, brothers, that our fathers were all under the cloud, and all passed through the sea, and all were baptized into Moses in the cloud and in the sea, and all ate the same spiritual food, and all drank the same spiritual drink. For they drank from the spiritual Rock that followed them, and the Rock was Christ." Paul refers to all Israel drinking the same *spiritual* [*pneumatikos*] drink, the water that came from the *spiritual* Rock, which was Christ. Does Paul's apostolic authority extend to this kind of spiritualizing interpretation? Should Christians today go and do exegetically likewise? Whose discourse is it, what is it really about, and what is the appropriate context in which to interpret it?

Can Evangelicals sing the rock with Paul? Greg Beale acknowledges that New Testament authors often appear to use the Old Testament "non-contextually" (by which he means in disregard of the original historical context), yet he believes that these instances are actually few in number, the exceptions that prove the rule.[25] F. F. Bruce complicates things, however, by distinguishing between grammatical-historical and theological exegesis, saying "the whole canon provides a theological context," and suggesting that the history of the Bible's reception as Scripture in the church constitutes "a further context."[26] Will the real determining context please stand up?

### Singing Falsetto? The Agony and the Allegory

Evangelicals have been loath to "sing the rock" (i.e., interpret the Old Testament christologically). To most evangelical biblical scholars, spiritual interpretation resembles a species of allegorizing whereby the meaning is other than [*allos* = "another, different"] what was said [*agoreuein* = "to speak openly"]. Explicit prophecies are one thing, but when it comes to texts that, in their original context, appear to refer to the immediate historical context, the exegetical law is clear: "Thou shalt not commit allegory."

The church fathers' reading practice is quite different. Many noted a correspondence between the manna and the water that nourish Israel in the wilderness and the bread and wine (themselves symbols for Christ's body and blood) that nourish the church, another pilgrim nation.[27] Almost any mention of wood in the Old Testament could, with a little interpretive ingenuity, be made to refer to Jesus' cross, as Justin Martyr does with Moses' staff.[28] Indeed, Augustine observes with respect to Numbers 20:11 that "The double striking prefigures the two pieces of wood on the cross."[29] The main problem with such suggestions, according to evangelical biblical scholars, is that there seem to be no criteria for distinguishing legitimate from illegitimate interpretations. Absent the original context, there are no constraints—no air traffic control—with which to rein in flights of exegetical fancy: "allegory (in general) rests on parallels between *ideas* and can become too often self-generated and arbitrary."[30]

Allegorical interpretation nevertheless continues to receive learned and spirited defenses. For example, Robert Louis Wilken insists that with regard to Scripture, "the task of interpretation is never exhausted by a historical account. The text belongs to a world that is not defined solely by its historical referent."[31] Allegory pertains to this "other" meaning (i.e., the spiritual sense), namely, the "Christological" dimension of the Old Testament that comes to light only retrospectively: "Context needs to be understood to embrace the Church, its liturgy, its way of life, its practices and institutions, its ideas and beliefs"[32]—precisely the point Swinburne was making in speaking of meaning determined by future context.

What *is* Paul doing with Numbers 20? No one view on the New Testament use of the Old Testament holds sway among Evangelical biblical scholars. Some insist that the New Testament authors find only what the Old Testament authors originally intended, though they may "apply" that single meaning in new ways. Others say that the New Testament authors, through rabbinic techniques like "midrash" or "pesher," discover meanings in the Old Testament texts that their human authors did not intend. Still others maintain that the Holy Spirit intended a "fuller" meaning (*sensus plenior*) that Paul eventually discerns.[33] Richard Longenecker argues, against the second and third possibilities, that we cannot replicate the way the New Testament authors read the Old Testament because we are not inspired as they were.[34]

The main points of contention concern whose discourse it is (Moses' or Paul's), what it is about (earthly or heavenly realities), and to whom it is addressed (ancient Israel or the church). With regard to the first point, let us say provisionally that Paul does not change the *verbal sense* of Numbers 20 (i.e., its semantic content) but identifies its ultimate referent. When Paul says "the Rock was Christ," he is not changing *what* the human author of Numbers says but rather specifying what that author was (unknowingly) talking *about*. This explains "how a text can 'deepen' in meaning *without departing from its inherent* [i.e., literal] *sense*."[35]

If Evangelical exegetes are to practice spiritual interpretation, they will need to be able to distinguish it from the kind of allegorizing that relocates textual meaning to a higher (divine) level, effectively dislocating it from its original human discourse. While allegorizing as a reading strategy can be applied to almost any text, there are no non-canonical texts to which the church fathers applied the category *spiritual sense*. This suggests that the "rule" governing Christian allegory pertains to Scripture alone. Indeed, the Old Testament "is a stumbling block for the application of general hermeneutical understanding to the tasks of reading biblical texts well."[36] Allegorizing becomes problematic, then, insofar as it resembles a general hermeneutical strategy by which later readers find new meanings in texts *unrelated* to the human authorial discourse. If allegorizing is to have an Evangelical future, it will be important to show that it is neither free-wheeling nor deregulated, but rather ruled by the literal sense and the event of Jesus Christ: "the conflation of figural reading with allegorical interpretation as it has been classically derided simply blocks understanding of what Christian interpretation of Hebrew Scripture . . . is all about."[37] The way forward is to distinguish between an allegorical hermeneutics in general and what we may term, by way of contrast, a special allegorical—or better, typological—interpretation that I shall in due course rename "transfigural."

## *IV. Can Evangelicals Sing the Rock?* Ressourcing *the Reformers*

### What Protestants May Contribute

It is true that Protestants have sometimes sided with the modern masters of suspicion. Biblical exegetes in particular were embarrassed to introduce their Fathers (and their antiquated ontologies) to their peers in the academy. *However, this desire to "kill the Fathers" is a pathology of Protestantism, not its essential principle.*[38] There are simply too many examples of Protestant theologians, from Calvin to Bavinck, who hold the fathers in high regard. Nor ought we forget that it was Barth's discovery, *ressourcement*-style, of Heppe's compendium of Reformed dogmatics that enabled him to complete his break from Protestant liberalism.

Martin Luther hated what he called allegories, yet he nevertheless found Christ in the Old Testament: "All the genuine sacred books agree in this, that all of them preach and inculcate [*treiben*] Christ."[39] There is a fly, however, in this Protestant ointment. If exegesis focuses on textual meaning rather than events, the critics say, then to think of typology as a form of exegesis is to commit a category mistake: "Typology is not an exegesis or interpretation of a text but the study of relationships between events, persons, and institutions recorded in biblical texts."[40] By way of preliminary response, let me make three points, corresponding to the three aspects of discourse mentioned earlier (i.e., who is speaking, about what, and to whom). First, I take typology to be a form of theological interpretation that responds to something unique to the biblical text, a special rather than general hermeneutic that is particularly attentive to the divine authorial discourse and its organic unity.[41] The second point is related to the first: if our goal is understanding biblical discourse, then we have to discover not only what is said but also what it is said about. And finally, doing justice to typology requires us to expand our notions of historical context, recognizing that later readers also figure among the divine addressees.

**Reading the Rock: From Basil and Chrysostom to Calvin and Clowney**
The Reformers did not invent typology, as the following quote from Basil's
fourth-century *Treatise on the Holy Spirit* makes clear: "The type is a mani-
festation of things to come through an imitation (*mimesis*) allowing us to see
in advance the things of the future in such wise that they can be understood. Adam is thus 'a figure of him who is to come,' the rock is Christ
typically (*tupikos*), and the water from the rock is the type of the quickening
power of the Logos."[42] Chrysostom says that a type is like a black and
white outline. We have a general idea, but we need the coloring to make
the picture clear and distinct. Israel's manna from heaven and water from
the rock are "outlines" of the bread and wine respectively that comprise the
Lord's Supper.

Cyprian criticizes these Eucharistic interpretations, preferring to connect
the water from the rock to the water that streamed from the pierced side of
Christ: "Every time that water alone is mentioned in the Holy Scripture, it
refers to Baptism."[43] The association of the water from the rock with baptism
rather than the Lord's Supper is the more common Patristic interpretation, 1
Cor. 10:4 notwithstanding.[44]

We here come to what Frances Young calls the problem of "cross-
referencing."[45] There is a conflict of interpretations, even among the Fathers,
over what the water from the rock means. Theodoret, for example, offers the
following expansive gloss on 1 Cor. 10:2–4: "The things of former time were
types of the later. . . . The sea is the type of the baptismal font, the cloud of
the Holy Spirit, and Moses of Christ our Saviour; the staff is a type of the
Cross; Pharaoh of the devil and the Egyptians of the fallen angels; manna of
the divine food and the water from the rock of the Savior's blood."[46] Let us
call such attempts at detailed point-by-point interpretation as Theodoret's
"bad type." The temptation is to dismiss it as deregulated allegorizing, when
it fact it is governed, albeit rather loosely, by the Rule of Faith.

Young argues that the attempt to distinguish typology from allegory is
born of modern historical consciousness.[47] These are deep waters, and I can
only dog paddle. I am aware of Lewis Ayres's concern that systematic theologians borrow Trinitarian capital—the *result* of Patristic exegesis—but seek
to distance themselves from the *processes* of Patristic exegesis.[48] While Ayres
and I agree that theology is fundamentally contemplation of Scripture, I am
less inclined to take descriptions of Patristic exegesis as normative for biblical
interpretation today.[49] He may be right historically about the difficulty of
distinguishing allegory and typology, but I believe some such distinction is
both necessary and legitimate. I therefore propose to "reform" (not reject!)
Patristic figural interpretation. The guiding assumption is that Protestants too
are part of the church "catholic." The way forward—call it "good type"—is to
recover not modern historicist assumptions but rather the Protestant Reformers' habit of following typological *trajectories* (i.e., the broad sweep of
redemptive history), as opposed to compiling allegorical *inventories* (i.e., a list

of detailed correspondences). Note that the focus in making inventories is on the multiple referents of individual words; by contrast, what comes to the fore in following trajectories is the importance of following the whole discourse.

How, then, does Calvin interpret what Paul is saying about the water from the rock? First, he rightly sees that Paul appeals to Israel's experience in order to warn his Corinthian readers not to repeat Israel's mistake (i.e., idolatry). The Israelites were God's people too; they too had "the same tokens of God's grace"[50]—"They all ate the same spiritual food and drank the same spiritual drink" (1 Cor. 10:3–4a)—yet they did not escape divine judgment. By "same tokens of God's grace," Calvin is referring to baptism and Eucharist. In the manna and the water from the rock "there was a sacrament which corresponded with the sacred Supper."[51] Modern biblical scholars may here demur, insisting that we cannot read a Eucharistic meaning back into Paul: "[Paul] is not arguing that the Red Sea crossing was a sacrament."[52] Yet Calvin asks: "Why then does Paul turn earthly benefits into sacraments, and seek to find some spiritual mystery in them?"[53] Because, he answers, God is showing himself to be a deliverer from earthly and heavenly distress alike. The manna and the water from the rock had a material role to play in preserving Israel, yet it also served "for the spiritual nourishment of souls."[54]

In Calvin's view God neither conflates nor separates but rather joins together the sign and the reality it indicates: "The rock was Christ" (1 Cor. 10:4). He gives the name of the *thing* (*res*) to the *sign* (*signum*). The Rock is not literally (i.e., materially, metaphysically) but spiritually Christ. The rock signifies Christ not by arbitrary human convention but through a divine ordination which ensures that the thing indicated is really, albeit mysteriously, present.[55] The point of the sacraments is to "lead us from the contemplation of the earthly element to the heavenly mystery."[56] The earthly participates in the heavenly "because the Lord, by the secret power of his Spirit, fulfills what he promises."[57]

What is going on here? Calvin's main concern is not to identify the hidden or deeper meaning of every element in Exodus and Numbers; he is not composing an allegorical inventory. He is concerned rather with discerning the deep continuity in the way God relates to his people (i.e., he is tracing a typological trajectory that shows both sameness and increase). The real point Calvin wants to make is not sacramental but covenantal: both the old and the new people of God have similar privileges and responsibilities.

Fast forward five hundred years to Edmund Clowney, a great-great-great-evangelical-grandchild of the Protestant Reformers, whose book *The Unfolding Mystery* argues that the Old Testament is filled with signs—the law, the tabernacle, the whole history of the covenant—that point to Christ: "The story of redemption in the Old Testament is the story of Jesus."[58] Like Calvin, Clowney sees the manna and the water from the rock as a type of God's spiritual provision for his people. He views the people's quarrel with Moses about having no water to drink in Exodus 17 as a covenant lawsuit lodged against Moses, and ultimately against God (the name of the place, Meribah, is related to the legal term *rib*). What happens next is in Clowney's opinion "one of the most amazing incidents in Scripture."[59]

God instructs Moses to take the rod (a symbol of judicial authority, used to beat criminals) with which he had struck and turned the Nile to blood: "Behold, I will stand before you there on the rock at Horeb, and you shall strike the rock, and water shall come out of it" (Exod. 17:6). And so it does. What strikes Clowney, however, is that God stands before Moses and the elders of Israel like a criminal in a dock, a dock made of rock. Moses strikes, and later sings, the rock, praising God for taking on himself the sanction for the people's rebellion. When Moses struck the rock, life-giving water poured out. When Jesus was crucified, blood and water poured from his side (John. 19:34). Jesus had earlier prophesied that anyone who thirsts should come to him to drink, and that from the hearts of those who believe in him "will flow rivers of living water" (John. 7:38). John helpfully informs us that Jesus was talking about the Spirit (John. 7:39). Clowney connects the typological dots: "The water that Christ gives is the water of the Holy Spirit. . . . The Spirit of life is given through Christ's death."[60] Clowney can even explain why Moses was judged so severely for striking the rock again (this time twice) in Numbers 20: "Only once, at His appointed time, does God bear the stroke of our doom."[61]

### Validity in Typological Interpretation: The Formal and Material Protestant Principles

I leave to others to decide whether typology existed as a distinct exegetical method among the church fathers, or whether its distinction from allegory marks the difference between the schools of Antioch and Alexandria.[62] Yet even Young, who problematizes the distinction, goes on to distinguish an "ikonic" (intratextual) mimesis that preserves the narrative coherence between type and antitype from a merely "symbolic" (extratextual) mimesis that imposes a system of non-historical, non-narrative connections between referents.[63] Whatever we decide to call it, I submit that the Reformers put this Pauline and patristic practice of finding Christ in the Old Testament on surer ground by providing a better theological warrant.

We get a glimpse of what this warrant is in Samuel Mather's 1705 work *The Figures or Types of the Old Testament, by which Christ and the Heavenly Things of the Gospel were Preached and Shadowed unto the People of God of Old.*[64] Mather proposes four rules for understanding a genuine type, which he defines as "a Shadow of good things to come."[65] The first rule is that only God can author a type: "It is not safe to make any thing a Type merely upon our own fancies and imaginations; it is God's Prerogative to make types."[66] Second, types are not only signs, but also seals, visible promises that communicate the good things that are to come.[67] Third, types "relate not only to the Person of Christ; but to his Benefits, and to all Gospel Truths and Mysteries."[68] And fourth, there is both a resemblance and a difference between type and antitype. Stated in contemporary terms: the meaning of the type is neither identical (*idem*) with its original historical sense nor wholly other (*allos*) to it, but rather stands in creative continuity (*ipse* identity) with it.[69]

Peter Leithart defends typology on the grounds that "An event of the past can acquire new properties as related events unfold."[70] If I shoot someone and the person dies from the wound a month later, the past event is no longer a shooting but a killing. In similar fashion, the meaning of the biblical text changes too: "Typological reading is simply reading of earlier texts in the light of later texts and events."[71]

I am not inclined myself to say that meaning changes. It is not that typological discourse adds a second, spiritual sense but rather that it *extends* the literal sense. To quote Patrick Fairbairn: the typical meaning "is not properly a different or higher sense, but a different or higher application *of the same sense*."[72] Or, as I prefer to say, the new referent (i.e., "the rock is Christ") is a different and higher (i.e., Christological) *realization* of the same semantic content. Calvin's and Clowney's typological readings simply follow the "Scripture interprets Scripture" principle, ensuring that the focus throughout remains on the unified drama of redemption, with its two-beat rhythm of salvation through judgment.[73] Typological exegesis therefore discovers the plain sense of the author, yet it also discovers that the human authors tell more than they can know, for they are not always cognizant of the ultimate referent of their discourse.[74] It is only when we read the plain sense of the human author in canonical context that we discern the divinely intended "plain canonical sense," together with its "plain canonical referent": Jesus Christ.

What is Protestant about the typology I have in mind is the insistence on the correspondence of word (same sense) and Spirit (same economy, different referent). It is not a matter of "signs" corresponding to two kinds of "things" as much as a single discourse serving as the medium for more than one illocutionary act. The human locutions and their semantic content do not change, but the divine illocutions and their historical referents (and, as we shall see, addressees) do. For example, the Day of Atonement is a type of Christ's death because the verbal sense in both cases has to do with the forgiveness that comes from atonement; the referent, however, concerns the blood of bulls and goats on the one hand and the blood of Jesus Christ on the other.[75] It is not that a new meaning has been added, but rather that the original meaning has finally achieved its Christological *telos*. The typological sense is not the "other" of the literal but the "same" (*ipse*); the typological meaning *is* the literal meaning of the discourse when viewed in canonical, which is to say redemptive-historical context. It is therefore misleading to reduce God's authorial discourse to that of the original human author's. On the contrary, divine discourse pertains to what God is now saying about Christ to the church, yesterday and today.

We can now make explicit the logic governing best typological practice. The formal principle of Protestant spiritual interpretation derives from its confession of divine authorship: read the biblical parts in light of the canonical whole (i.e., as a unified divine discourse). Divine authorship also gives rise to the material principle of spiritual interpretation: read God's involvement in Israel's history as elements in a unified history or theodrama whose climax and end is Jesus Christ. Even more succinctly: read Scripture in redemptive-historical context.[76] The typology the Protestant Reformers practiced ultimately presupposes neither *linear* nor *sacramental* but rather *redemptive* history, where type is related to antitype as anticipation is related to its realization, promise to fulfillment. The rule, then, is never to dislodge the spiritual sense given to persons, things, and events from the biblical narratives in which they are emplotted. In the words of Hans Frei: "figuration or typology was a natural extension of literal interpretation. It was literalism at the level of the whole biblical story and thus of the depiction of the whole of historical reality."[77] To be sure, not every piece of wood figures the cross. It is the redemptive-historical context that both enables and constrains the spiritual sense. *What spiritual significance things have is not a function of their sheer createdness but rather their role in the ongoing drama of redemption.* Typology is ultimately a matter of *theodramatic mimesis*, in which later things, persons, and events recapitulate earlier ones in a way that highlights their *ipse* identity.[78]

"Theodramatic mimesis" is my catch-all term for the intersection of divine authorial discourse, the *ipse* continuity/discontinuity of verbal sense and reference, and the redemptive-historical context of both text and contemporary readers. To speak of the redemptive-historical context is to see typological unity as intrinsic to Scripture itself rather than an imposition by an interpretive community. It is also to remember that Scripture not only describes but also plays a part in the triune economy of revelation and redemption: typological interpretation is a matter of verbal sense and Spirited reference, a means by which the Holy Spirit leads readers through earthly shadows to the incarnate heavenly reality of Jesus Christ.

The Protestant principle, so understood, is less a wound in than a gift to the body of Christ. At their evangelical best, Protestants have something positive to contribute to the church catholic. Their insight into the conjunction between divine discourse and redemptive history provides a framework with which to account for best Patristic interpretive practice. Protestantism need not be something from which the church has to recover. On the contrary, its emphasis on divine typological discourse in redemptive-historical context represents a net gain for spiritual—which is to say, theological—interpretation of Scripture.

## V. Ascending the Mount: "Transfiguring" Biblical Interpretation

Thus far we have been "singing the rock" on the plains with Paul, using Protestant insights to reclaim best Patristic interpretive practice. It is now time to ascend the mountain with Peter, James, and John, to see what Patristic theologians have to contribute to Evangelical Protestants. The episode of Jesus' transfiguration is one of the most striking pictures we have in the New Testament of heaven on earth. Moreover, thanks to 2 Peter and Patristic commentators, it also provides important insight into the "to whom" of Scripture's divine discourse.

### What Does Transfiguration Have to Do with Spiritual Interpretation?

Why Transfiguration? I confess that its verbal proximity to "figuration" is part of the attraction, though the connection ultimately goes much deeper than etymology. The real justification for associating the Transfiguration with biblical interpretation is Paul's comment about the rock being Christ. In Augustine's words: "No Christian will dare say that the narrative must not be taken in a figurative sense. For St. Paul says: 'Now all these things that happened to them were symbolic [τυπικῶς]' "[79]—a prefiguring of the future. Paul explicitly states that the story of Israel's wilderness wanderings was written "for our instruction, on whom the end of the ages [τὰ τέλη τῶν αἰώνων] has come" (1 Cor. 10:11).

To speak of the "end of the ages" is to invoke eschatology, the *telos* of redemptive history and hence the heart of spiritual interpretation. Indeed, one might describe the typological trajectory of "water from the rock" in terms of its archaeology and teleology respectively. One needs both moments in order to expound its "plain canonical sense."

The Transfiguration has hermeneutical significance; it eventually helps the disciples, and us, to discern the plain canonical sense of the Old Testament. It is therefore a key that unlocks the Old Testament, signified by the presence of Moses (the Law) and Elijah (the prophets): "[The Transfiguration] stands as a gateway to the saving events of the Gospel, and is a mirror in which the Christian mystery is seen in its unity. Here we perceive that the living and the dead are one in Christ, that the old covenant and the new are inseparable, that the Cross and the glory are of one, that the age to come is already here, that our human nature has a destiny of glory."[80] In the Transfiguration, the disciples experience the "end of the ages" and the grandeur of God.

### A Brief Theological Interpretation of the Transfiguration

The transfiguration is a mini-summa that recalls God's presence in the history of Israel and anticipates the consummation of the covenant: the glory of God's presence in his people and all creation. As such, it provides program notes as it were for understanding the whole narrative sweep of Scripture.

The focal point of the event is Jesus' face, that bodily place where one's personal identity shines through. Matthew and Mark use the Greek verb μεταμορφόω to describe the transfigural change in his face and attire, which become radiant. The literary context of the event is also significant. All three Synoptic Gospels have the same sequence: Peter's confession; Jesus' prediction of his passion; Transfiguration. In each case, Jesus' statement to his disciples that some will not taste death until they see the kingdom of God immediately precedes the account of his Transfiguration (Matt. 16:28; Mk. 9:1; Lk. 9:27). All three accounts mention the presence of Elijah and Moses as well, and Luke tells us what they were talking about: "his departure [*exodus*], which he was about to accomplish at Jerusalem" (Lk. 9:31).

In resolving the riddle of Jesus' identity, the Transfiguration also provides us with a paradigm for understanding what typology, as a form of spiritual interpretation, is and does. John Chrysostom asks, "What does 'transfigured' mean? It means that He disclosed a little of the Godhead and showed them the indwelling deity."[81] The Transfiguration is not a change from one substance to another but the event where Jesus is better seen for what he always has been. In the words of St. John Damascus: "He is transfigured . . . not by receiving something he is not, but by revealing to his intimate disciples that which He really is."[82] Something similar happens when the divine discourse shines through the human authorial voices of the Old Testament: Christ's physical body is to his transfiguration what the literal sense is to its spiritual rendering. It is not a matter of leaving the body, or the verbal sense behind, but of penetrating more deeply into their intrinsic nature. The glory (i.e., the divine discourse) that was formerly implicit has become explicit.

### Transfigural Interpretation

According to 1 Peter, the Old Testament prophets themselves wondered what their prophecies referred to—the "about what" of their discourse—"inquiring about the person or time that the Spirit of Christ within them indicated when it testified in advance to the sufferings destined for Christ and the subsequent glory" (1 Pet. 1:11). Paul says the Exodus and wilderness stories "were written down for our instruction" (1 Cor. 10:11), yet it is Peter who informs us that it was revealed to the prophets "that they were serving not themselves [nor their original readers] but you [later interpreters]" (1 Pet. 1:12) when they "testified in advance" [προμαρτυρόμενον] to the passion and Parousia of Christ. To acknowledge the prophets as proclaimers of divine discourse is ultimately to acknowledge the church as the addressee "to whom" God presently speaks in Scripture.

2 Pet. 1:16–21 further explains this Petrine insight with an important gloss on the Transfiguration. As a result of what the disciples saw and heard (especially the voice from heaven declaring "This is my beloved Son"), Peter says "we have the prophetic message more fully confirmed [βεβαιότερον]" (2 Pet. 1:19, ASV), a "more definite" grasp of the plot of the drama of redemption. Stated differently: because of the Transfiguration, we now know what the Old Testament prophets were talking *about*.

This "Spirited" referent (for this is how we should now think of the spiritual sense) is the "glory" of the literal sense: the *divinely* intended meaning. Typology is less a matter of *sensus plenior* than of *sensus splendidior*—the "how much more" glorious referent that the letter signifies when seen in the radiant light of the event of Jesus Christ. As the transfiguration displays the glory of the Son in and through his flesh, so "transfigural" interpretation discovers the glory of the prophetic word in the "body" of its text. De Lubac has it right: "the Old Testament lives on, transfigured, in the New."[83]

Spiritual interpretation is ultimately a matter of a *transfigural* reading that discerns the mystery of God's glory in the body of the text, the earthiness of history. Just as the Transfiguration changes only the form, not the essence of Jesus, so the New Testament changes only the referent of the Old Testament, not the semantic content ("sense"). Nothing less than the voice from heaven ultimately interprets the prophecies in relation to Jesus' divine person and work: "*The transfiguration is God's own exegesis of the prophetic word. . . .* The transfiguration reveals to us the proper understanding of the origin and interpretation of holy scripture."[84] The Transfiguration is, as it were, *God's own spiritual interpretation of Scripture—God's own glorious extension of the literal sense* (i.e., the human authorial discourse).

Some conceptual fine-tuning is now in order. In what Erich Auerbach calls "figurative" reading, the spiritual meaning supersedes the literal meaning: "one can state the meaning apart from the representation without loss."[85] This is the Protestant worry about allegorizing when it functions as a general hermeneutic. By contrast, "figural" reading, a special hermeneutic, preserves the literal sense and historical reality of the biblical narrative: "The intelligibility of biblical narrative for the figural reader lies in the perception of divinely constructed figural relationships between persons and events in the world, not in the reader's perception of merely semiotic relations between sensible images and abstract concepts."[86] The persons, events, and institutions of the Old Testament "have meaning and significance because they are the idiom in which God acts and speaks."[87] The lesson of the Transfiguration is that Christian interpreters must read the law and the prophets as divine figural discourse: "the enacted intention of God to signify" Jesus Christ.[88]

David Dawson views Origen as offering figural rather than figurative interpretations. Whereas allegories work with a binary opposition between a literal, embodied, and historical reality and a superior nonliteral spiritual reality, for Origen "the letter, like the body, is the unsubstitutable site of the Spirit's transformation."[89] Origen intends his figural interpretations to bring readers to greater self-awareness of their own place within the ongoing process of spiritual transformation: "Where Origen most excels . . . is in his awareness that classical Christian life is a life of continual transformation of what already is into something different."[90] Scriptural figures find their fulfillment in the context of God's ongoing theodrama; today's readers of Scripture—we upon whom the end of the ages has come—do too.

There is something important here with which evangelical Protestants who view the Bible as God's word ought to agree. We too "figure" in the story. The figures that characterized Israel now define the church and her mission: we are "a chosen race, a royal priesthood, a holy nation" (1 Pet. 2:9) in our time and place as Israel was in hers. We have been transferred into the story of Jesus Christ, emplotted into his narrative, drafted into the drama of redemption. We too, the divine addressees of Scripture, are being transfigured, transcending history not in the sense of leaving it behind but of participating in the mystery—the glorious theodrama—in its midst.

Spiritual interpretation is ultimately a matter of reading for the Spirit's intended transfigural meaning, *an intention that includes the reader's transfiguration*. Transfigural reading is a matter of beholding the glory of the Lord in the face (i.e., literal sense) of the biblical text; this exegetical renewal of our minds is one means the Spirit uses to effect our own transfiguration, "from one degree of glory to another" (2 Cor. 3:18). Recovering this expanded hermeneutic—the awareness that the Spirit uses Scripture to form interpreters into active actors in the theodrama—may well be the main Patristic contribution to Protestants today.

*VI. Concluding Ontological Postscript: "If Anyone Knows Why These Two Should Not Be Wed . . ."*

This article began by "earthing" spiritual interpretation, arguing for the priority of the literal sense on the grounds that salvation is not an otherworldly escape from earthly existence but a bodily and historical accomplishment attested by embodied historical witnesses. I then suggested that spiritual interpretation is a kind of "typing" that discovers new referents implicit in the verbal sense of many Old Testament passages, referents that come to light when those texts are read in broader redemptive-historical context (i.e., the event of Jesus Christ). Finally, I proposed a new label ("transfigural") for the particular typological interpretation displayed in 1 Cor. 10 and elsewhere, one that allows us to see that the New Testament readings of the Old Testament do not change the sense but rather specify a more glorious referent.

Transfigural interpretation discerns how divine discourse *transfers* and *transcends* what is said about something to Israel to the gospel of Jesus Christ addressed to the church. Transfigural interpretation is spiritual because it proceeds from the Holy Spirit's authorial transfigural intention, an intention that includes presenting Christ to us and uniting us to him.

### "They're Playing Our Song": The Marriage of Literal and Spiritual, Heaven and Earth

What are the implications of transfigural interpretation with regard to the Song of Songs? Can I pass the Swinburne test and say whether it is reasonable for Christians to read the Song in terms of its original meaning only? The final paragraphs in an overly compressed article are hardly the place to take a final exam, so I shall have to confine myself to three brief comments, corresponding to what I have said above about earthing, typing, and transfiguring interpretation.

First, the Song means what it says: it really is poetry that celebrates human love and faithful sexual intimacy. Like Adam, it is a Song of the earth, an ode to physical joy.

Second, the Song's "nuptial metaphor" is also about God's love for Israel.[91] Though Longman says there is "absolutely nothing in the Song of Songs that hints of a meaning different from the sexual meaning,"[92] Provan thinks there is good reason to assume that the text may be about both human and divine-human love.[93] Ellen Davis argues that the Song is the "most biblical" of all the biblical books because throughout it is in conversation with other biblical words, themes, and texts that speak of God's troubled relationship with Israel, his inconstant bride, and because it provides a positive counterpoint to the prophets inasmuch as its garden love scenes depict "the reversal of that primordial exile from Eden."[94]

Third, the Song in its transfigural intention is about Christ's love for the church. Bonhoeffer's comment is apt: "I must say I should prefer to read it as an ordinary love song, and that is probably the best 'Christological' exposition."[95] This is so because God transfigurally intends human marriage, instituted in Genesis 2, to signify the union of Christ and his bride: "This mystery is profound . . . it refers to Christ and the church" (Eph. 5:32). Marriage is a figure (*tupos*) made in heaven, instantiated on earth, and fulfilled in mystical union with Christ. The literal details of the Song are not to be interpreted singly, much less explained away, but are rather to be taken together as a holistic description of the kind of marital, covenantal love that characterizes Christ's union with the church.[96] In the final analysis, the Song of Songs is the Song of the Rock, Christ's own voice shining through the Spirit into the depths of our own hearts to unite, transfigure, and transform.[97]

## The Marriage of Catholic and Evangelical? Towards a Covenantal Ontology

What are the implications of this transfigural approach for the marriage of Evangelicals and Catholics, at least as concerns the theological interpretation of Scripture? It should be clear that the transfigural readings I have set forth here, while affirming the literal sense, are a far cry from methodological naturalism. Luther and especially Calvin were *ressourcers* themselves; the best Evangelicalism is a catholic Evangelicalism.[98] While I share with the *nouvelle théologie* a concern for participation in the heavenlies, my own preference is for a covenantal rather than a sacramental ontology. This, I submit, is what an evangelical Protestant *ressourcement* has to offer *la nouvelle théologie*. Again, space permits only three brief comments:

First, by covenantal ontology I am thinking of the way in which being in Christ restores right relatedness between Creator and creation: "if anyone is in Christ, he is a new creation" (2 Cor. 5:17). We do not simply participate in being; we participate in *him*. Yes, we participate in the pre-existent Logos simply by virtue of existing, for "All things were made through him" (John 1:3; cf. 1 Cor. 8:6). This existence, however, is not yet what Scripture calls "life." God's life-giving presence is not a generic "being-thereness" but an active being-there-for-you in communicative action before which unholy creatures can only tremble.[99] To be "in Christ" is thus to be caught up in grace through faith into Christ's headship and history, into the communicative activity of Father and Son through the Spirit, that ceaseless activity in which the three persons share their light, life, and love. Covenantal ontology is a matter of sharing in this eternal life of communicative activity through union with Christ.

Second, the Eucharist, as the prime celebration of this new union and communion, is indeed a real participation in Christ. The nature of this participation, however, is theodramatic and covenantal: in sharing the Supper, we proclaim the earthly work of Jesus Christ and participate in his ascended humanity and Sonship.

Third, transfigural interpretation is a matter of participating in the prophetic and apostolic witness to Christ as well.[100] Indeed, theological interpretation is ultimately a matter of the reader's martyrological participation in a prior triune communicative action oriented to communion. Theological interpretation of Scripture is a covenant privilege and responsibility in which saints participate as witnesses of the communicative action of God's love for the world. As such, it cannot but be a transfiguring experience. Indeed, the effective history of God's Word and Spirit is a matter of transforming meaning and readers alike from one degree of glory to another by making increasingly explicit the eschatologically new at the heart of the redemptive-historical. Evangelicals and Catholics will agree, I hope, at least in this: exegesis is not an operation we perform on dead texts, but an ascending of the mountain to hear the voice of the living God, to see the face of Christ, to sing the choruses of the Rock.[101]

## NOTES

1   Aquinas, *Quodlibet* VII q. 6 a.1. See also his *Summa Theologica* I.1.10.
2   Annie Dillard, *Living by Fiction* (New York, NY: Harper & Row, 1982), p. 136.
3   Hans Boersma, *Heavenly Participation: The Weaving of a Sacramental Tapestry* (Grand Rapids, MI: Wm. B. Eerdmans Publishing Company, 2011), p. 87.
4   See Langdon Gilkey, "Cosmology, Ontology, and the Travail of Biblical Language," *Journal of Religion*, Vol. 41 (1961), pp. 194–205.
5   Boersma, *Heavenly Participation*, p. 2.
6   Matthew Levering, *Participatory Biblical Exegesis: A Theology of Biblical Interpretation* (South Bend, IN: University of Notre Dame Press, 2008), p. 6.
7   Paul Ricoeur, *Hermeneutics and the Human Sciences* (Cambridge: Cambridge University Press, 1981), p. 138.

8    Cf. Bernard Ramm: "Calvin's *Commentaries* are considered the first real scientific, philological exegesis of Scripture in the history of the Church" (*Protestant Biblical Interpretation:
A Textbook of Interpretation*, third revised edition, [Grand Rapids, MI: Baker Book House,
1970], p. 117). By the eighteenth century, however, the secular academy pushed this to its
pathological extreme, resulting in the disenchantment (i.e., "desupernaturalization") of
Scripture (see Michael C. Legaspi, *The Death of Scripture and the Rise of Biblical Studies*
[Oxford: Oxford University Press, 2010]).

9    Nicholas Wolterstorff, *Divine Discourse: Philosophical Reflections on the Claim that God Speaks*
(Cambridge: Cambridge University Press, 1995).

10   Lewis Ayres prefers to speak of the "plain" rather than "literal" sense precisely because
the latter has in modern times been restricted to human authorial intent. Ayres defines
the plain sense as "'the way the words run' for a community in the light of that community's techniques for following the argument of texts" (*Nicaea and its Legacy: An
Approach to Fourth-Century Trinitarian Theology* [Oxford: Oxford University Press, 2004],
p. 32).

11   Paul Ricoeur notes that language has a referent "only when it used" by a speech agent
(*Interpretation Theory: Discourse and the Surplus of Meaning* [Fort Worth, TX: Texas Christian
University Press, 1976], p. 20).

12   Cf. Gerhard Preyer and Georg Peter: "only in the context of a speech act does a sentence
express a determinate content" ("Introduction: The Limits of Contextualism," in *Contextualism in Philosophy: Knowledge, Meaning, and Truth* [Oxford: Clarendon Press, 2005], p. 4).

13   Richard Swinburne, *Revelation: From Metaphor to Analogy*, second edition, (Oxford: Oxford
University Press, 2007), p. 287.

14   *Ibid.*, p. 266.

15   *Ibid.*

16   So Philip Schaff, *The Principle of Protestantism*, Lancaster Series on the Mercersburg Theology, Vol. 1 (Eugene, OR: Wipf & Stock, 2004), p. 225.

17   Swinburne, *Revelation*, p. 273.

18   The Council of Chalcedon forbade the literal interpretation of the Song in 450.

19   Ayres holds that there are no objective criteria for deciding what counts as "good" figural
or spiritual exegesis, only criteria internal to a particular interpretive practice and tradition
(Ayres, *Nicaea and Its Legacy*, p. 38).

20   Tremper Longman, *Song of Songs*, The New International Commentary on the Old Testament (Grand Rapids, MI: Wm. B. Eerdmans Publishing Company, 2001), p. 36.

21   *Ibid.*, p. 28.

22   See Marvin Pope, *Song of Songs*, The Anchor Bible, (Garden City, NY: Doubleday & Co.,
1977), pp. 89–229 for a comprehensive survey of the various possibilities.

23   Longman, *Song of Songs*, p. 36 (my emphasis).

24   Ellen F. Davis, *Proverbs, Ecclesiastes, and the Song of Songs* (Louisville, KY: Westminster John
Knox Press, 2000), p. 231.

25   G. K. Beale, "Did Jesus and his Followers Preach the Right Doctrine from the Wrong Texts?
An Examination of the Presuppositions of Jesus' and the Apostles' Exegetical Method," in
Greg K. Beale, ed., *The Right Doctrine from the Wrong Texts? Essays on the Use of the Old
Testament in the New* (Grand Rapids, MI: Baker Books, 1994), p. 389.

26   F. F. Bruce, "Interpretation of the Bible," in Walter A. Elwell, ed., *Evangelical Dictionary of
Theology* (Grand Rapids, MI: Baker Book House, 1984), pp. 558–565.

27   See Hendrik F. Stander, "The Patristic Exegesis of Moses Striking the Rock (Ex. 17:1–7 &
Num. 20:1–13)," *Coptic Church Review*, Vol. 12 no. 3 (1991), pp. 67–77.

28   Justin Martyr, *Dialogue with Trypho*, ed. Michael Slusser, (Washington, DC: Catholic
University Press of America, 2003) ch. LXXXVI.

29   Augustine, *Tractate on the Gospel of John* 26.12.2; cf. 28.9.4.

30   Anthony C. Thiselton, *First Corinthians: A Shorter Exegetical And Pastoral Commentary*
(Grand Rapids, MI: Wm. B. Eerdmans Publishing Company, 2006), p. 150.

31   Robert Wilken, "In Defense of Allegory," *Modern Theology*, Vol. 14 no. 2 (1998), p. 201.

32   *Ibid.*, p. 209.

33   These more or less correspond to the three views represented by Walter C. Kaiser, Darrell
L. Bock, and Peter Enns, *Three Views on the New Testament Use of the Old Testament* (Grand
Rapids, MI: Zondervan, 2007).

34  Richard Longenecker, *Biblical Exegesis in the Apostolic Period*, second edition, (Grand Rapids, MI: Wm. B. Eerdmans Publishing Company, 1999), pp. 193–198.

35  Darrell L. Bock, "Single Meaning, Multiple Contexts and Referents," in *Three Views on the New Testament use of the Old Testament*, p. 125. I argue below that the divine meaning does not contradict but *transfigures* the human authorial discourse.

36  Richard S. Briggs, "'The Rock was Christ': Paul's Reading of Numbers and the Significance of the Old Testament for Theological Hermeneutics," in Stanley E. Porter and Matthew Malcolm, eds., *Hermeneutics, Paul, and Theology* (Grand Rapids, MI: Wm. B. Eerdmans Publishing Company, 2012).

37  David Dawson, *Christian Figural Reading and the Fashioning of Identity* (Berkeley, CA: University of California Press, 2001), p. x.

38  John Webster counters the worry among many today that Protestants fatefully divide the natural from the supernatural (and then compound the error by locating church tradition in the former) by suggesting that Protestant doubts about "intrinsicist" ecclesiologies are actually rooted in a concern to distinguish God's perfect life in himself (i.e., uncreated being) from the church and its existence in time (i.e., created being). The Scripture principle simply affirms "the non-continuity between the divine Word and the church" (John Webster, "*Ressourcement* Theology and Protestantism," in Gabriel Flynn and Paul D. Murray, *Ressourcement: A Movement for Renewal in Twentieth-Century Catholic Theology* [Oxford: Oxford University Press, 2012], p. 9).

39  Preface to the epistles of James and Jude in Luther, "September Testament" (1522), English trans., see *Luther's Works*, Vol. 35, edited by Jaroslav Pelikan, Hilton C. Oswald, Helmut T. Lehmann, and Christopher Boyd Brown, (Saint Louis, MO: Concordia Publishing House, 1955), p. 396.

40  David L. Baker, "Typology and the Christian Use of the Old Testament," in Beale, ed., *The Right Doctrine from the Wrong Texts?*, p. 324.

41  "A type is a form of analogy that is distinctive to the Bible. Like all analogies, a type combines identity and difference." Edmund Clowney, *The Unfolding Mystery: Discovering Christ in the Old Testament* (Phillipsburg, NJ: P&R Publishers, 1988), p. 14.

42  Cited in Jean Daniélou, *From Shadows to Reality: Studies in the Biblical Typology of the Fathers* (London: Burns and Oats, 1960) pp. 188–189. Cf. Frances Young: "'Types' are forms of *mimesis*, the *mimesis* of a story or act, of a *drama*, a thing done, a life lived" (*Biblical Exegesis and the Formation of Christian Culture* [Cambridge: Cambridge University Press, 1997], p. 209).

43  Cited in Daniélou, *From Shadows to Reality*, p. 195.

44  See, for example, Tertullian: "It is this water which gushed forth from the rock which followed the people. If the stone was Christ, then undoubtedly Christ has sanctified the water of baptism" (*De Baptismo* IX, 208, 16). Daniélou's conclusion is also worth noting: "It is, then, in types of the Sacraments that we find the core of the Patristic interpretation of the Exodus." (Daniélou, *From Shadows to Reality*, p. 197).

45  Young, *Biblical Exegesis and the Formation of Christian Culture*, p. 136.

46  P.G. LXXX, 257; cited in Daniélou, *From Shadows to Reality*, p. 194.

47  Young, *Biblical Exegesis and the Formation of Christian Culture*, pp. 152–53.

48  Ayres, *Nicaea and its Legacy*, p. 386.

49  *Ibid.*, p. 416.

50  Jean Calvin, *Commentary on the Epistles of Paul to the Corinthians* Vol. 1, trans. by John Pringle, (Edinburgh: Calvin Translation Society, 1848), p. 313.

51  *Ibid.*

52  Ben Witherington, *Conflict and Community in Corinth: A Socio-Rhetorical Commentary on 1 and 2 Corinthians* (Grand Rapids, MI; Wm. B. Eerdmans Publishing Company, 1995), p. 219.

53  Calvin, *Commentary on the Epistles of Paul to the Corinthians* Vol. 1, p. 314.

54  *Ibid.*, p. 315.

55  "Those things ordained by God borrow the names of those things of which they always bear a definite and not misleading signification, and *have the reality joined with them*" (Calvin, *Inst.* IV.xvii.21; my emphasis).

56  Jean Calvin, *Commentary on a Harmony of the Evangelists* Vol. 3, trans. by William Pringle, (Edinburgh: Calvin Translation Society, 1846), p. 209.

57  *Ibid.*

58  Clowney, *The Unfolding Mystery*, p. 116.
59  *Ibid.*, p. 122.
60  *Ibid.*, p. 126.
61  *Ibid.*
62  Young claims that typology is a modern construct (*Biblical Exegesis and the Formation of Christian Culture,,* p. 152). For a helpful overview of the state of the question, see Benjamin J. Ribbens, "Typology of Types: Typology in Dialogue," *Journal of Theological Interpretation*, Vol. 5 (2011), pp. 81–96.
63  Young, *Biblical Exegesis and the Formation of Christian Culture*, pp. 209–212. De Lubac draws a similar distinction between a merely symbolic (*allegoria verbi*) and a historically based "Christian" allegory (*allegoria facti*). Andrew Louth prefers to speak of allegory rather than typology, but he too recognizes the difference between spiritual interpretations concerned with *words* and those concerned with *things*. See Andrew Louth, *Discerning the Mystery: An Essay on the Nature of Theology* (Oxford: Clarendon, 1983), pp. 114–120. For an excellent account of the debate between Daniélou and de Lubac over the respective merits of typology and allegory, see Hans Boersma, *Nouvelle Théologie & Sacramental Ontology: A Return to Mystery* (Oxford: Oxford University Press, 2009), ch. 5.
64  Samuel Mather, *Figures or Types of the Old Testament*, second edition, (London: N. Hillier, 1705).
65  *Ibid.*, p. 53.
66  *Ibid.*, p. 55.
67  *Ibid.*
68  *Ibid.*, p. 56.
69  Whereas *idem* pertains to numeric identity (i.e., self-sameness), *ipse* refers to the kind of narrative identity that characterizes persons (i.e., same self) and, as such, connotes constancy rather than reduplication.
70  Peter J. Leithart, *Deep Exegesis: The Mystery of Reading Scripture* (Waco, TX: Baylor University Press, 2009), p. 41.
71  *Ibid.*, p. 74.
72  Patrick Fairbairn, *The Typology of Scripture* Vol. 1 p. 3, cited in Bernard Ramm, *Protestant Biblical Interpretation*, p. 224.
73  "The correspondence of the *tupos/antitupos* is not between 'bare' or 'neutral' historical events, persons, or institutions, but one that is soteriologically 'charged.' The Old Testament *tupoi* are *salvific* realities, and they find their fulfillment in the *soteriological* work of Christ and/or in the new covenant *soteriological* realities issuing from Christ." Richard M. Davidson, *Typology in Scripture: A Study of Hermeneutical* tupos *Structures* Andrews University Seminary doctoral dissertation series Vol. 2, (Berrien Springs, MI: Andrews University Press, 1981), p. 400.
74  See Robert Plummer, "Righteousness and Peace Kiss: The Reconciliation of Authorial Intent and Biblical Typology," *Southern Baptist Journal of Theology*, Vol. 14 (2010), pp. 54–61.
75  I take this example from Ribbens, "Typology of Types," pp. 87–88.
76  The Reformers' emphasis on redemptive history as the primary context for spiritual interpretation, rather than some other scheme, may be a distinctly Protestant contribution, and one that fits well with the Reformers' general tendency to privilege soteriology over metaphysics.
77  Hans Frei, *The Eclipse of Biblical Narrative: A Study in Eighteenth and Nineteenth Century Hermeneutics* (New Haven, CT: Yale University Press, 1974), p. 2.
78  Ribbens helpfully distinguishes three kinds of typological or ikonic mimesis: christological, tropological/example, and homological/pattern ("Typology of Types," pp. 90–94).
79  Augustine, *De Genesi ad litteram* 1, 1.
80  A. M. Ramsey, *The Glory of God and the Transfiguration of Christ* (London: Longmans, Green and Co, 1949), p. 144.
81  John Chrysostom, Homily 21, *De Imperio, Potestate et Gloria*.
82  St. John Damascene, *Homily on the Transfiguration*, cited in Peter Chamberas, "Transfiguration of Christ: A Study in the Patristic Exegesis of Scripture," *St. Vladimir's Theological Quarterly*, Vol. 14 (1970), p. 55.
83  Henri de Lubac, *Scripture in the Tradition*, translated by Luke O'Neill with an introduction by Peter Casarella, (New York, NY: Crossroad Publishers, 2000), p. 175.

84   Douglas K. Harink, *1 & 2 Peter*, Brazos Theological Commentary on the Bible (Grand Rapids, MI: Brazos Press, 2009), pp. 159–160.

85   John David Dawson, "Figural Reading and the Fashioning of Christian Identity in Boyarin, Auerbach, and Frei," *Modern Theology*, Vol. 14 no. 2 (April, 1998), p. 188.

86   Dawson, *Christian Figural Reading*, p. 11.

87   Dawson, "Figural Reading," p. 187.

88   *Ibid.*

89   Dawson, *Christian Figural Reading*, p. 74.

90   *Ibid.*, p. 214.

91   Paul Ricoeur and André LaCocque, *Thinking Biblically: Exegetical and Hermeneutical Studies* (Chicago, IL: University of Chicago Press, 1988), pp. 265–300.

92   Longman, *Song of Songs*, p. 36.

93   Iain W. Provan, *Ecclesiastes, Song of Songs*, The NIV Application Commentary Series (Grand Rapids, MI: Zondervan, 2001), p. 242.

94   Davis, *Proverbs, Ecclesiastes, and the Song of Songs*, p. 232.

95   Dietrich Bonhoeffer, letter to Eberhard Bethge, June 2, 1944, in *Letters and Papers from Prison*, edited and translated by Eberhard Bethge, (London: SCM Press, 1971).

96   Malachi 2:14 mentions marriage in covenantal terms. See Gordon Hugenberger, *Marriage as a Covenant: Biblical Law and Ethics as Developed from Malachi* (Leiden: E. J. Brill, 1994).

97   For a further development of this reading, see J. Christopher King, *Origen on the Song of Songs as the Spirit of Scripture: The Bridegroom's Perfect Marriage Song* (Oxford: Oxford University Press, 2005).

98   "Catholic Evangelicalism" calls attention to the importance the magisterial Reformers accorded church tradition as the history of effects of the Spirit's leading the church into all truth. For a further development of the Scripture/Tradition relationship, see Kevin J. Vanhoozer, *Drama of Doctrine* (Louisville, KY: Westminster John Knox Press, 2005), chs. 5–6.

99   For a fuller treatment of this theme, see Kevin J. Vanhoozer, *Remythologizing Theology: Divine Action, Passion, and Authorship* (Cambridge: Cambridge University Press, 2010), ch. 4.

100  Cf. John Webster: "The church and its acts come to be thought of as witness to the presence of God rather than as internal to that presence or as modes of its extension and embodiment" (Webster, "*Ressourcement* Theology and Protestantism," p. 15).

101  My thanks to Mark Bowald, Andrew Cowan, James Gordon, Douglas Harink, Steve Pardue, Darren Sarisky, Daniel Treier, Hank Voss, and Martin Warner for their comments on an earlier draft.

# INDEX

---

*Heaven on Earth?: Theological Interpretation in Ecumenical Dialogue*, First Edition.
Edited by Hans Boersma and Matthew Levering.
© 2013 Blackwell Publishing Ltd. Book compilation © 2013 Blackwell Publishing Ltd.